JMGardner
1951.

MAURICE TO TEMPLE

A Century of the Social Movement
in the Church of England

SCOTT HOLLAND MEMORIAL LECTURES
1946

MAURICE TO TEMPLE

A Century of the Social Movement
in the Church of England

SCOTT HOLLAND MEMORIAL LECTURES
1946

by

MAURICE B. RECKITT

FABER AND FABER LIMITED
24 Russell Square
London

First published in mcmxlvii
by Faber and Faber Limited
24 Russell Square London W.C.1
Printed in Great Britain by
Latimer Trend and Co Ltd Plymouth

To

WILLIAM G. PECK, S.T.D.

To whom this book owes much,
but its author more

CONTENTS

9

PREFACE

These Lectures do not set out to provide even an outline of the history of the subject of which they treat. For this students must go to the sources, some of which are listed in the select bibliography at the end of this book. What I have sought to provide is a commentary upon and an interpretation of the development of Christian thought about the problems arising out of the relation of the Church to the social life of the time, and action resulting therefrom, during the last hundred years.

One aspect of the subject, however, I have not attempted to explore. The vast complex of activities covered by the term 'social service' has been to a pre-eminent degree inspired by the faith and devotion of Christian people. Much of what it is now generally accepted as natural that the State should undertake on behalf of its weaker members was initiated by the Church. The challenge of such activities to the assumptions and operations of a secularized society was, however, implicit rather than explicit. I have interpreted my subject as confined to movements which were seeking not so much the immediate rescue of the victims of a godless industrialism and a soulless urbanism, as the reconstruction of society on Christian principles. In the movements here discussed the Church is seen as at issue with the world in Westcott's sense of the term, 'society organized apart from the thought of God'.

I would emphasize that my concern is solely with activities within the Church of England. This is not because I under-rate the significance of the social movements promoted here by

Preface

Roman Catholics and by the Nonconformist bodies, but for the opposite reason that I think (i) that such movements are of an importance which demands a separate treatment, and (ii) that they require to be dealt with by one who knows them from the inside, as no member of another communion can claim to do.

No student of this subject can fail to be supremely indebted to three books: Dr. W. G. Peck's Hale Lectures, *The Social Implications of the Oxford Movement*; Mr. G. C. Binyon's, *The Christian Socialist Movement in England*, and Dr. C. E. Raven's, *Christian Socialism, 1848–1854*. The extent of my own debt to these authors will be obvious to anyone familiar with their work. I have further to thank Dr. Peck and Mr. Binyon for advice and suggestions in regard to the subject of this course, but it must not be assumed that their judgment on all points covered by these lectures would coincide with opinions expressed here.

I cannot mention all those among my friends who have made suggestions of which I have been glad to avail myself, but I must record my thanks to Dr. Stephen Liberty for material relating to Wordsworth's social outlook; to Brother George Every, S.S.M., for information about Charlotte M. Yonge; and to Canon Donaldson for reminiscences of his early days in the movement. What I owe to Canon Widdrington in this respect, as in many others, is immeasurable.

It only remains to thank the Chairman, Fr. E. K. Talbot, C.R., the Secretary, Fr. Martin Jarrett-Kerr, C.R., and the Trustees of the Scott Holland Memorial Trust for giving me this opportunity of recalling the centenary of the movement initiated by Ludlow and Maurice; and Canon E. S. Abbott and the authorities of King's College, London, for their generous hospitality to the lectures and to the lecturer.

M.B.R.

November, 1946

❧ I ❧

A DOORSTEP IN QUEEN'S SQUARE: 1846

It is just a hundred years since 'a small, slightly built man of gentle manner', twenty-five years old, 'with a finely shaped head and brown eyes of peculiar brightness', appeared for the first time on the doorstep of a house in the north-west corner of Queen's Square, Bloomsbury. The owner of the house, a widower, who had only been established there for some six months, had spoken of his new venue, as few or none would do now, as 'this very quiet and antiquated square', and no doubt he had chosen it for this reason as being an appropriate spot in which to pursue the study of theology which was his vocation. But it was not about theology that the young man and a friend were calling by invitation. The young man had been for three years a barrister of Lincoln's Inn where his host had recently been appointed Chaplain, and he had come to ask for his counsel and help in a scheme for 'bringing to bear the leisure and good feeling of the Inns of Court upon the destitution and vice of the neighbourhood'. The barrister, already familiar with and impressed by his Chaplain's preaching, no doubt expected much from this interview, but if he did he was disappointed. The lonely widower, never at any time a man of sanguine temperament and always self-distrustful in practical affairs, was still prostrated by the loss of his wife and 'without spring to answer any appeal' such as his caller had in mind. 'A good man but very unpractical' was the visitor's verdict after his call. Nothing, it seemed, had come of it. Yet what was in fact to come of it is, in a real sense, the theme of this whole course of lectures.

13

Maurice to Temple

The name of the barrister was John Malcolm Forbes Ludlow and that of his host John Frederick Denison Maurice, and the centenary of their first meeting is one which could not have been passed over without impiety. The greatness of Maurice is perhaps more widely recognized to-day than at any time since his death, though that we still have no adequate study of his teaching and its significance is surely the most curious and the most deplorable *lacuna* in English theology. But of Ludlow, the true founder of the movement the development of which we are to trace, so far as any single man was or could be that, scarcely anything seems to be generally remembered to-day. 'One of the greatest and best men of our time—I speak advisedly', as E. O. Greening, who knew him well, declared, Ludlow was also one of the most modest, and as he lived to so great an age, dying at ninety in 1911, none of his contemporaries was left to pay testimony to him, and his life was too uneventful to have provoked a biography. It is one of the most conspicuous merits of Dr. Raven's definitive study of the first years of the movement which Ludlow initiated that it has brought out his unique place in it; for he was unique, not only as having precipitated it, but as supplying an element in it without which it would have been something less than it was. To describe that element by so vague and indeed protean a term as 'Democracy' is perhaps hardly satisfactory. It was, however, a faith not only in the people's cause but in the people themselves which Ludlow had in a sense and to a degree that his colleagues, or most of them, had not; he had it from the beginning and he never lost it. Educated in Paris, he had witnessed and welcomed the revolution of 1830 as a boy of nine, and early made acquaintance with the writings of the social philosophers who contributed to the ferment by which it was inspired and which it inspired in its turn. He was a disciple of Fourier in particular, and this influence is obvious in Ludlow's life-long advocacy of the worker's rights and responsibilities as producer in association with his fellows. Ludlow had mixed with workers on a footing of equality in a guild of French Protestants for the relief of distress, and when he came to England at the age of seventeen, after a brilliant studentship at the

A Doorstep in Queen's Square: 1846

Collège Bourbon, he quickly associated himself with the Corn Law agitation then at its height. The young man on the doorstep in Queen's Square did not merely want to work *for* the people; he wanted to work *with* them, and with the movements they were making for themselves. Ludlow indeed exemplified in its finest form the new social consciousness which was shaping itself as the new reign with its new problems confronted a new England with a seriousness which in itself was somewhat new.

For a serious age it was. It is curious that the term 'Early Victorian' should have become synonymous with smugness and complacency, for these are characteristics of the penultimate rather than the opening decades of the reign, the mood of those years against which Kipling's *Recessional* was a protest. Earnestness in the first Victorian decades there certainly was, but that is another matter. It pervaded every department of life, and was, as we might expect, nowhere more evident than in the sphere of religion. It would have been inconceivable to Newman or to Maurice that religious issues should be debated in the language and in the mood which Scott Holland, Charles Marson and G. K. Chesterton were to bring to them fifty years later. The solemnity of the period, exhibited as much by scientists, sociologists and even novelists as by theologians and ecclesiastics, is a feature which cuts it off as sharply from that which preceded it as from our own century. That Queen Victoria was 'not amused' was taken by those unorthodox historians, the authors of *1066 and All That*, as the clue to the understanding of her reign, and it is a significant fact that wit did not long survive her accession. Theodore Hook died in 1841, Barham of the *Ingoldsby Legends* and Sidney Smith four years later; and for anything like them we have to wait nearly fifty years till the age of Whistler and Wilde. Regency wit gave way to that sort of fantasy which is the escapist compensation for Victorian seriousness, ushered in by Lear's *Book of Nonsense* in this very year—1846, and reaching its climax twenty years later at the summit of the Victorian Age in the adventures of the child who followed a white rabbit into Wonderland and a black kitten through the looking-glass.

What were the causes of this new access of solemnity? I think they were mainly two. In the first place, the initial decade of Victoria's 'sixty glorious years' was, in fact, among the most inglorious in English history. The huge industrialist experiment upon which such confident hopes were founded was not going according to plan. Instead of distributing boundless wealth, it was multiplying poverty upon an unexampled scale and in the most repulsive forms. The realization of this came upon the country with a startling suddenness, caused in large part by the controversy over the new Poor Law. In 1833, said Douglas Jerrold, no one was thinking about the poor, and in 1839 no one was thinking about anything else. In the former year two pronouncements had been made of a strikingly dissimilar character. Robert Owen, declaring to a meeting on May 1st, that date so recurrently provocative of sociological enthusiasm, that 'we dismiss all envy and jealousy from the new world, in which all will partake of the advantages derived from the excellences of each', went on to 'proclaim to the world the commencement on this day of the promised millennium, founded on rational principles and consistent practice'. (A year later his Grand National Consolidated Trades Union lay in ruins, and the unhappy labourers of Tolpuddle were on their way to join the convicts of Australia.) In July John Keble proclaimed no millennium but the national apostasy implicit in the State's interference with the affairs of the established Church of Ireland—a curious starting point for an Anglo-Catholic revival. Neither of them was worrying about the social problem; Owen because he believed that he had solved it, Keble because it would not have occurred to him that such matters were fit subjects for the consideration of the Church.

But by 1839 it was different. Richard Oastler, a Tory Churchman, was abroad in the land, campaigning against the 'new Bastilles'; the bleak, tenacious Shaftesbury was trying to persuade Parliament that Britain's industrial prosperity did not depend, as the new medicine men of Political Economy were understood to declare, on factory children working a ten-hour day or infants of five pulling trucks through mine passages too

narrow for grown men. But in fact industrial prosperity was far
from evident by 1839. A serious slump set in with the beginning
of the new reign, one of the gravest of those 'commercial crises'
which habituated the nineteenth century to see in boom and
slump an 'act of God', so that the trade cycle became accepted
as the 'sorrowful wheel' of Western civilization. In 1839 the
Charter, which Lovett had produced for his handful of serious-
minded London artisans in the previous year, suddenly became
the rallying point of an insurgent populace and was for the first
time presented to Parliament. The Free Trade League, to which
Ludlow attached himself, competed with the Chartists for the
attention of the new street-corner audiences. Not all were so
confident that change would be for the better. Carlyle characteristically declared to Caroline Fox in 1842 that 'to me the
world seems all going wrong and tending irresistibly to change—
which can't but be for the worse'. But whether optimists or not,
men were developing a social conscience. Soon there began to
appear the new sociological novels, initiated by Mrs. Gaskell
and Charles Kingsley, which were to prompt Thackeray's complaint that a day had come when only those who wrote with a
purpose were held to be 'good for anything'. And the worldling
Greville declared 'we are now overrun with philanthropy and
God knows where it will stop'.

A suspicion of error is not the same thing as a conviction of
sin, though it often serves as a preparation for it. The England
of 1846 had got no further than the first stage, but the apprehension that there might be a catch somewhere in the 'progress'
on which it had come to count so confidently was as destructive
to light-heartedness as the realization of the existence of a moral
flaw in it would have been. Yet the solemnity of the age was due
to something more and something deeper than anxiety over an
economic setback or even than a sense of social failure. It was
due, above all, to the widening of the intellectual horizon. As
the 'fifties wore on the economic outlook improved, despite the
slump of 1857, and events at Scutari and Cawnpore gave more
immediate cause for anxiety. But the real issues, the problems
that weighed upon men's minds and spirits most profoundly

and brought this new seriousness into the Early Victorian world, were not those that arose in politics or economics. They were the upshot of the new atmosphere in which men's understanding of their place in nature had to be formed. Time began to stretch backwards to hitherto unimaginable aeons, space became more and more illimitable. Scientists may have guessed at these things already and even begun to establish them as something more than speculations, but it was only now that they began to communicate their discoveries to an audience which half a century before scarcely existed, that middle class which paced the long galleries of the 'palace' erected in Hyde Park in 1851 and found its mind opening on vistas longer still. In 1858 Wallace and Darwin simultaneously proclaimed the doctrine of Natural Selection; in the next year *The Origin of Species* inaugurated the great debate upon the nature of Man which was the real issue in that battle of false antithesis inaccurately described as the conflict between science and religion. These were high themes, and men were ready enough to agree with the transatlantic poet who told them that life was real, life was earnest, whether or not they concluded that the grave was not its goal. The new learning of the biologist and the naturalist might or might not be deemed impious in its inferences, but it was not so in its manners. Darwin was no Bradlaugh, whose day had not yet dawned.

But in 1846 all this lay ahead, and Kingsley had not begun to pen those reflections on the marine life of the Devon seashore with which he interlarded his later stories. We are still in an age of theology. And at the heart of the theological conflicts, implicated in them and yet so largely transcending them, was Frederick Denison Maurice. Indeed, up to the date when Ludlow called on him he had seemed to have a mind for little else. And it was not till the spring of 1848 that Ludlow's letters from revolutionary Paris kindled that spark in the Chaplain of Lincoln's Inn which was to fuse theology and sociology into a single inspiration, and recover after two centuries of virtual apostasy a social witness for the Church of England.

That Maurice is ideologically the *fons et origo* of what we, inevitably yet inadequately, call the social movement in the Church of England cannot be doubted for a moment. Yet this phrase, 'social movement', has come to have such connotations as to make it not a little misleading to treat of so great a figure in such a connection. Maurice and Kingsley turn up as a pair of benevolent inseparables (for there is hardly ever a mention of Ludlow) in all our text-books and general histories, promoting working-class associations, worrying over drains, and stimulating adult education; and they appear, thus linked and thus occupied, so continually, that it is all too easy to forget that when we are dealing with Maurice we are not concerned with a social reformer who happened to be a clergyman and therefore 'animated by the Christian ethic', as the familiar phrase goes. We are considering the life and utterances of a theologian, a prophet, perhaps a saint, certainly one of the most significant figures in the history of English religion. As a matter of fact, though Maurice himself declared that 'as a child anything social and political took a hold of me such as no object in nature, beautiful or useful, had', there is not much to suggest that he had any more spontaneous interest in what we call social questions than Keble or Newman had shown, until he was challenged by Ludlow to face what was implied in them. His greatness is indicated by the fact that under the impact of Ludlow's letters from Paris in March 1848 he responded to this challenge, and not merely by setting on foot or supporting this or that good work, though he was always insistent that action must follow on conviction. His greatness lay in his capacity to see and to show that his theology was deep enough to answer all the questions which a secularized economic development and a secular idealism alike had raised. Maurice's capacity to be what he was and to lead as he did arose from no special interest in or knowledge of social questions, but from a profound grasp of the answers which God in Christ had already given to them.

Through decades not scant of theologians, but very barren of Christian social teachers, it was not unnatural that Maurice who was so pre-eminently the one should have loomed even larger as the other. There are still lessons in the sphere of social

and political principle to be learnt from Maurice, though they
are nowhere set out very systematically in his writings and sermons. They are not so set out because they were essentially
deductions from and implications of that which meant so much
more, not only to him, but to those living amidst the world's
problems whom he inspired—the theology and, above all, the
interpretation of the Bible which it was his mission to expound.
'I am a theologian and have no vocation except for theology',
he wrote to Ludlow in 1852, when the social activities of the
movement were at their height. 'To preach the Gospel of the
Kingdom, the fact that it is amongst us, and is not to be set up
at all, is my calling and business.' Nearly twenty years later,
at the end of his life, Maurice is to be found emphasizing the
same point. 'Every hope I had for culture, for the reconciliation
of opposing schools, for blessings to mankind, was based on
theology.' When we look to Maurice as a Christian Socialist, we
should see him, as it were, as an iceberg where the socialism (to
accept the term he then so bravely accepted) is represented by
the mass which towers above the water-line, but is itself supported by the far vaster sub-structure which we do not see. So
regarding him, we may say in a special sense that the things
which are seen are temporal, but the things which are not seen
are eternal. Yet it is no less important to remember that they are
in essence the same things, or indeed more precisely the same
thing. As the iceberg is a single substance, so Maurice's teachings
on the truths of earth and heaven are an undivided whole. As
he himself declared, in one of his Lincoln's Inn sermons, 'Let
us not try to sever, for they are inseparable, those principles
which affect the problems of earth from those which affect the
Kingdom of Heaven. All unrighteous government whatever,
all that sets itself against the order and freedom of man, is hostile
to Christ's government, is rebellion against Him, in whatsoever
name and by whatsoever instruments it is administered.' And
he goes on to give a characteristic warning of how easily and how
often religious interests and religious duties can act as such
instruments, bidding us to remember 'the innumerable crimes
for which religion has been the plea for the last eighteen hundred

years', nor unfortunately do the facts of history since his day restrain us from correcting this to 'nineteen hundred'. Nothing does more to emphasize the 'oneness' of Maurice's teaching than the fact that every exhortation of his that our social life should be seen as a part of the Kingdom of Christ is matched by a warning that our religion ceases to be authentic directly its interests are conceived as—or subconsciously assumed to be— something withdrawn from the total interests of mankind—a 'vested interest' of the spirit, or (still worse) of the ecclesiastical organization.

Such warnings will always be necessary, though the context in which they will call to be given will vary with the nature of the challenge which the world at any particular moment is offering to the Church. And the danger will often be less that Church leaders will be too spiritless to accept such challenges than that they will not be alert enough to perceive them. This was conspicuously the case in the Hungry 'Forties, when great souls like Keble, Newman and even Maurice himself at this time, were too much preoccupied with the authenticity of that Faith they were commissioned to preach to notice what was happening to the body, soul and spirit of the common man. Yet what was in fact happening was a matter of the most urgent pastoral concern, for it was rendering the new proletariat, which was the most significant product of the new industrial tech- niques, almost impervious to the preaching of any faith whatso- ever. We speak of men as too poor to keep body and soul to- gether, but in fact it is the affluent who are most prone to this form of schizophrenia; beneath a certain level of subsistence it needs a literally superhuman heroism to keep a soul alive at all. And in the forties of the last century vast numbers of our people had been thrust below that level. It is therefore not sur- prising to find that the 'Official Census of Religious Worship', taken in 1851, having noted that 'a regular church attendance is now ranked amongst the recognized proprieties of life', went on to remark that 'it is observable how absolutely insignificant a portion of the congregation is composed of artisans'. Of that stratum which fell below even the artisan's level we may conjecture that the proportion was not merely insignificant but nil. But among the less destitute workers the neglect of religion was not merely a natural upshot of a degraded condition; it was based chiefly upon a conscious hostility to its constituted guardians, and to the Church of England most of all. Nor is there any mystery about the main reason for this. The Hammonds say roundly that 'the chief cause of the Church's unpopularity was . . . the feeling that the Church gave its sanction to all the injustices and abuses that degraded the poor and outraged their self-respect. . . . For the Church, *like every other part of the system of aristocratic government*, had been corrupted by the abuses that come thick and fast when the sense of property is stronger in any body of men than the sense of duty.'

This is indeed a terrible indictment, but perhaps the most interesting part of it is the assumption that the Church of England at this time was merely a 'part of the system of aristocratic government'. It is interesting because it points to the social implications of that essentially spiritual movement launched in this very 'age of the Chartists' to demand the disentanglement of the nation's Established Church from her other established institutions. Keble and Newman's 'ideal of a Christian Church' in launching the Oxford Movement was something a good deal less inclusive in its implications than that set forth by their disciple W. G. Ward a dozen years later. But in such a matter as this *c'est le premier pas qui coûte*, and that is why the first step of 1833 should always be seen as having so vast a significance not only for the Church as a whole, but equally for students of our subject, even though Newman might seem to say—as he did in another connection—'one step enough for me'. It will be necessary to say more on this subject, and there is indeed much more to be said than can be said in these lectures. Let me be content for the moment to quote some words of Dr. S. C. Carpenter's on the Oxford Movement:

'Within it lay a momentous challenge. What is the impact of Christ upon the individual, the nation and the world? If Pusey is right about Holy Baptism, if Keble is right about Eucharistic doctrine, this makes a difference in the realm of economics,

politics, citizenship and public health. . . . There will be things
in the story [of the Movement] which will seem to the reader to
speak a limited concern. The critics will be right. The concern
was limited. *But it was a concern with an unlimited thing.*'

True and important as this may be, the new spiritual impulse was doing nothing as yet to clothe the naked and feed the
hungry of the ragged and hungry 'forties, still less to challenge
the assumptions and interests which made and kept men so.
Carlyle was not unjustified of his complaint in *Past and Present,*
'that certain human souls living on this practical earth should
think to save themselves and a ruined world by noisy theoretic
demonstrations and laudations of *the* Church, instead of some un-
noisy, unconscious, but *practical*, total heart and soul demonstrations of *a* Church'. We may be tempted to regard the antithesis as misleading, but we can hardly dismiss the criticism as
irrelevant. It is simply impossible for us, as it was surely impossible for Ludlow as he stood on Maurice's doorstep, to look at
the society which man had made and to look at the Church
which Christ had founded, as England exhibited both in 1846,
and not to feel that here was displayed not one great moral
failure but two.

Yet we have to be careful here, for the danger of such indictments as that of the Hammonds is that they may lead us to over-
simplify a somewhat complex matter. It is easy enough for us
now to see, and to say, how grievously the Church failed at this
time; indeed it is generally even easier to be moral after the
event than it is to be wise. But we shall mistake both the character of the problem by which the Church was confronted in the
early nineteenth century and her failure in face of it if we see that
failure as manifested merely by complacency, heartlessness and
greed. These things were present no doubt, but they are not the
most significant elements in the situation. It is arguable that
the failures from which the Church always suffers most are the
consequences not of the sins of bad men but of the shortcomings
of good ones. It was not the cold-hearted prelates, the greedy
pluralists and the clerical worldlings who cast away—or at any
rate failed to seize—the Church's opportunity at this critical

time; it was the saintly Wilberforce and the spiritually introverted Clapham Sect, the no less saintly Keble and the ecclesiastically introverted Oxford Movement. It may seem captious indeed to murmur a complaint against men like these, whose whole lives were a dedication to the causes which they believed themselves to have received at God's hands. Yet it is impossible to resist the conviction that the Church which, though from so diverse an inspiration, they so devotedly served, long suffered, and indeed has not yet recovered, from the consequences of the failure of such men to understand all that was involved in the challenge of their changing times. This challenge they saw as materialism, an unbalanced absorption with the things of this world; not wealth and comfort only, but the lure of power and pride and pleasure. The challenge was real enough, but their attitude to it was inadequate, partly because it was negative only and based on too limited an understanding of God's will and purpose in creation, and partly because it was not related to what was happening to man at that time. When, for example, Wilberforce wrote, about 1820, 'I declare my greatest source of difference with the democrats is their laying and causing the people to lay so great a stress on the concerns of this world as to occupy their whole minds and hearts and to leave a few scanty and lukewarm thoughts for the heavenly treasure', we have no need and no right to regard him, as Cobbett so frankly regarded him, as a canting old humbug. Wilberforce was in truth the most sincere of men; the real charges against him are not, as they might often be with others in such a case, those of hypocrisy or a callous complacency, but on the one hand an absence of any notion of social justice as a good in itself and a fulfilment of God's will for His world, and on the other a total lack of imagination as to the situation of the great majority of his fellows in the new industrial civilization. Wilberforce was in his own rather 'sectarian' way an other-worldly man, but he was so on the basis of an assured worldly position. For him to expect such an outlook, even so far as it can be accepted as a validly Christian one, from the new proletarian of the new towns was fantastic, and totally opposed to the realism of the Gospel to which he paid such ceaseless homage. No wonder that, as his latest biographer, Mr. Coupland, says, 'nothing that Wilberforce might achieve for suffering humanity in other lands could ever placate the Radicals' hatred of his "other-worldly" attitude to the English poor'.

Confronted by the rise of Capitalism some three hundred years or so earlier, 'the social teaching of the Church had ceased to count', said Mr. Tawney in his classic contribution to these Lectures, 'because the Church itself had ceased to think'. Confronted by the rise of industrialism, the Church failed to count because in relation to this sphere of human activity she had not begun to think. Devout men entirely failed to realize what was going on, because the Divine Society to which they belonged had long ago surrendered so large a measure of initiative to the world it was its mission to combat. How much was lost by this apostasy is well indicated by a saying which Carlyle reports of the brilliant John Sterling, the brother-in-law of Maurice and his companion at Cambridge. 'Has not the Church', Sterling flashed out in some undergraduate debate twenty years before our centenary, 'a black dragoon in every parish, on good pay and rations, horse meat and man's meat, to patrol and battle for these things?' Unfortunately Carlyle does not tell us *what* things; whether Sterling was pointing out that the Church was the only institution in the land with a representative everywhere pledged to patrol and battle for charity and justice we cannot be sure, and a more sinister interpretation is possible. But in fact this was the situation, if the Church had been equipped to take advantage of it. To say that her 'black dragoons' were not so equipped, theologically or sociologically, is to put it very mildly. 'The rich know nothing of the poor', said one of the members of the famous Health of Towns Commission in 1845; and if the clergy of that time were not always to be counted among the rich, and were often forced to know a great deal more about the poor than most other members of the class from which they chiefly sprang, they understood all too little of the causes of their poverty, and all too seldom concerned themselves with the possibility—or even with the need—of its remedy.

After 1833 there was a further complication. As the social
situation grew ever worse, those most sensitive to the spiritual
claims of Christianity, the Evangelicals and the Tractarians,
were diverted from facing that situation by their conflicts over
the nature of that Divine Society to which, in their different
ways, they gave such devoted allegiance. And while they con-
tended a new religion, and something very like a new priest-
hood, was stealing away the souls and minds of Englishmen, a
religion of canonized acquisitiveness and authorized fatalism,
commended by its doctors the Economists, who claimed, and at
any rate were believed to have proved, that henceforward men
might act in a purely self-regarding spirit with a good conscience,
since everyone would, sooner or later, be the better for it.
'Avarice', said David Hume explicitly, 'is the spur of industry'.
Protests against this doctrine there were, but they were fitful
and unco-ordinated, while the new sociology advanced with an
impressive show of enlightened unanimity. The first and in some
ways the most prophetic of these protests came from one who
called himself a Churchman, though he had little good to say
of the Church and made no very obvious attempt to live by its
life. Cobbett has been as often dismissed as a reactionary since
his death as he was dismissed as a revolutionary while he was
alive, but in truth he was nothing so doctrinaire as either, but a
realist who saw what was happening and made himself
generally unpopular by pointing out what it was. He did more,
he saw what the consequences of the silent proletarianization of
England would be; as Chesterton, in his study of Cobbett, puts
it, 'he saw what we see, but he saw it when it was not there'.
As he looked at the Industrial Revolution he may not have seen
the way out, but at least he saw the way in. Though Cobbett
is often stigmatized as a romantic, he was never so romantic as
were the new apostles of Progress, who were always explaining
how rich men were to become as the result of the new discoveries
and techniques. Cobbett's reply to this sort of talk was in effect
to ask, 'which men?' and to answer the question himself by
pointing to the few who were becoming richer and how they
were doing so, while the vast majority were becoming in all

respects poorer. But though he moved men he founded no movement; he had a following, but no followers; yet if he was, in some sense, a Voice crying in the wilderness, at least he knew that a wilderness it was. He was in no danger of mistaking the England of the Reform Bill for the Promised Land, despite its so handsome promises.

As we look back upon the appalling abuses which our social system exhibited in the first half of the nineteenth century, and recall at the same time the resolution and the single-mindedness required—and so largely forthcoming—to combat and to eradicate them, we may be puzzled not that the reformers should have had so much against which to contend, but that they should have found so little for which they could combine. A lonely reformer in an age of callousness and cynicism is a familiar phenomenon enough. But a dozen lonely reformers in an age in which benevolence and earnestness were by no means unusual is scarcely what we should expect to find. Yet it is what, in fact, we do find. Cobbett was lonely. Chesterton has pointed out that he 'hardly had a friend outside his family; and it is doubtful whether there had ever been one human being who really understood what he meant . . . nobody stood exactly where he stood or saw the world exactly as he saw it.' If Wilberforce was not precisely lonely he sometimes found himself left rather severely alone. Coleridge was not indeed left to talk alone, but the author of *The Constitution of Church and State* was left to stand alone, since few understood and fewer shared his 'Idea of each'. Nor was Carlyle left to talk alone, but he would have disliked the idea that he did not stand alone; and indeed those who would have stood beside him were apt to find that on their arrival he was somewhat disposed to walk away from where he had been standing and stand somewhere else. Shaftesbury was a lonely figure, one of the loneliest in the whole public life of his time, though he moved all his life in movements and spoke often to applauding crowds. 'I feel sadly alone', he said in 1841, 'I am like a pelican in the wilderness or a sparrow on the housetops. I have no one with whom I can take counsel, no one to aid me, no one to cheer me.' Robert Owen, again, was a man of many movements, yet it is not his movements which endure in our memory but the man himself, and the movements at the head of which he seemed for a time to stand went forward without him and away from him, leaving him high and dry, high in naïve ideals, dry in his arid blend of rationalism and sentimentalism. And Maurice, beloved and revered by his own little circle as he was, and as few men have been, was nevertheless a lonely figure; misunderstood as a theologian and basely misrepresented as a reformer; his ineradicably dogmatic teaching interpreted as latitudinarianism, his Christian sociology presented as sanctified progressivism.

The man of reforming mind to-day is not only puzzled by all this; he is apt to be irritated by it. It does not fit into that outlook upon affairs on which he relies to furnish him with an interpretation of history, whether past or present. He starts out by expecting to find a single and clear-cut reform movement marshalling the forces of progress; instead of this he finds progress 'advancing', in the Chestertonian phrase, 'in all directions'. There is only one explanation of this which he is ready to accept: the reformers were unworthy of their role. If they had been men of self-forgetting tolerance and constructive statesmanship, they would have been ready to 'gang up' against 'the forces of reaction' and carry the People's Cause to an early and triumphant victory. And no doubt there is some justice in this stricture. No one would call Cobbett tolerant, or Shaftesbury wide-minded, or Robert Owen a political realist, or Maurice a practical statesman. They had, one and all, their limitations, as men are wont to have, and some of these were moral limitations. There might well have been more co-operation among co-operators, more sociality among socialists, even no doubt more Christianity between Christians. To say, however, that better men even than these might have done better work even than they did is not to make a particularly original or illuminating commentary on what they did do. The 'progressive' critic, moreover, forgets two things. In the first place, he forgets that a man faced by some great evil is not likely to make much impression on it if he is principally concerned to be tolerant, wide-

28

minded and statesmanlike. That is not the sort of person a reformer can well afford to be, even if his temperament and his
convictions incline him to be, which is not very likely. And in the
second place, the critic forgets, or omits to notice, that the reformers did not drop all their differences to work for the same
thing, for the sufficient reason that they did not want the same
thing. To say that Cobbett did not want the same sort of world
that Wilberforce wanted is to put it a good deal more mildly
than Cobbett himself put it; indeed, he rated it as a principal
advantage of the New World, geographically speaking, that it
contained no Wilberforces. 'Think of that', he repeated. 'No
Wilberforces!' Yet no one, not even Wilberforce himself, can
take away from this persistent champion of the slave the glory
of having led and maintained the assault against an evil that
some of the most pious men of his day had contrived to tolerate
and even to defend. Coleridge, in his second *Lay Sermon*, attacked the 'overbalance of the commercial spirit' in phrases
which Carlyle could hardly have matched for incisiveness; yet
the sage of Chelsea, though anxious not to 'be unjust to this
memorable man', found something in the sage of Highgate
which he could not tolerate: 'did he not too', says Carlyle,
'procreate strange Centaurs, spectral Puseyisms, monstrous
Illusory Hybrids and ecclesiastical Chimeras—which now roam
the earth in a very lamentable manner!' Carlyle despised and
feared what Coleridge despised and feared, but he was not seeking what Coleridge was seeking; they had a common enemy,
but neither a common inspiration nor a common aim. And when
we come to Robert Owen and Anthony Ashley the convergence
of interest and divergence of philosophy is striking indeed. Two
more single-minded men never lived; both saw what their contemporaries refused to see—or more often perhaps refused to
look at—that the new discoveries and the new technics which
were presumed and proclaimed to be about to raise men to new
heights of achievement were, in fact, plunging the great
majority of them into new depths of degradation. Yet it would
be somewhat fantastic to suggest that the rationalist and the
evangelical should have set aside the little matter of the existence

of God—on which, indeed, Owen was every bit as much exercised as Shaftesbury—to work together, not indeed for specific factory reforms, as they well might have done, but for that 'new moral world' which, if it could ever have existed outside Owen's imagination, would have filled the conservative Shaftesbury with a highly moral aversion.

The truth is that in the spiritual and intellectual conditions of the age it was impossible for reformers, animated as they were by so diverse inspirations and illuminated by no enduring doctrine of man and society, to 'get together'. But it was a good deal less impossible for those whose interests they were attacking from so many angles to do so. Indeed, it was so far possible that they had to a large extent already done so, and what Cobbett consistently and characteristically called 'The Thing' was the result. Political philosophers, no doubt, can find plenty of material for discussion of Tory traditions and Whig principles, but in the England of the Combination Acts and of Peterloo this was very far from being the sort of discussion which was going on at the dinner tables of the governing class. It was there that the virtues, for lack of which the reformers are so often rebuked, were being exhibited. Pitt seemed, to the Abolitionists at any rate, to have become only too tolerant in the matter of the slave trade in his later years; the Whigs were quite ready to be 'realistic' about the liberties which Sidmouth and Castlereagh took with civil liberty; the Tories were not all so prejudiced in their preference for money made by enclosures as to grudge the new manufacturers the fortunes they were beginning to make by trade. It did not need a philosophy to defend privileges established for generations, and in so far as it needed one to defend wealth more recently obtained by 'enterprise' the political economists had already begun to provide it. To attack the abuses of the new plutocracy, based upon enclosure and machine production and money power, as a whole, it was necessary to see plutocracy as a whole, which perhaps only Cobbett did, and to understand it as a whole, as even Cobbett did not. To persuade oneself of the necessity to defend it as a whole, however, it was necessary only to profit from it. To fight for it effectively no more inspiration was required than a common instinct founded on self-interest would furnish. To fight against it effectively there was needed a common outlook founded upon a common faith. And that faith did not exist.

Despite what has so far been said as to the diversity of the reforming impulse, however, with the end of the Napoleonic wars there can nevertheless be discovered three strains in the movement of protest against what Dr. Peck has well described as 'the ossified defence of an impossible *Status quo*'. Two of these strains were personified by Coleridge and Bentham respectively; the third at first appeared to be represented by Cobbett, so far as Cobbett can ever be said to have represented anything but himself, but soon seemed, if only for a short time, to be much more effectively represented by an entirely different sort of man —Robert Owen. This third movement was that out of which Chartism sprang and from which the contemporary working-class movement has grown. Its origins were confused, but what is perhaps chiefly distinctive about it is that it was trying to create not so much a new sort of public opinion about public affairs as a new set of people to hold it, nothing less indeed than a new political class. It was therefore apt to be poorly regarded —or, more often, not regarded at all—by the sort of people who had become accustomed to treat public opinion as a monopoly of their own. Such people did not any longer look for intellectual leadership to politicians; after the deaths of Burke, Pitt and Fox it had plainly become impossible to do so. Brilliant as Canning was, he was not really a leader; respectable and even admirable as Wilberforce was (errors and omissions excepted) he was not primarily a politician. After 1815 men looked for political philosophy not to politicians but to philosophers. 'Every thinking Englishman', said J. S. Mill, in 1840 (but it was perhaps still more true in 1830) 'is by implication a Benthamite or a Coleridgean'. The distinction was, indeed, as Mill explained, of some importance. 'By Bentham men have been led to ask themselves, in regard to any ancient or recent opinion, "Is it true?" and by Coleridge, "What is the meaning of it?" ' Both questions, of course, are worth asking at any time, and never more so than in a period when ideas and institutions are ceasing to correspond with social and economic realities, but it is rare that both are asked by the same sort of people. Of Coleridge and his influence it will be necessary to say more hereafter. But we may notice in regard to Benthamism that it led to a mood in which men were unwilling to look beyond their immediate advantage and were tempted to suppose that by the successive eradication of what were, practically considered, anachronistic abuses, a reformed society could be trusted to arise, as it were, spontaneously on a basis of self-interest. Bentham's reforms have been somewhat summarily described by a contemporary historian, Mr. E. L. Woodward, as 'a series of political gadgets', but the philosophy behind them having a more or less explicitly hedonist basis, its influence was more far-reaching than the character of the reforms themselves might have suggested. In fact, says Dean Church, in his *History of the Oxford Movement*, writing while Bentham's influence was still a vivid memory, Utilitarianism 'made desperate attempts to take possession of the whole field of morals', and a later historian of the Movement, Dr. Peck, has said that its effect 'was all in the direction of finding secular solutions for the problems of the soul'. Bentham himself would hardly, one supposes, have denied this, since he declared that 'the Clergy are a body of inspectors and moral instructors who form, so to speak, the advance guard of the law. The expense of their support ought to be referred to the same branch of the administration with justice and the police, viz. the support of internal security.'

Security, according to Bentham, was the most fundamental of all the 'principles of legislation'. We to-day, who have seen a continent rocked and racked by the ruthless struggles arising from civil faction and the ideological passions of 'Right' and 'Left', can perhaps find more justification for this standpoint than we might have done before the events of 1944 in Greece, of 1936 in Spain and of 1917 and after in Russia. Bentham lived within the shadow of the French Revolution, which had furnished a shock from which the British governing class of that generation never recovered its nerve. Yet when men seek, as

they must in the social as in any other sphere, to provide for
security, it is well that they should ask themselves, 'security for
whom and for what?' Bentham's answer was not so much 'order'
(which reply may in any given case be hypocritical but is
always in a measure defensible) as 'property'. 'In consulting the
grand principle of security, what ought the legislator to decree
respecting the mass of property already existing? He ought to
maintain its distribution as it is actually established.' And this
is said at a moment when that distribution had lately been and
was still being violently disturbed by forces which 'enlightened'
philosophers were the first to justify, whether in the interests of
landlordism or of capitalism. 'The grand principle of security'
was not invoked, and Bentham would have been the last person
to invoke it, to prevent the disturbance of the countryman's
property by the enclosures. To

> *leave the larger felon loose*
> *who steals the common from the goose,*

was somehow supposed to work out for the greatest good of the
greatest number, even no doubt including the geese, among
whom the Utilitarians would hardly have hesitated to include
the dispossessed yeomen.

In the last resort, therefore, the progressive Utilitarians lined
up with the enlightened Economists to produce a new rationale
for the men in possession, including, it is only fair to add, a
substantial number of new men who were moving into possession.
But even these apologists were less concerned to defend the new
possessors of the new machines for what they had so far done
than for what they confidently predicted they and their system
would do one day. Right through the first half of the nineteenth
century, capitalist industrialism was regarded by all those who
gave themselves time to reflect upon it as intolerable except as a
transitional stage to something else. Social thinkers were often
ready to welcome the capitalist for the blessings of the new state
of society which his enterprise and abilities were 'about to usher
in'; for what he actually had ushered in they could not pretend

C

to find much enthusiasm. The new energy and the new technique were so impressive in themselves, however, that it was
generally felt that despite a few moral and aesthetic flaws, a
society which could command such resources must necessarily
have a great and noble future. The avarice and the callousness
which the Industrial Revolution displayed, the submergence of
beauty, the contempt for personality and the cult of self, were
regarded as transient irrelevances in a process fundamentally
benevolent; they were not recognized as a chief part of the
driving force which was carrying out the changes from which so
much was hoped. A few, like Robert Owen, did realize that the
new machine lords were drawn from 'the most ignorant and
ruthless section' of the population, but even they believed that
their anti-social proclivities would be subdued, not so much by
statutory penalties as by 'the irresistible spirit of the age'. A
boundless optimism about the future of 'associated production',
by which most people meant not any sort of co-operative principles, but merely work in factories, enabled many of the sages
of the early years of the century to overlook, or at any rate to
minimize, the horrors resulting from the aggregations which
plutocracy was in fact calling into being. But if their optimism
and credulity may seem to us now fatuous in the extreme, they
were not for the most part so fatuous as they are sometimes
represented. Theirs was not an acceptance of things as capitalism
and industrialism had so far made them, but as they fondly believed that it was going to make them. They were welcoming the
new forces, but they did not think of them as having yet created
a normal and fundamentally static social order of a new kind.
Blind they may have been, but they were not as blind as all
that.

Yet even from the beginning there were dissentients from this
sanguine view, and it is the two different schools of dissentients
which Coleridge and Southey, on the one hand, and first
Cobbett, then Owen and then the Chartists on the other, represented. The tragedy for their day was that these two sets of
dissentients could not contrive to act or even to consult together;
the problem for our day is to understand why this was so, and

what consequences have flowed from it. From the one side, Coleridge, though far indeed from Tractarianism himself, did much to inspire the Tractarians' suspicion of commercialism, but he did not succeed in inspiring them to act against it. As Paine said of Burke in a very different connection, they pitied the plumage but forgot the dying bird. Newman confessed that 'he had never considered social questions in their relation to faith and had always looked upon the poor as objects for compassion and benevolence'. From the other side, there were many men like Hetherington, the moderate Chartist, who were trying to inspire the masses to work for their own liberation from Mammon, not only physically but spiritually, who did not challenge the Church to be true to her mission; they merely denied that she had one. Perhaps it is the chief greatness of Ludlow and Maurice and Kingsley that, with whatever limitations and whatever mistakes, they recognized, as Churchmen explicitly, a responsibility and an opportunity which good Christian men before them of so many schools of thought had refused to admit or failed to see. If it was a tragedy that this recognition should have had to wait till 1848, it would have been a disaster had it had to wait any longer. From that disaster the Christian Socialists saved both the Church and the nation.

Recalling all this, the widening breach between Church and people, the dangerous misery that lay all around, the hardly less dangerous prosperity that lay ahead, we are surely not wrong to see in the young barrister on the doorstep in Queen's Square a figure of great significance for the religious and social future of his country. For Ludlow was calling (in much more than the conventional sense of the phrase) upon the only man in the Church of England at that moment capable of supplying not only a personal inspiration but a theological foundation for the movement delayed indeed too long, yet not, by God's mercy, to be delayed altogether too late. In 1846 the decisive moment had not indeed arrived, and the 'good man' seemed merely 'unpractical'. But eighteen months later, with the spectacular failure of the workers' hopes, that moment did arrive, and with it a new catalytic agent, another good man who was by no means unpractical, though he was often imprudent. Kingsley, already known to Maurice as a correspondent, comes into the picture, and the great triumvirate of theologian, country priest and reforming layman is established. The Movement begins— and moves. But before we can see whither it moves and what it moves we must look more closely at some other of the forces which had been, and still were, struggling to reawaken alike the conscience of England and the soul of her dormant Church. For as we peer through the smoke and grime of the thirty years which followed Waterloo we see that this was an age of some- thing more than steam and coal and iron. It was, far more significantly, an age of prophets, priests and poets, through the mouth of whom God was speaking to the people of this bruised and blackened land.

❧ II ❧

PROPHETS, PRIESTS AND POETS

It is a strange phenomenon, yet one so familiar that even Christians have come to take it for granted, that save for Coleridge and Southey at the beginning, all the lay prophets of the nineteenth century, though they spoke often in the name of God, spoke not only from outside the Church but in disregard of the Church. Carlyle, Ruskin, Matthew Arnold, William Morris, Samuel Butler, Bernard Shaw—all these men who were telling a complacent age some part of the truth about the progress and civilization of which it boasted, were indeed rebuking the world, which is, of course, one function of the prophet. But what is less often noticed, but is in fact the really surprising feature in the situation, is that they were not, except incidentally, rebuking the Church. There was indeed no lack of persons to do this: earnest atheists like Bradlaugh, who believed that the Church was at best perpetuating an illusion and at worst perpetrating a swindle; earnest ethicalists like Stanton Coit and the founders of 'Labour Churches', who aspired to preserve the congregation and the preacher while eliminating that which for eighteen centuries had brought them together. But these were the minor figures; the true prophets did not attack the Church, because they were too busy attacking what they saw to be effectively false and evil, and they deemed any direct attack on the Church superfluous. It is, of course, a commonplace that this separation of the prophets from the Church was very bad for the Church. It has been less often seen—and would even now be seldom admitted—that this was bad also for the prophets. No doubt it spared them the embarrassment of being implicated in the blindness—and worse—of the historic institution through which organized religion was preserved and communicated. The Church—to adopt a contemporary idiom—did not cramp their style. But for the same reason it did nothing to form their style, or to restrain their style, with the result that the style tended to run riot and obliterate the message. The world soon came to be more interested in the *way* Carlyle and Ruskin and even Shaw said things than in the things they said, and this fact is surely connected with a certain justifiable dubiety about their authority for saying them. For a pronouncement made without reference to a recognized mode of belief is only an opinion after all. To anathematize the commercialism, the vulgarity, the ugliness, the meanness, the mass-mediocrity of Victorian civilization was the accepted thing for nineteenth-century critics and philosophers, who came to be tolerantly regarded in the same light as the fleas which were good for a dog since they kept him from 'brooding over being a dog'. Free speech is one condition of a healthy society, but it is not sufficient to heal a diseased one. For when the prophet speaks it should be to do more than proclaim his own convictions: his keynote is not 'Believe me', but 'Thus saith the Lord'.

But it may be asked, if the moral reformers and the social critics neglected the Church, was this not because the Church herself was neglecting to take in hand or even to consider those matters upon which the secular prophets were so strongly moved to deliver themselves? I say 'it may be asked', but in fact, of course, this question has been asked almost *ad nauseam*, and generally in the manner described in our Latin grammars as 'expecting the answer, "yes".' It looks a simple question enough, but, as I suggested in my previous lecture, it is really an extremely complex one, and this lecture will in effect be largely devoted to the discussion of it. Nor is such a discussion merely an academic one, for the problem has not by any means been disposed of, despite the efforts made by what we call the Christian social movement to grapple with it from the days of Maurice down to our own. I have sought myself to crystallize the problem thus: how can the Church play the game if she is not to be consulted about the rules? The centuries in which the Church exhibited herself as a formative social influence, those centuries to which her own social movement has increasingly come to look back in the effort to discover the elements of a Christian sociology which may yet be relevant to the contemporary situation, were precisely the period in which not only the rules but the very meaning of the game of life were expounded by the Church. The rules were accepted because the interpretation of life from which they sprang was accepted. They might be broken, since men in what we call the 'ages of Faith' were no more immune from the temptations of avarice, ambition, selfishness and irresponsibility than they were before it, or have been since; but over a large and important field of human relations they were the only rules there were. How this state of things came to an end was the subject of the first and greatest course of lectures given under the auspices of this foundation. We can interpret the process as we will. It was all the Church's fault: she was, when the strain came, slothful, ignorant, corrupt, rent by irrelevant heresies and needless schisms. It was not the Church's fault: her teaching was flouted by a godless world, seduced by new opportunities for the indulgence of pride and power. It was nobody's fault: the problems of a rapidly expanding national and international economy were insoluble by any existing agency, and could only be understood in the light of a science still to be born. I am not here concerned with such controversy; I desire only to point out that the society clamouring for and against 'reform' in the quarter of a century before 1846 was not one in which either the defenders or the critics of its alleged abuses were judging matters with reference to any doctrine of a supernatural origin and destiny for man. The problem in its essence was to be stated some hundred years later in a document published by the Church Union, which sought with some exactitude to limn the outlines of 'A Christian Realm'.

'The Church is God's appointed instrument for saving mankind. But it is not her mission nor is it within her power to save the world on its own terms. She cannot offer salvation to nations or to individuals except upon the condition of repentance. She cannot get society out of trouble which it has brought upon itself by its refusal to acknowledge the standards which she exists to proclaim. Nor is it her vocation to add moral force to social purposes in which religion is regarded as merely instrumental.'

I am not, of course, suggesting that there could have been no better answers to this problem in the half century which followed Waterloo than those which Christians sometimes found, or thought they had found—but more often failed to look for. I am only contending that the problem was there, and that it was there for the earnest Christian who honestly desired to improve matters, even more than for the complacent or the selfish or the 'pietistic' Christian who was content to let things remain as they were, or resigned to such an imagined necessity. The Church may be held to have forfeited her right to be consulted about the terms upon which progress and prosperity were being sought in the newly industrialized England; she may have had few or no qualifications for offering an informed opinion on the subject; but in fact the assumptions on which the rationalization of the social process was being proposed were at least as dubious from any Christian standpoint as were the anachronistic privilege and unimaginative conservatism by which it was being resisted. The latter was the exhausted and degenerate Toryism from which Cobbett had revolted in disgust; the former was the 'liberalism' which Newman so greatly dreaded, with its self-sufficiency, its repudiation of the supernatural, and 'the opinion that dogma is a matter of opinion'. In essence, says Dr. Peck, 'it was the belief that the human future might be constructed upon a basis of sheer experimentalism. It was a basis which, denying dogma, denied any spiritual significance, any mystical essence, in human personality and society. Such secularized humanism, devoid of any firm dogma of man, comes at length to regard only the phenomenal values of personality. As it demolished the old aristocracy, it looked like a charter of freedom. A man must now prove his worth for this world. In the result it is unable to convince any man that he is worth very much. It brought the modern plutocracy and the consequent confusion and loss of human value and direction.'

Having recognized the nature of the challenge presented to the Church, however, we have to be on our guard against supposing that there was no better way of responding to it than was in fact attempted in any quarter before 1848. The Evangelicals dismissed the social problem by denying the reality of it, as so many Christians have done, with less excuse, since their day. Wilberforce wrote thus of the matter in that book of his which, despite its insufferable complacency in face of the miseries being endured by the destitute masses of his day, was nevertheless a courageous protest against the despiritualized conformity which masqueraded as Christianity at the end of the eighteenth century:

'If any country were indeed filled with men, each thus diligently discharging the duties of his own station without breaking in upon the right of others, but on the contrary endeavouring, so far as he might be able, to forward their views and promote their happiness—all would be active and harmonious in the goodly frame of human society. There would be no jarrings, no discord. The whole machine of civil life would work without destruction or disorder and the course of its movements would be like the harmony of the spheres.'

Anything less like the harmony of the spheres than the movements of society in the new towns at this time it would be difficult to imagine, and if the uprooted peasants, and the ruined hand-loom weavers, and the pitiable children, 'diligently discharging the duties of their station' for twelve hours a day, had been as other-worldly and altruistic as Wilberforce himself genuinely sought to be, the several virtues of their individual characters could have produced no 'goodly frame of human society'. The Evangelical revival was not without its social effects. M. Halevy, in an oft-quoted verdict, has opined that it not only 'invested the British aristocracy with an almost stoic dignity and restrained the plutocrats newly risen from the masses from vulgar ostentation and debauchery', but that it 'placed over the proletariat a select body of work people enamoured of virtue and capable of self-restraint'. But as the nineteenth century wore on that self-restraint began to wear thin, and the virtue of which such a 'select body of work people' as was represented, for example, by Lovett's London Working Man's Association, was showing itself enamoured, was something different from the dutiful resignation preached by the Evangelicals. Indeed, their influence had lost its vitality by the 'twenties, when the first stirrings of reform began. There was a prophet abroad in the land with a 'New View of Society', a view which soon led him to a 'Denunciation of All Religions'. Robert Owen's hostility to church and chapel alike seems to have arisen less from any indignation over their moral and social failures than from a conviction of their irrelevance. His prescription was simple: 'man's character is made for him and not by him'; improve his environment and he will automatically improve. Nor was this merely a matter of theory with Owen: he claimed to have proved it. Why ask men to live for the New Jerusalem in another world when they might have New Lanark in this?

At a moment when the average Englishman's environment had been rendered more discouraging than it had been since the Glacial Age, Owen's teaching could hardly be dismissed as irrelevant; and a Church which was alive at once to a Christian doctrine of Creation and to the realities of the time would have been content to expose its limitations only after espousing the positive element of truth which it contained. It is a main count in the indictment against those who impose sub-human conditions upon their fellows that they thereby prevent them from discovering what men's true problems are. It was, of course, an unreal simplification to say, as in effect Owen said, 'look after the slums and men's sins will look after themselves'. The truth is, in the first place, that slums are themselves an embodiment of sin, as being a misuse of materials God gave to men for a better purpose, and secondly, that while men are imprisoned in such conditions they are scarcely free to know, and still less to confess themselves sinners at all. But this was very far from being the sort of reply which most of those who accounted themselves religious gave to Owen's 'Denunciation', which, says Mr. Cole, in his Introduction to the *New View of Society*, 'was seized upon and quoted against him in every accent of horrified surprise . . . largely as a stick wherewith to beat his growingly unpopular doctrines'. Indeed, as Ludlow said later, 'instead of seeking to understand the Movement, to distinguish in it between what was genuine, living and hopeful, and what was false, excessive, dangerous, they looked on bewildered or joined with its opponents to hoot and crush the whole thing down'.

There were Christians, however, who did make the effort to distinguish between what was true and what was merely naïve in Owen's proposals. The most notable was Southey, who in his *Colloquies on the Progress and Prospects of Society* called him that 'happiest and most beneficent and most practical of all enthusiasts', while attributing his failure to what he described, in a singular but not inappropriate phrase, as a lack of 'the organ of theopathy'. And this appreciation comes as late as 1829, many years after Owen had been dropped by the influential and the respectable, who had been momentarily impressed by his success as a benevolent employer. Though there was never anything like a school of Christian Owenites, there were three types of people who did not feel it necessary to denounce their religion in order to support some part of what Owen taught and did. First, there were the men who associated themselves with the agitations which arose out of the democratic movements which from 1825 onwards Owen inspired. Notable among such was Dr. Arthur Wade, Vicar of Warwick, a mountain of a man, who headed the great procession of petition against the scandalous sentences imposed upon the Dorchester Labourers, and bluntly declared that to withhold God's bounty from those who want 'is the highest treason against heaven'. A more academic type was represented by John Minter Morgan, a layman and a prolific writer, who backed Owen from the first, claiming that his teaching could be interpreted in a sense which would revive the Christian social ideals of earlier times, and who protested against the 'apprehensions that the existing state of society is a dispensation of Providence, not to be altered by human exertion'.

'Would it not', he pertinently added, 'become us rather to obey the commands of the Deity than thus to ascribe to His laws the imperfections of human institutions?' Finally, there were the Christian workers in the early experiments in Co-operation which Owenism inspired. Of these the most notable is Dr. William King, of Brighton, one of the saints of Co-operation and editor for some years of its leading journal, *The Co-operator*. He was, perhaps, the most theologically minded, as he was certainly the most practically influential, of those Christians who responded to Owen's challenge. There is some evidence that he was influenced by Maurice in his later years, and since a summary of his main tenets was published in *The Christian Socialist* in 1851, he may himself have exercised some influence on Maurice's movement twenty years after his own journal had ceased to exist.

The chief significance of Owenism for our study is that it represented the strongest, or at any rate the most loudly proclaimed, repudiation of the fatalism by which social and economic thinking was pervaded at this time, largely as a legacy of the conclusions of a clergyman of the Established Church. Thomas Malthus had been influential because he had encouraged his contemporaries to believe what the more powerful among them had only too much interest in believing, that any socially-organized alleviation of the misery of the masses would make matters worse by increasing their numbers at the expense of their subsistence. Here we have 'the economics of scarcity' at their crudest, and Owen, by implicitly repudiating the idea that the world was constructed on such a design, was, for all his humanitarian rationalism, nearer to a Christian doctrine of Providence than the ordained priest. Blind as Owen's optimism was, he was right in seeing and insisting that whatever the problems with which the new discoveries were confronting mankind, the scramble for gain and power was not the only, to say nothing of the best, way by which those discoveries could have been exploited. If it needed something more than a rational enlightenment and a hygienic environment to produce the co-operative commonwealth which for Owen was always just round the corner, it ought to have been obvious to the faithful churchman in the new towns that what had, in fact, grown up round the corner from his begrimed parish church was at variance with every article of his belief about God and Man.

Why then was it not obvious, or alternatively, if it was, why was there nothing that the Church could say to illuminate the matter or do to alter it? These are legitimate questions, and it is not a sufficient answer to them to say that Owenism was impious and Utilitarianism at bottom a hedonist philosophy. The guilt of the Church at this time did not lie in her refusal to throw herself heart and soul into the reform movements which were beginning after 1822 to challenge the moral, social and political stagnation of England, for in truth there was not much heart in them and no soul at all. Her guilt lay in finding no alternative to an identification with utopian illusions or materialistic trends other than a dull and ignorant complacency in face of the evils with which, however defectively, the reformers set themselves to cope. No wonder that the mass of the people deduced that, in the bitter phrase of the Hammonds, 'Christianity was not a standard by which to judge the institutions of society, but a reason for accepting them'. The bishops gained nothing for the cause of the religion they were so handsomely endowed to foster by their resistance to the Reform Bill; as the *Morning Chronicle* said at the time, they merely 'challenged a public attention to their base record, unredeemed by a single virtuous act'. Dean Hook may have been wrong in thinking that 'by not heartily throwing themselves into the cause of Reform, the clergy lost a magnificent opportunity of attaching the people to the Church'. Attachment to the Church in any real sense is hardly likely to result from mere gratitude for the conferment of earthly benefits. But the opportunity which *was* lost was a twofold one: the opportunity to prove that the Church was not part and parcel of a set of vested interests bound up with an obsolete political and social system; and the opportunity to show that she understood better than either those resisting all change or those proposing it, what was mistaken about the purposes on which men had set their hearts, and in what directions a true social regeneration was to be sought.

There was the less excuse for the more official spokesmen of religion since a prophetic witness had been borne for decades against the influence of commercialism by men who had not only a right to be listened to but a power to secure that they were so. A penetrating social critic of this century, Ramiro de Maeztu, has asserted that the validity of any social order may be judged by the degree to which it fulfils the requirements of the physician and the priest. He might have added 'and of the poet'. And of all cultured men in the early decades of the nineteenth century the poets showed perhaps the least disposition to be satisfied with the conduct of human affairs. Wordsworth, Southey and Coleridge had all begun as revolutionaries; if in the era of the Reform Bill they were more commonly accounted reactionaries, at any rate by their juniors, it was due to two circumstances. In the first place, they had suffered, along with so many of their generation, a violent shock to their political hopes by the development of the French Revolution. If to be young in 1789 was 'very heaven', it was only the more discouraging to be ten years older in 1799, with the Terror and the Directory behind, and an imperial dictatorship in prospect. Younger men were not tormented by such memories. When Shelley

met Murder on the way,
he had a mask like Castlereagh,

and not like Robespierre, still less like Napoleon, who had about him after 1820 the aura of defeat by 'the forces of reaction'. The second and more profound reason for the distrust with which the Lake poets watched the development of what were accounted to be the 'progressive' forces of their age was partly based on an aesthetic revulsion against what industrialism was doing to countrysides, the loveliness of which had never been more beautifully celebrated than by themselves. But it was founded still more on a discernment of the destruction of a 'way of life', the truth and beauty of which they were pre-eminently equipped to understand. Their hostility to much that was being

46

so blindly acclaimed by the dominant forces of their time sprang no doubt primarily from such insights, but it was not aesthetic only or mainly. All three men were animated in varying modes and measures by something more than 'natural religion'; they were, in fact, in their later lives at any rate, Churchmen, and it is hard to understand why their fellow-churchmen paid so little heed to what they had to say about all that an increasingly godless civilization was doing to man.

It is perhaps with some surprise that we recall that Wordsworth was still alive in 1846—alive indeed and kicking against

> *the wrongs to universal ken*
> *daily exposed,*

as he had written in a sonnet only four years earlier. Wordsworth's great poetry is not to be found in his productions of these years, but his social protest is still being proclaimed there. And, indeed, the voice that speaks in the sestet of this sonnet is something stronger than that of J. K. Stephen's 'old, half-witted sheep':

> *Rest not in hope Want's icy chain to thaw*
> *By casual boons and formal charities;*
> *Learn to be just, just through impartial law;*
> *Far as ye may, erect and equalize;*
> *And what ye cannot reach by statute, draw*
> *Each from his fountain of self-sacrifice.*

There is a note here to justify Wordsworth's claim, made about this time, and reported by Crabb Robinson in his *Diary*, that 'I have no respect for Whigs, but I have a great deal of the Chartist in me'. But there is nothing new about this. Thirty years before the poet had made one of the strongest, and in some circles at any rate, most influential, denunciations of the horrors of his time. *The Excursion* may seem to-day for the most part a pedestrian performance, in more senses than one, but the attack upon the mangling of childhood in the ever-encroaching factories has not lost its power to move the reader. The worker's

47

birthright now is lost.
Economists will tell you that the state
thrives by the forfeiture—unfeeling thought,
and false as monstrous. . . .
Can hope look forward to a manhood raised
on such foundations? 'Hope is none for him',
the pale recluse indignantly exclaimed,
'and tens of thousands suffer wrongs as deep'.

Such also was the verdict of another poet who chose (and perhaps in his case fortunately) to make his contributions to social criticism through the medium of prose. Twenty years after the publication of *The Excursion* Southey wrote to John May:

'I have gone through the whole evidence concerning the treatment of children in factories, and nothing so bad was ever brought to light before. The slave trade is mercy to it. . . . This white slavery has arisen in our own days, and is carried on in the midst of this civilized and Christian nation. Herein it is that our danger consists. . . . In the manufacturing districts, where the wages of the adults are at a starvation rate and their children are literally worked to death—murdered by inches—the competition of the masters being the radical cause of these evils, there is a dreadful reality of oppression, a dreadful sense of injustice, of intolerable misery, of intolerable wrongs, more formidable than any causes which have ever moved a people to insurrection. Once more I will cry aloud and spare not. These are not times to be silent.'

To do Southey justice, not only the horrors but the heresies of the Industrial Revolution were themes upon which he was never silent for long. The chill detachment of its official apologists drove him to fury. 'As for the Political Economists', he wrote, in a letter quoted later in *The Christian Socialist*, 'no words can express the thorough contempt which I feel for them. They discard all moral considerations from their philosophy and in their practice they have no compassion for flesh and blood.' It was an opposite mood and a totally different approach for which, he thought, the times were calling. For effective

reform 'a degree of generous and virtuous excitement is required, which nothing but religious feeling can call forth'. It
was this feeling which inspired the volume in which Southey's
social criticism comes nearest to a formulation. The *Colloquies
on the Progress and Prospects of Society* is one of those unfortunate
books far better known for what a famous critic has said about
them than for what they say for themselves. Macaulay's attack
on it is one of the classics of denigration and the book certainly
afforded targets for his scorn. Southey's latest biographer, Mr.
Jack Simmons, who is also his champion, finds in his political
utterances 'much prejudice, much short-sightedness, much
ignorance and some absurdity', and Macaulay was justified in
suggesting that he seemed 'to have an instinctive apathy for
calm and moderate men'. But returning to this controversy
after the lessons suggested by a century of industrial evolution,
it is precisely the calm and moderation of the Whig rather than
any extravagances of the Tory that one finds so infuriating.
In reading Macaulay's essay, with its smug declaration that
'this island is now the richest and most highly civilized spot in
the world', it is easy to forget that any such appalling abuses as
the child jobbery and child slavery against which Southey was
tilting in print and Ashley in Parliament had ever existed,
harder still to realize that the condition of England exposed by
Wordsworth in the poem of 1812, and lingering on to be pic-
tured by Disraeli in the novels of thirty years later, was going on
under Macaulay's eyes as he framed his ironic periods. But
Southey's analysis of all this was not the product of emotion only.
He saw clearly that 'it is the tendency of the commercial and
more especially of the manufacturing system to collect wealth
rather than disperse it', and it was on the basis of this analysis
that, against the fashionable *laissez-faire*, he called for more
power in the government and a higher rate of taxation to
counteract the consequences of the process. Indeed Southey has
perhaps a better claim to be considered the progenitor of
Christian Socialism than any of those to whom the title has
been affixed. If he was not so fully Christian in theological
doctrine as Maurice, he was a good deal more of a Socialist in

D   49

political policy; the high Tory of 1829 sometimes sounds surprisingly like the Labour politician of 1946.

A dozen years before the publication of the *Colloquies*, however, a voice had been raised against 'the overbalance of the commercial spirit, taken as the paramount principle of action in the nation at large'. It is not in any utterance of Southey's but in Coleridge's *Lay Sermons* that Max Beer, the historian of the Socialist movement in this island, hears 'the first voice of Christian Socialism'. In his view the Tractarians, 'Young England', and the group round Maurice were 'all of them, without any exception, either directly or indirectly, under the influence of Coleridge'. Indeed, this can hardly be denied, though the specific character of that influence varied in each case, and is not perhaps in any instance chiefly traceable to *Lay Sermons*. Yet it is these disquisitions which are most germane to our present purpose, for it is here that Coleridge throws down the challenge not only to the philosophy of Mammon, but to those professing Christians who were offering no opposition to it, or even attempting to accommodate their religion thereto. 'The distinguished and world-honoured company of Christian Mammonists', he writes, 'appears to the eye of my imagination as a drove of camels, heavily laden, yet all at full speed, and each in the confident expectation of passing through the *eye of the needle*, without stop or halt, both beast and baggage.' No wonder, then, that he doubted 'whether religion in its present state and under the present conceptions of its demands and purposes, does, even among the most religious, exert any efficient force of control over the commercial spirit'. But Coleridge is doing something more in these 'Sermons' than protesting against the spread of avarice. He is contending against the whole quantitative and mechanical valuation of life, not only as it was exemplified by the greedy manufacturers, but as it was systematized and proclaimed by the Utilitarian philosophers, who were in effect providing them with a ready-made apologia. 'Men', he wrote, in a notable phrase, 'ought to be weighed not counted. Their worth ought to be the final estimate of their value.' At a moment when the complete establishment of the wage-system was depersonalizing the workmen of England so that they reappeared in the national economy merely as 'hands', he declared that:

'On the distinction between things and persons all law, human and divine, is grounded. It consists in this: that the former may be used as mere means; but the latter must not be employed as the means to an end without directly or indirectly sharing in that end.'

And writing on the effects of unemployment more than a century before the 'World Depression' of our time, he said, 'I shall perhaps be told . . . that in a free and trading country all things find their level. But persons are not things . . . neither in body nor soul . . . does man find his level.' Coleridge saw indeed with prophetic clarity that under the impact of economic principles avaricious in spirit and determinist in philosophy, men were sinking below the level of Man.

Coleridge's courage and insight in all this are wholly admirable. Yet he failed to rise to the height of the challenge by which the times were confronting men who felt and thought as he did, because while he saw the falsity and the danger of the direction in which society was moving, he did not face the fact that movement there would have to be. As an American commentator, Dr. C. K. Gloyn, shrewdly remarks, while 'portraying the *status quo* as the embodiment of an unfolding idea, his political theory [of which there is no time now to speak] tended to sanctify . . . the prevailing institutional life of society'. Coleridge was thus conservative in the bad as well as in the good sense of the term; he mixed a wise anxiety to preserve the nation's power and opportunity to grow from its own moral and historical roots with too much concern for the particular blossoms—and even weeds—into which those roots had happened to sprout at a specific moment of history. 'Like all conservative patriots', says the critic I have quoted, 'he tended to revere unduly the institutions of a single nation at a particular time.' The danger which ever lies in wait for the conservative rises from his predisposition to mistake traditional and specific crystallizations for eternal verities, and to assume that those good things which disruptive forces threaten can only be preserved in the forms in which they have so far been known. Churchmen in particular have found, and still find, it difficult to distinguish between the philosophy of Progress against which they will commonly have to argue, and the achievements of progress with which they will somehow have to reckon if they are to match themselves with and not evade their responsibility to their own time.

This difficulty was one which confronted the Tractarians, and it cannot be said that they coped with it very successfully. The case against them cannot be better put than it was by Maurice in 1837 when he said, 'their error, I think, consists in opposing to "the spirit of the age" the spirit of a former age, instead of the ever-living and acting spirit of God'. Abundant excuses can indeed be made for them, not the least of which derives from the circumstance that theirs was so emphatically an Oxford Movement. Into the *hortus inclusus* which Oxford was in the eighteen-thirties, still in very truth what Mr. Belloc satirically called it three-quarters of a century later,

a kind of Fold or Pen
wherein to herd a lot of Learned Men,

a city at that time without industries or suburbs, reached only by coach, little penetrated from the harsh new world of the Industrial Revolution. 'It was scarcely possible', says Mr. Woodward, in his volume on *The Age of Reform,* 'for sensitive and clever men like Keble, Pusey, Newman or Hurrell Froude to understand the world of George Stephenson or Feargus O'Connor or Edwin Chadwick. The fascination of Oxford was too much for them . . . the domination of ecclesiastical subjects and religious beliefs was a real domination; everything else was seen at second hand.'

The matter is, of course, rather more complex than this and it is one to which a great deal more discussion deserves to be— and indeed has been—devoted than can even be summarized here. The question involves much more than the movement's opposition to Liberalism, to which Maurice, who was always critical of the Tractarians, was at least equally opposed and for the same reason that it was 'emphatically anti-theological'. Newman, indeed, in his poem entitled 'Liberalism', while he stigmatizes its devotees as 'men of presumptuous heart', admits that they have hold of some part of Christian truth:

> *Ye have caught some echoes of its lore,*
> *As heralded among the joyous choirs;*
> *Ye heard it speak of peace, chastised desires,*
> *Good will and mercy*—and ye heard no more.

The failure lies in the absence of all other-worldliness. The stanza ends:

> *But as for zeal and quick-eyed sanctity,*
> *And the dread depths of grace, ye pass them by.*

It would be unfair to complain of the Movement as von Hügel does, perhaps with some justice, of Pusey 'and many of his following', that it was 'really not Catholic' because 'incapable of taking any interest in anything that was not directly technically religious'. To speak thus of the Movement as a whole would be to go too far, though it is true that it was in some respects more ecclesiastical than truly Catholic, and that, for example, we find a much closer approach to acceptance of the essentially Catholic idea of Natural Law in the writings of Maurice than in those of any of the Tractarians. The trouble was that in their just suspicion of the world, as it was manifesting its spirit in their time, they turned to its challenges rather a defiant back than a courageous face. They were not hesitant in their denunciations of that spirit which they plainly stigmatized as Mammon worship. 'The special political evils of the day', said Newman, 'have their root in that principle which St. Paul calls the root of all evil.' But their very awareness of this peril, in an age which was providing all sorts of new ideological justifications for acceptance of its pretensions, perhaps made it the more difficult for the Tractarians to make any specific claim for justice for those who were the victims of the resurgent *pleonexia*. They dreaded unloosing the same spirit upon and multiplying the same opportunities among the masses as were already corrupting the new rich. They would have been glad enough to see the mighty pulled down from their seats, if they could have perceived any way in which the humble and meek could be exalted without falling into the same corruptions as were depraving the prosperous. It was natural enough for such a one as Owen, who believed that man was solely the product of his environment, to strive, above all, that that environment should be so reconstituted as to influence every individual for his own good. And since the poor suffered most in this respect, improvement of their lot was obviously the first thing needful. But for men with so strong a sense at once of the gravity of sin and of the reality of individual responsibility as Newman and Pusey had, the social problem newly precipitated in their time was a great deal more complex, and, in fact, they never really faced it. While ready enough to denounce the deceitfulness of riches for those who enjoyed them, they seem at times to have been disposed to congratulate the poor, as Wilberforce had, that at least they were spared the danger of the temptations to which the wealthy were exposed. Their failure here largely derived no doubt from their being so much preoccupied with the necessity of recovering for the Church a consciousness of her divine vocation before she was overshadowed by the advancing secularism of the age. But this preoccupation blinded them to the truth that the social order must have a moral validity of its own if the world has indeed been created by God for any purpose beyond the affording of a *raison d'être* for the Church by provision of an opportunity for her resistance to it.

Truth, even Christian truth, can be dangerous when the assertion of it leads men not into battle with evil but away from it. Insistence upon the gravity of sin and emphasis upon the world as a vale of tears could not justify indifference to the removal of such serious occasions of sin as industrialism was then multiplying or failure to wipe away the tears of those who suffered from it. A godless rationalism was not the only alternative to the passive vindication of a theocentric order. The year in which Keble's sermon launched the Oxford Movement was the year in which Ashley opened the first of his campaigns for a ten-hour day. Ashley was, of course, a Tory churchman, though one as far from Tractarianism as a Christian man could be, yet we do not find much evidence that even Hurrell Froude, who in his impatience with the 'Z's', the Establishment men of the old school, evinced certain radical tendencies, showed any interest in his crusade. But before the victory of Ashley's principle in 1847 in the great Factory Act, of which Marx subsequently declared that 'it was the first time that in broad daylight the political economy of the middle class succumbed to the political economy of the working class', a new note had been sounded from the Tractarian camp. W. G. Ward's *Ideal of a Christian Church* is a book far better known for its consequences than for its contents, and the furore which it caused had, ostensibly at any rate, nothing to do with those features of it which give it to-day its chief interest and significance. For, as we read it now, what strikes us is not its 'Romanism', which was somewhat exaggerated at the time, but its challenging social teaching, which appears to have gone almost unnoticed. Here, four years before 'Christian Socialism', is England's first volume of modern Catholic sociology. A whole lecture could easily be devoted to outlining and illustrating the social philosophy of this almost forgotten book, which must now be passed over in a few pages. Declaring that 'England is one vast mass of superficial splendour, covering a body of festering misery and discontent', Ward contends that 'a pure Church could *not* have co-existed with such tremendous evils', evils that he analyses at some length. But he adds, 'ever since the schism of the sixteenth century the English Church has been swayed by a spirit of arrogance, self-contentment and self-complacency . . . which has stifled her energies, crippled her resources, frustrated all the efforts of her most faithful children to raise her from her existing degradation'. How different the role of the ideal Church of Ward's imagination:

'Let us suppose, however, an ideal Church to be suddenly

placed in charge with a country in which such a state of things had been allowed to grow up unchecked. What a scene presents itself to the imagination! How careful at once her inquiry what may be those branches of labour in which, whether from the kind or the amount of toil, the leading of a Christian life would be impossible; and how stern the prohibition, enforced by all spiritual sanctions, against any of her children engaging in those branches! . . . Then what employment would she make of her spiritual censures in directing them against the oppressors of the poor, what loud and clamorous appeals to our civil rulers; what addresses to those of her own children who are influential in a worldly point of view.'

All this is very characteristic of Ward, for whom ecclesiastical authority had an unusual, perhaps we may say an abnormal attraction. Magisterial denunciations and 'spiritual censures' suggested the very possibilities which ultimately made the 'Roman obedience' an irresistible magnet to him, even though he had declared in his book that he found in that communion 'at present no sufficient model to follow' in Christian sociology, and 'no attempt to point out the nature or the remedies of any of the great social evils which have grown up during the past three centuries'. But though his mind dwelt too exclusively perhaps on prohibitions, Ward was seeking something essentially constructive, nothing less indeed than 'a full and systematic moral theology' to cover 'questions of right and wrong connected with the various employments of man in our present state of society, or again with international morality'. He is quite specific about this:

'It happens (he says) that almost every different trade or profession seems to have its own maxims and generally immoral ones. . . . If the Church is really to possess a sound moral theology, and inculcate precepts based on it, it is included as part of this, that she should have a view, and should proclaim it, on the moral value of these maxims; that she should authoritatively declare what sort of causes a barrister ought to plead, and what sort of books a bookseller ought to sell. . . .

'When subjects have been discussed so closely connected with right moral action as the question, to what extent the duty of a barrister to his client supersedes his general duty to society;— the very idea seems never to have occurred to any of her authorities that it is a matter with which, as a national Christian Church, she has any concern or interest.'

This strikes a very modern note; nothing of this kind was heard in any explicit form until the rise of the new Christian sociologists three-quarters of a century later. Modern, too, in another way is the lesson driven home in the following passage:

'A friend of mine was told by an eminent London physician whose practice had been in cases of insanity that he considered the chief causes in England to be (1) The unsettled state of religion [this recalls a famous dictum of Jung's]. (2) The pressure of our commercial system upon weak minds, both from the ruin in which it sometimes involves whole families, and from the constant strain upon the faculties in the endeavour to *get on*.'

The cry of the Hungry 'Forties rings out again and again in Ward's book; some of his denunciations of the National Church and its 'sinful and unpardonable dereliction of duty' read almost as if written by a Chartist atheist. But one note is not to be found in the book—that of democracy. Ward is all for vindicating the poor, protecting the poor, even raising the poor; but, like all the Tractarians, he never seems to have conceived the possibility of a society in which 'the poor' as a class had ceased to exist. Here his outlook was far indeed sociologically, as it was still more so ecclesiastically, from that of the young barrister whom we left on his chaplain's doorstep. Ludlow by no means approved of the Tractarians and it is unlikely that he read Ward's book. He is much more likely to have read another book being much discussed at this time, a book which told of the Two Nations into which England had become divided, and which seemed for a moment to announce the arrival of a new party in the councils of the English ruling class. But it was not *Sybil*, nor yet *Coningsby*, nor even their author himself, who kindled the first spark of 'Young England', but a Tractarian who ended as Ward did. It was F. W. Faber who inflamed the youthful John Manners to declare as an undergraduate that 'we have now virtually pledged ourselves to restore—what? I hardly know, but still it is a glorious attempt'. This sentence, so reminiscent of the verdict on 'a famous victory', is suggestive of an epitaph for a movement which got no nearer to a real battle than a sham tournament ruined by the rain. Yet it had its moments of insight, crystallized in John Manners' judgment that 'this is clear, nothing but monastic institutions can Christianise Manchester'; and at least 'Young England' rallied in Parliament to Ashley's championship of young Englishmen belonging to that other nation of which Disraeli wrote.

One author we know that Ludlow read, and Carlyle's *Past and Present*, written but three years before, would doubtless be much in his mind at this time. This writer's influence on the group round Maurice, and on Maurice himself, is known to have been great. A contemporary writer, Mr. S. Sagar, has well said of Carlyle that

'his thunderbolts shattered the glass of the eighteenth century gentleman's library, letting into that snug, not to say stuffy, apartment, the fresh wind of reality. . . . Utilitarian ethics, profit and loss philosophies, cash nexus the sole bond between man and man, Parliamentarianism—these things have never sounded quite the same since Carlyle spoke. . . . He was a Calvinist without the theology, but he was very decidedly a Calvinist with a protest—a protest against the world which Calvinism had produced.'

Such a protest Maurice, who had himself begun as a Calvinist, found a better way to state than the iconoclast who, in *Sartor Resartus*, could see only 'a Church gone dumb with old age which only mumbles delirium prior to dissolution'; but he found, in the attempt to do so, inspiration in the writings of one of whom Mr. Sagar observes that 'he felt as strongly as any man that has ever lived that the bonds of society were religious, that man could not believe in man unless he believed in something higher than man'.

Another voice, silent then for four years, which greatly influenced the Christian Socialists, was that of the 'great-hearted, high-minded, wrong-headed man', as Dr. S. C. Carpenter describes him, who was Tom Hughes's schoolmaster. 'Is Dr. Arnold a Christian?' asked Newman ironically; and indeed Arnold's readiness to dispense both with the supernatural claims and with the spiritual sanctions of the Church was so evident, that the question was not unjustified. Yet there was much that was prophetic about Arnold's Christianity, despite his unbalanced insistence on its value as a cultural instrument, and Ludlow had probably noted the passage in which he had declared in 1832:

'I cannot understand what is the good of a national Church if it be not to Christianize the nation and introduce the principles of Christianity into men's social and civil relations; and expose the wickedness of that spirit which seems to think that there is no such sin as covetousness, and that if a man is not dishonest, he has nothing to do but make all the profit of his capital that he can.'

And we cannot doubt that Ludlow was a reader of that still rising young novelist of whom already in 1842 Daniel Webster had said that 'he had done more to ameliorate the condition of the English poor than all the statesmen that Great Britain has sent into Parliament'.

That Ludlow was a reader of Dickens we may indeed feel sure. But one book written at this time he had pretty certainly not read, for though published in Germany in the previous year, 1845, it did not appear in an English translation till forty years later, and then only in New York. This country had to wait till 1892, when the 'New Unionism' was conferring a new status on the lower strata of her proletariat, to read Friedrich Engels's account of *The Condition of the Working Class in England in 1844*. The book is, of course, a revolutionary classic; a virile, if tendentious, story of the jungle stage of industrialism, written, as Engels admitted in his preface to the 1892 edition, just as it was about to pass away. The conditions which the book describes have been made familiar to present-day readers by such modern classics of social history as the Hammonds have provided to shock our sensibilities, but not, it may be hoped, to inflate our self-satisfaction. For there is a subtle danger in the contempla-

tion of outmoded social abuses. Sickened by the filth, barbarity
and injustice of the eighteen-forties, we may be tempted to
thank God that our age is not as other ages were, even though
we live with the spiritual, moral and material desolation of a
continent at our doorstep as a consequence of Europe's most
spectacular catastrophe. We are apt to congratulate ourselves,
despite all this, on a century of moral progress and the victories
achieved by the 'social conscience'. We are not without some
justification if we do so, but this is not the whole story, and it
was certainly not the interpretation which Engels put upon
events in 1892. The Materialist Conception of history is a
dangerous drug, but like other such drugs it can be salutary
if taken in small doses. An extract from Engels's Preface may
perhaps supply one. The co-author of *The Communist Manifesto*
(which was written a year after Ludlow's call on Maurice, and
four months before its upshot in the birth of 'Christian Socialism'
with Kingsley's Manifesto) sets no store upon the 'social conscience'. He points out that 'the revival of trade, after the crisis
of 1847, was the dawn of a new industrial epoch'. He goes on to
outline its features: the effect of Free Trade; the discovery of
vast new goldfields; the development of Colonial and Asiatic
markets; the opening up of the United States; above all, new
means of communication—all this led to an enormous world-
market 'grouped round one manufacturing centre—England'.
And he continues:

'No wonder England's industrial progress was colossal and
unparalleled, and such that the status of 1844 now appears to
us as comparatively primitive and insignificant. And in proportion as this increase took place, in the same proportion did
manufacturing industry become apparently moralized. The
competition of manufacturer against manufacturer by means of
petty thefts upon the workpeople did no longer pay. Trade had
outgrown such low means of making money; they were not
worth while practising for the manufacturing millionaire, and
served merely to keep alive the competition of smaller traders,
thankful to pick up a penny wherever they could. . . . Moreover the larger the concern, and with it the number of hands, the

greater the loss and inconvenience caused by every conflict between master and men; and thus a new spirit came over the masters, especially the large ones, which taught them to avoid unnecessary squabbles, to acquiesce in the existence and power of Trade Unions, and finally even to discover in strikes—at opportune times—a powerful means to serve their own ends. The largest manufacturers, formerly the leaders of the war against the working class, were now the foremost to preach peace and harmony. And for a very good reason. The fact is, that all these concessions to justice and philanthropy were nothing else but means to accelerate the concentration of capital in the hands of the few, for whom the niggardly extra extortions of former years had lost all importance and become actual nuisances. . . . Thus the development of production on the basis of the capitalistic system has of itself sufficed—at least in the leading industries . . . to do away with those minor grievances which aggravated the workman's fate during its earlier stages.'

This is not the place to discuss whether, or how far, the development which Engels here describes affords a basis for the condemnation of 'the Capitalistic System itself' with which he follows it, or alternatively for a justification of that. Nor could the young barrister standing on Mr. Maurice's doorstep be expected to speculate before he rang the bell on the possibility of these at any rate relatively salutary developments occurring spontaneously on such a scale and at such a speed as to make it superfluous for him to trouble his chaplain about the matter. The conditions as Ludlow knew them, and was moved to take issue with them, were not those of 1892 when Engels wrote his reminiscent Preface for English readers. (Ludlow had just retired after a life of service to the working class, from his post as Registrar of Friendly Societies at this date, yet still had another twenty years of vigorous mental activity before him.) He was living in 1846, in or near to the very conditions which Engels had just described to his German readers in the body of his book. He was not the sort of man to wait for economic progress to clean up the muck of a world which, as he believed, God had

made and man had marred, or to counsel either the Church to
which he belonged or the workers in whom he trusted to do so.
And it is certain that he would not have agreed in 1892 that the
'concessions to justice and philanthropy', to secure which his
whole life had been dedicated, would all have come about any-
how as 'means to accelerate the concentration of capital in the
hands of the few'. It so happens that we have a record of his
impressions of the transformation in the conditions of the people
given in this very year in evidence before the Royal Commission
on Labour. 'I think', he said, 'the condition of the working
class has changed immensely, but not so much, I am happy to
say, as the change in public opinion on the subjects relating to
that. I find now that boys and girls fresh from school are at a
point of advancement in relation to this question which in 1848
we could not bring grown-up people to. I think the change has
been something perfectly marvellous.' Even allowing for the
optimism common in advancing age, we cannot but agree with
him. The Hungry Forties of the nineteenth century have been
repeated in many parts of Europe by the Hungry Forties of the
twentieth century, when industrialism has dissipated its vast
inheritance in two great wars largely because it has not learnt
how to overcome its contradictions without such cataclysms.
But in 1892, though the accumulation of that inheritance was
already provoking dangerous international rivalries, the outlook was still encouraging; and not crumbs only but whole
loaves and even a few cakes were falling from the rich man's
table. Nor was it only a careless affluence which accounted for
the flow. However 'naughty' the 'Nineties may have been,
they were not lacking in social compunction, and so much
'leisure and good feeling' had been brought to bear on 'destitution and vice' since Ludlow's errand of 1846, by Settlement
worker and benevolent employer, and more indirectly by reforming legislation, that to the more complacent and superficial
churchman the 'social question', as men were still wont to call
it, might seem to have found its answer. That the Guild of Saint
Matthew and even the Christian Social Union were clamouring
for a very different sort of answer would not do much to shake

such a one's conviction that grave social abuses were a thing of the past. But he would not have been very ready to admit that either Communist agitators like Engels or Christian reformers like Ludlow were to be thanked for it.

It is not difficult for men of a conservative habit of mind to admit that progress has been achieved in the field of social and economic relations. They may even stress the matter in support of the suggestion that the process has gone far enough. It is not so easy for them to face the fact that these victories were won as the result of the efforts of those stigmatized by their contemporaries as dangerous agitators, as even temperamental conservatives like Ashley and Maurice were regarded by those whose complacency they disturbed or whose self-interest they threatened. It is perhaps partly for this reason that it has been so widely agreed to regard Progress as a strictly abstract and anonymous phenomenon. This view may be conveniently linked with the assumption that man never *is* but always *was* oppressed, the advantage of this thesis being that generous sentiments and liberal opinions can be combined with a conscientious resistance to current proposals for change. Most commonly of all perhaps does this outlook develop with the onset of age. It is related of a certain Gladstonian Liberal who had been an enthusiastic advocate of what were once regarded as radical reforms, that in later life he was found to be in strong opposition to all projects for social improvement. Being reproached for having receded from his former standard of enlightenment and zeal, he warmly rebutted the accusation. 'The situation to-day is entirely different', he declared; '*there were great abuses then.*' This is a conviction to which men often come who might not be prepared to state the matter in such clear-cut terms. They are carried forward, whether by emotion or by reason or by both, into movements for the removal of 'abuses'; time goes by and the abuses are removed. They are by then at an age when generous sentiment, sanguine expectation and civic energy arise less spontaneously within them. They recall clearly enough that there were 'abuses then'; it is much less easy for them to admit, or even to perceive, that there may be abuses now. Ludlow thought in 1892 that 'the change has been something perfectly marvellous', as indeed it had, but he at least did not suppose that no further changes were necessary, and he kept his reforming ardour to the end.

The removal of obvious abuses, however, is seldom sufficient for the solution of basic problems. Dr. Gloyn, in his acute 'study of Anglican theory from Coleridge to Maurice', has pointed out that 'the problems which eighteenth-century development presented to intelligent and sincere nineteenth-century churchmen are the problems most disturbing to churchmen to-day'. These he enumerates as the secularization of life fostered by Rationalism; the relations of Church and State; the effect of the Industrial Revolution in breaking up what had been in large measure a functional order and producing the confrontation of the 'Two Nations' described by Disraeli; and the re-emergence, despite this, of the idea of the Nation. Reflection does indeed suggest that the spectacular events of this century, which have ushered in what is in effect a new phase of Western civilization, the Post-Christian era, are in large measure a logical consequence of the fact that these problems have gone for more than a hundred years unsolved. Perhaps the accumulated consequences of human error in Church and State were such by the middle of the nineteenth century that they could not have been solved. But at least they could have been faced; and faced not only in the realm of principle, as they partly were by this school of Christians or that, but on the plane of action. It is a main significance of the little movement which the Christian Socialists set on foot that they grappled with the abuses of their day as and where they found them, not as devoted Christian individuals, but in the name of the Church to which they were not afraid to claim that such a task had been entrusted. Others may have made a diagnosis more profound; others again may have discovered action more effective. But in an age of prophets, priests, poets and reformers, the group round Maurice found in a specific need a unique vocation. A gulf yawned between God's Church and God's poor, and they proved their fidelity by bridging it.

❧ III ❧

THE SEVEN YEARS: 1848–1854

(a) *1848 and Charles Kingsley*

The year 1838, a grave moment in the fortunes of England's new industrial society, was marked by two events between which it can have occurred to few of those who noted them to trace a connection. The People's Charter, a programme for the political enfranchisement of the masses excluded from the benefits of the Reform Bill of half a dozen years earlier, which had been elaborated by a group of eminently law-abiding London artisans, was publicly promulgated, and at once became the focus of an agitation which brought this country nearer to social revolution than it had been before or was to be again. The other event was less spectacular: the Chaplain of Guy's Hospital published a book, subsequently described by his biographer as 'a vindication of the position of the Catholic Church as the "spiritual Constitution" designed to maintain both human and divine relationships'. The connection between Lovett's Charter and Maurice's *Kingdom of Christ* was certainly not obvious. The man who was most clearly to perceive that connection was then an undergraduate in his first year at Cambridge, whose attention, understandably enough, had not yet been much given to such matters. Six years later Charles Kingsley wrote to Maurice, 'to your works I am indebted for the foundation of any coherent view of the word of God, the meaning of the Church of England, and the spiritual phenomena of the present and past ages'. And in 1849, amid the ruins of a decade of proletarian hopes, he could face an audience with the declaration: 'I am a Church of England clergyman—and I am a Chartist.'

E   65

Maurice to Temple

It was a declaration notable rather for its courage than for its accuracy. In fact Kingsley's enthusiasm for the Charter, and for a good many of those who clamoured for it, was severely restrained. 'You regarded the Charter as an absolute end', he makes one of his characters say in *Alton Locke*; 'you made a selfish and self-willed idol of it. And therefore God's blessings did not rest on it or you.' Yet for all the scoldings and lecturings of the working classes in which Kingsley felt it to be his duty to indulge, both in this novel and elsewhere, his deep understanding of their ideals and of their longings, and the solidarity that sprang from them, is evident, and it is chiefly this which prevents *Alton Locke*, despite its interminable soliloquies, its rhapsodical disquisitions and its impossible dialogue, from being altogether unreadable. 'Hunger and hatred', says Mr. G. D. H. Cole, a sympathetic historian of the period, in his *Chartist Portraits*, 'these were the forces that made Chartism a mass movement of the British working class', and the statement is true as far as it goes; but Mr. Cole would be the first to insist, as he has been the latest to make plain, that there was much more in it than that. All that was connoted by the word 'Chartism' was the dream of thwarted and desperate men, yet a dream it was nevertheless and not merely a blind mass-impulse. But as Kingsley makes Alton Locke say, 'to understand the allurement of that dream, you must have lain, like us, for years in darkness and the pit'.

In 1848 the significance of much that was implicit in Maurice's book of ten years before became plain, and its relevance, alike to the hopes and to the disillusions of the time, called those who perceived it to action. 'Almost the whole of Maurice's social teaching', says Dr. S. C. Carpenter, 'is found in principle as early as *The Kingdom of Christ*,' but what might have seemed academic on its publication could appear so no longer. Men like Kingsley and Ludlow might well have recalled such a passage as that towards the end of the book in which Maurice pleaded for an understanding of the plight of a generation which the Faith was failing to illuminate, or even to reach:

'Men feel that they are not merely lost creatures; they look up to heaven above them and ask whether it can be true that this is the whole account of their condition; that their sense of right and wrong, their cravings for fellowship, their consciousness of being creatures having powers which no other creatures possess, are all nothing. . . . If religion will give us no explanation of these feelings, if it can only tell us about a fall for the whole race and an escape for a few individuals of it, then our wants must be satisfied without religion. Then begins Chartism and Socialism and whatever schemes make rich men tremble.'

It was not only rich men who trembled in 1848; the whole state system of Europe, and much of its social order, were in convulsions. Maurice demanded that all this should be seen not as a merely political phenomenon but as one having a profound religious significance. 'Do you really think', he wrote, 'that the invasion of Palestine by Sennacherib was a greater event than the overthrowing of nearly all the greatest powers, civil and ecclesiastical, in Christendom?' Neither Maurice's temperament nor his philosophy was of a kind which would lead him to welcome revolution merely for being such; but he saw that amid the turbulence and destruction abroad in Europe, there were ideas and forces which were potentially constructive because they appealed rather to the higher than to the lower instincts of men. This theme was the burden of that letter which Ludlow wrote to him from revolutionary Paris, and which had, as he later declares, 'a very powerful effect' on him and on that course of sermons on the Lord's Prayer which he was then preaching at Lincoln's Inn. When Ludlow returned all barriers were broken down between them, and as national excitement rose to fever heat with the Chartist threat to march on Westminster, they prepared to meet whatever might be the upshot of the dreaded clash with a new word spoken in the name of the Faith and of the Church. And then, on April 10th, just as Ludlow had hastened to Paris two months before to see what truth its Revolution held for mankind, Kingsley rushed to London. The two men met and went together to witness the fiasco of Kennington Common, on that 'day to be forgotten—and forgiven', as Kingsley makes Alton Locke describe it, when the Charter went ignominiously to Westminster in a cab through the rain, and the heart went out of England's revolutionary movement, which was not to know revival for forty years.

In that moment Kingsley and Ludlow saw that the workers' defeat was the Church's opportunity. There was a vacuum to be filled, and what I have now to speak of is the noble effort to fill it made during the next seven years, from Kingsley's famous Placards of April 12th, through *Politics for the People*; through the conferences with the Chartist workmen ('they seem', wrote Maurice, 'to think very much of a clergyman being willing to hold conference with them in a friendly spirit, though they are accustomed to meeting Members of Parliament'); through the *Tracts on Christian Socialism*, and the launching of the trade associations, down to the establishment in 1854 of the Working Men's College. It is a heroic story, still too little known, even by those who should know it best, and who shall say what might not be the situation of the Church to-day if her response had been such that the effort could have been sustained? For the vacuum which was left by the collapse of Chartism was in the event filled by no religious movement, but by two crystallizations of a secularist materialism, the clash between which has done so much to bedevil the human situation since 1854. On the one hand there was the new capitalist prosperity, on which for the first time every class in the community began, in some degree, to cash in. And on the other, the challenge to it, half idealist and 'apocalyptic', half envious and power-hungry, which was at this moment promulgating its programme in the *Communist Manifesto*, and which we see to-day triumphant across a sixth of the world, the ghost of capitalism sitting crowned upon the grave thereof. A great opportunity for the Church of England offered itself for a moment in 1848. Three men perceived it, and stood together so far as might be to seize it. Their gifts were complementary, but in this year of revolution it was the fiery zeal of the young country rector which counted for most of all.

It is not altogether easy at this time of day to look back with any great liking on Charles Kingsley. He was perhaps the first of that long line of Impatient Parsons which Anglicanism brings upon itself from time to time by its surrender to shallowness and complacency, but who are themselves too much bounded by characteristically Anglican limitations to know where to look or upon what resources to draw to combat the evils which arouse their impatience. Kingsley had indeed a better hold upon the essentials of the Christian faith than his more irresponsible utterances might lead us to believe. Taught by one whom he never ceased to call his 'dear master', his religion never fell away into mere humanitarianism; he believed that 'the powerful and working element' in the Bible 'is just that which Christendom in all ages has held it to be—the account of certain "noble acts" of God, and not of certain noble thoughts of man'. He could say, like a contemporary Barthian, that

'If all that a man wants is a "religion", he ought to be able to make a very pretty one for himself, and a fresh one as often as he is tired of the old. But the heart and soul of man wants more than that, as it is written, "My soul is athirst for God, even for the living God".'

Kingsley was orthodox enough in essentials; he could even describe himself to his curate as an old-fashioned High Churchman, and this man declared that 'I have never known anyone speak more emphatically and constantly of the value of the Creeds and the efficacy of the Sacraments' and that 'his belief in Revealed Truth deepened and increased'. When we are tempted to see in Kingsley only a naturalist in a surplice, we should remember not only that he said—rather surprisingly—of himself, 'I am nothing if not a Priest', but that he was in fact, year in, year out, a devoted pastor to his people, and a notable preacher to the most diverse congregations.

But as we read his letters and listen to him speaking, we find ourselves wondering whether his recklessness, his intolerance and his astonishing provincialism can be excused as only the defect of his qualities, or whether what we salute as his zeal, his courage and a certain engaging Englishness are merely the happier aspects of fundamental weaknesses of spirit and of mind. His almost neurotic aversion from the ascetic element in religion led him to the perpetration of such extraordinary judgments (if that is the word for them) as those contained in a letter to Mill in 1870 in which he says that 'Christianity was swamped by hysteria from at least the third to the sixteenth century' and that 'there will never be a good world for women till the last monk ... is civilized off the earth'. His curious but all too characteristically Victorian combination of a 'Nordic' racialism with a governing-class condescension could lead him to declare that 'a French peasant grows up in barbarism and superstition. . . . No gentleman—and worse—no lady speaks to him or his from the cradle to the grave; and his civilization is impossible.' It is difficult to believe that anyone could inscribe a poem of welcome to a 'wild north-easter' if he had not ulterior reasons for attaching almost mystical value to anything Norse, or could stigmatize a range of mountains as 'Popish' because it ran down the middle of a country of whose system of ecclesiastical government he violently disapproved. This racial obsession crops up in the oddest places, as in the famous Placard to the workers of April 1848, in which he addresses them as 'Workmen of England! *Saxons!*' as if this very dubious derivation gave them some special title to what those 'men who are drudging and sacrificing themselves to get your rights; men who know what your rights are better than you know yourselves' were promising them.

Ludlow is commonly said to have collaborated in the production of this Placard, but it is difficult to trace his hand in it, for Ludlow was essentially a democrat, whereas the whole tone of the document is 'trust disinterested reformers of the governing class to know what is good for you and to get it'. If the 'Young England' group had not broken up by 1848 one might surely expect to have found Kingsley allied with it, for he was much closer to its spirit than to that of Ludlow and Neale, who were prepared, against whatever disappointments, to work alongside and even within the workers' movements, movements which Kingsley never really trusted. 'The only advice I can give', he said to a working-class inquirer in 1856, 'is, Emigrate but never *Strike.* . . . I am very sad about all these matters; but all I can recommend is, *peace* and making the prudent use of wages when they are to be got'. This is hardly the sort of counsel likely to inspire an oppressed class with the passion to achieve its liberation; and it is perhaps significant that he gave it in the same year as he wrote the famous epistolary poem to Tom Hughes proclaiming it the role of 'honest Englishmen' to 'help lame dogs over stiles'. This, indeed, Kingsley was always ready to do; he never turned away from an appeal, least of all an appeal from an underdog; but when such a dog got on its own feet and showed some determination to jump over the stile itself, Kingsley was apt to become alarmed.

Impatient Parson, Muscular Christian, 'Blue Domer' ('I am not fond, you know, of going into churches to pray'), proponent of a 'British Christianity', apostle of social benevolence—Kingsley sometimes appears as the originator of all the fallacious and unbalanced enthusiasms by which so many good men in the Church of England have been misled and so much laudable energy has been dissipated. But one familiar charge against him cannot surely be made with justice. It is sometimes suggested that Kingsley deserted the movement he had done so much to launch, and deserted it because he had lost faith in it. He himself, at the end of his life, complained that 'Radical Cockneys howl at me as an aristocrat and a renegade'. We may have our reservations about Kingsley, but charges of desertion will hardly bear examination. It has to be remembered that Kingsley was neither a professional theologian (though he conscientiously and sometimes disastrously sought to be an amateur one), nor a trained social reformer, nor had he lived long in London whence 'movements' are, more or less, necessarily controlled. Maurice was a theologian and a teacher and could continue to be so whatever happened to the social experiments he had inspired. Ludlow, Neale and Hughes were laymen of independent means, in a position to pursue their vocation of service to the working class, as they so nobly did, in good times and bad, until they had largely contributed to put the workers' movements on their feet. Kingsley was a country priest; he had the care of the rural poor under his direct charge, and he refused to separate the care of their bodies from the care of their souls in an age when there were none too many who were concerned to look after either.

We may laugh a little at the spectacle of the rector marching round his parish with great bottles of gargle to help his people ward off the new menace of diphtheria, or refusing to pray for fine weather because he believed that a wet season was needed to drain the land and forestall a return of the cholera he had seen work such dreadful havoc. Such interests and activities do not contribute much to the development either of Christian sociological thought or of democratic movements. But Kingsley had said all he had to say on purely social topics by 1851; *Yeast* and *Alton Locke* were worth-while not because of their artistic merits (which are not high) but because they came just when they did and their message came home to men's hearts and minds as it did. Endless repetitions of them would have been intolerable and unreadable—and unread. Parson Lot had had his smack at the Political Economy of Mammon in *Cheap Clothes and Nasty*, and though he showed himself more respectful to the 'science' in his latter years, he never took back a word of that. We can surely forgive him for saying in 1857, 'Politics and Political Economy may go their way for me. If I can help to save a few thousand working people and their children I may earn the blessing of God.' And because in the twentieth century sanitary reform no longer seems a very exciting subject, are we to say that he did not?

More interesting is the question whether Kingsley lost the social faith which animated him in early years. There is no real evidence of this. For what was that faith? It was certainly not a faith in democracy—whether as we in England understand the word now, or as such a man as Ludlow understood it then, for Kingsley had never shared that faith. In the famous Placard of 1848 he urged the workers to trust for leadership to such as himself, 'men who know what your rights are better than you know yourselves'. He was not really interested in their movements, as Ludlow and Neale were; he was more concerned that they should unite, as he urged, with the Church and the gentlemen against the shopkeepers and the Manchester School, than that they should unite with each other, and he was as suspicious of the trade unions as any other member of his class at that time.

The Seven Years: 1848–1854

His sometime curate believed him to be 'democratic in his opinions rather than in his instincts . . . when he advocated democratic measures, it was more as a means to an end than because he altogether liked the means'. Tom Hughes has an interesting passage in his Prefatory Memoir to *Alton Locke* in which he explains how unhappy Kingsley was made by finding himself at odds with the aristocracy to which he temperamentally, and in some degree by birth, belonged, and by having to mix with 'reckless and eccentric persons' such as were drawn to the Co-operative Movement, which nevertheless 'entirely approved itself to his conscience and judgment'. That approval he never withdrew. Some years after the breakdown of the Associations he said, 'the failure of a hundred schemes would not alter my conviction that they are attempts in the right direction. . . . For it is my conviction that not self-interest, but self-sacrifice, is the only law upon which human society can be grounded with any hope of prosperity and permanence.' The antithesis was not indeed a very illuminating one, for both motives may and should have their place in man's economic action, individual and corporate. But seeing that this was the conviction which had led him to take the stand he had taken nine years before at the cost of considerable unpopularity (the incurring of which he disliked more than most of his colleagues) and that he never went back on it, criticism of Kingsley as a deserter can only be based on a misunderstanding of what was in fact the cause in which he had enlisted and the spirit in which (whatever its limitations) he had done so.

Not only did Kingsley retain his faith in that capital article of their belief which he and his colleagues called 'the principle of association', but he applied it in a direction beyond that to which it occurred to them to apply it. The Christian Socialists were not really interested in politics in either the wider or the narrower sense, though Maurice had the makings of a truly organic political philosopher and Tom Hughes lived to become a Liberal M.P. Kingsley was like them in this; there are scarcely any references to what we should commonly call politics in his correspondence, and the few that refer to current political controversies do not suggest that he had or wished to have much to contribute to them. But there is a passage in that Preface to the 1854 edition of *Alton Locke* addressed 'To the Working Men of Great Britain', which does show evidence that Kingsley might have had something of consequence to teach in this field if he had thought out the matter more clearly. He has been saying, almost in his old vein, that 'the Charter, now defunct, was just as wise and righteous a "Reform Bill" as any which England has yet had or was likely to have'. But he goes on:

'I frankly say that my experience of the last five years gives me little hope of any great development of the true democratic principle in Britain, because it gives me little sign that the many are fit for it. Remember always that Democracy means a government not merely by numbers of isolated individuals, but by a Demos—by men accustomed to live in Demoi, or corporate bodies, and accustomed, therefore, to the self-control, obedience to law, and self-sacrificing public spirit, without which a corporate body cannot exist: but that a "democracy" of mere numbers is no democracy but a mere brute "arithmocracy", which is certain to degenerate into an "ochlocracy" or government by the mob, in which the members have no real share.' Kingsley is saying this by way of rebuke to the workers for wasting their 'endurance and courage' in strikes instead of 'developing the organization of the Trades Unions into its true form, Association for distribution, from its old, useless and savage form of Association for the purpose of resistance to masters'. This is disappointing, not because Kingsley shows here his failure to perceive the limits of the Co-operative movement in the liberation of the workers from the wage system, for these limits were a good deal more difficult to perceive than they are now, after a century of experience. It is disappointing because Kingsley makes no differentiation between the economic and the political function. That there are lessons of civic value to be learnt by all attempts on the part of groups of men to handle affairs for themselves is no doubt true; but a nation is not a multiple store, and the problem which modern democracy has certainly not yet solved is how to get men in large numbers to think in any true sense politically, i.e. with that minimum of informed objectivity about affairs of which most of them can have no direct experience which the exercise of a truly responsible share in government demands. Kingsley's apprehensions of a 'brute arithmocracy' may have had their origin less in a purely disinterested apprehension of the manipulation of a 'massified' public opinion and more in that governing-class-consciousness by which he was so thoroughly permeated; but he spoke more truly than he knew, or could know, in an age when the techniques of mass hypnotism had scarcely begun to be developed. But it is perhaps worth remarking that of the four focuses from which such political capacity as the working class displayed as it developed in the half century between the date of Kingsley's Preface and the appearance of the Labour Party as a substantial element in parliamentary life, the Co-operative movement was perhaps the least important. Trade Unionism, instead of being the 'old useless and savage form of Association', which was all that Kingsley could see in it, became a veritable complex of 'Demoi'; the Nonconformist bodies contributed much; Local Government still more. It may indeed seem curious that Kingsley should have had nothing to say about local government in this context, though we must remember that its democratic opportunities at this date were far fewer than they are to-day. For though local politics set men problems distinct from those presented by national politics, they are problems of a political order. If in 1854 statesmanship—and the sort of 'statesmanship' which was allowing Aberdeen and Lord John Russell at this very moment to blunder into perhaps the most superfluous war in English history—was necessarily assumed to be a permanent monopoly of aristocrats, a man of foresight might at least have perceived the possibilities of self-government latent in the control of those affairs which lay within the view, and largely within the experience, of men whom in other respects even Kingsley was prepared to trust with no small measure of responsibility. Nevertheless, his perception that a true democracy cannot be merely 'atomistic' and that the essence of an authentic social structure is not an individual franchise but the vitality and

inter-action of 'associations', spontaneous or functional or both
—this was substantial truth of the kind to which the liberal
democrats of his age, as of our own, were dangerously blind.

But as we look back on him now we may be led perhaps to
decide that it is not as a theological or a social or a political
teacher that Kingsley has his chief significance. Indeed that
Sanitary Reform which has sometimes been held to have seduced
him from the sterner pursuit of social justice, may actually reveal
to us what was his most original contribution to the thought of
the movement with which his name will be for ever linked. For
Kingsley, uncertain as a theologian, limited as a poet, diffuse as
a novelist, capricious and sometimes preposterous as a historian,
at once too reckless and too cautious as a reformer, was by grace
a devoted pastor and by every instinct a naturalist. When he
said in 1859, 'I am tired of most things in the world. . . . I shall
try henceforth to teach a sound theology through physics', he
was obeying a genuine intuition, indeed four years earlier he
declared that 'my theological creed has grown slowly and
naturally out of my physical one'. This was the sort of theology
he understood; one which too many of his contemporaries
neglected; one which with the re-emergence of Natural Law
concepts among theologians is only to-day being rediscovered.
But Kingsley had the right instincts about it. Already in *Yeast*
he is taking the landlords to task for their treatment not only
of their tenants but of their land.
'Had our forefathers had no more enterprise than modern landlords, where should we all have been at this moment? Everywhere waste! Waste of manure, waste of land, waste of muscle,
waste of brain, waste of population—and we call ourselves the
workshop of the world!'
His hero speaks of
'that huge black-mouthed sewer, vomiting its pestilential riches
across the mud . . . hurrying to the sea vast stores of wealth,
elaborated by Nature's chemistry into the ready materials of
food,'
and another character asks,
'Did I not warn you of the folly and sin of sinking capital in

foreign countries while English land was crying out for tillage, and English poor for employment?'

Such passages, owing to the recovery of a viewpoint disastrously submerged by the forces Kingsley was combating, strike quite a contemporary note, though their religious implications are only very incompletely and confusedly drawn out in the novel. But Kingsley could be much more explicit on the matter than this. He is always telling those who will listen to him that not only is God's revelation to be sought in the working of Nature but that His laws are to be looked for there. 'Nature', he told the Ladies' Sanitary Association (a delightfully Victorian title) 'is fierce when she is offended and kind when she is obeyed.' For him, sanitary reform represented not only service rendered to man but obedience due to God.

It is surely this element in his outlook on society which led Kingsley, seemingly alone in the group, to express serious misgivings about industrialism. Maurice never seems to have concerned himself with the question, while the rest appear to have accepted without hesitation the view of their time that large-scale production was in itself essentially a beneficent process, which only worked out badly (in so far as it did so) because men did not handle it in the right spirit. Such a view was not unnatural in a movement of Londoners, most of whom probably saw little or nothing of the great industrial hives of the north. Poverty they knew indeed, for London had plenty of that to show, and they worked devotedly to discover its causes and to assuage its consequences; but they did not see much of the effect of the great new machines upon the men whose life it was to feed them before they could feed themselves. Kingsley was a countryman, full of joy in the vocations and skills of the countryside, however bitter he might be at its injustices, and the contrast between these and the mechanical servitudes revolted him. As he says in his letter to a mill owner in 1862:

'That large bodies of men should be employed in exclusively performing day after day the same minute mechanical operation, till their whole intellect is concentrated on it, and their fingers kept delicate for the purpose, is to me shocking. . . . When I am told that the Lancashire system is perfect and ought to be permanent and helped towards permanence by the alms of a whole nation [the State aid called for in the cotton famine of 1862] I answer: it is not perfect at all. It is fortuitous, exceptional, transitional.'

'Fortuitous, exceptional, transitional'—here is the kernel of Kingsley's diagnosis. He saw the factory system as it had developed under the influence of a purely secular valuation of wealth—and of man—not, as most of his contemporaries did, as an irresistible manifestation of progress, which might yet be held in certain particulars to need reform; he saw it as something in itself abnormal. Kingsley was not an uncompromising 'ruralist'. He would not have said, as some of the more impetuous devotees of the 'husbandry' school to-day come near to saying with Jefferson, that 'generally speaking, the proportion which the aggregate of other classes of citizens bears in any state to that of its husbandmen, is the proportion of its unsound to its healthy parts and is a good enough barometer whereby to measure its degree of corruption'. But as he travelled each year in the late 'sixties from his country rectory to fulfil his duties as Canon of Chester, through the appalling spectacle of the Black Country, as he brooded on what he saw and heard of Liverpool, then in that diocese, his instinctive revulsion against the Manchester School was reinforced by the evidence of his senses. The outspoken sermon on 'Human Soot', given at Chester in 1870 on behalf of the Kirkdale Ragged Schools, is one expression of this; yet more striking is a deliverance in the following year:

'We had better, instead of boasting of our empire over Nature, take care lest we do not become parasites too troublesome to Nature, by creating, in our haste and greed, too many great Black Countries through which I have too lately passed, and too many great dirty warrens of houses, miscalled cities, peopled with savages and imps of our own mis-creation: in which case Nature, so far from allowing us to abolish her, will by her inexorable laws abolish us.'

It is in such words that Kingsley shows that, deceived as he was by many things on which he had to rely upon his intellectual judgment, he was not deceived by what his eyes revealed to him. The industrial system he was urged to admire appeared to him a violation of God's law for nature and for man, and what he saw he was not afraid to proclaim.

(b) *Maurice and Christian Socialism*

The great place taken by the three leaders of the movement has almost obliterated the memory of most of those who collaborated with them, though these were both more numerous and more notable than is now remembered. Some, like Tom Hughes and like Septimus Hansard, whose subsequent work at Bethnal Green is one of the slender links with the later movement, were Rugbeians, and others who were not could nevertheless be numbered amongst those whom Mr. G. M. Young, in his *Victorian England*, has described as 'the Arnoldians',
'a new type issuing from the Universities and public schools, somewhat arrogant and somewhat shy, very conscious of their standing as gentlemen, but very conscious of their duties too, men in tweeds who smoke in the streets, disciples of Maurice, willing hearers of Carlyle, passionate for drains and co-operative societies, disposed to bring everything in the state of England to the test of Isaiah and Thucydides, and to find the cause of all its defects in what, with youthful violence, they would call the disgusting vice of shop-keeping.'

Yet in so far as they were truly 'disciples of Maurice' they became something more significant and more profound than 'Arnoldians'. Dr. Raven is right in stressing that 'the true centre of their fellowship and the source of their strength lay, as they were the first to insist, not in the quality of their members so much as in the spiritual basis of their work'. And, humanly speaking, this was established and maintained by that great man under whose leadership they worshipped Sunday after Sunday in Lincoln's Inn Chapel and studied each Monday evening the word of God as he interpreted it. These meetings, Dr. Raven insists, were 'the effective symbol of their unity, the means whereby they received their inspiration . . . as the experience of God came into their lives the bonds which united them one to another became holy, and the venture upon which they were embarked was transfigured into the splendour of a crusade'. Thus it was that they came to feel for the man whom they plainly acknowledged to be their 'Master', 'a loyalty and an affection such as has been given to few in all the ages of the Church'.

It is the more important to insist upon the degree and the character of Maurice's leadership in that he lacked almost all the qualities generally held to be requisite for such a position. Ludlow called his self-distrust 'almost morbid', and his sensitiveness to his own shortcomings was such that coarser spirits, reading his self-reproaches, are sometimes puzzled to know what it can have been that he was making such a fuss about. To be conscious thus of 'guilt within' may be characteristic of those who fain would serve God best, but it does not breed the sort of self-confidence on which leadership is most commonly founded. Linked with this distrust of himself was an equal distrust of all formulations, or 'systems' as he was wont to call them; but without some such crystallization of conviction it is not easy to found a movement, yet if this be abjured how is propaganda to be spread and action to be taken? Maurice had a hatred of what was purely academic and he desired both propaganda and action, yet he shrank from sanctioning the instruments through which they could alone be put in hand. Again and again he imposed checks upon the enthusiasms which he had himself provoked, and interfered in the projects of more practical spirits in a manner that in any other group would have been resented as high-handed. The fact that high-spirited men like Kingsley and Ludlow, to name but two, not only submitted to leadership of this sort but accepted it as inhering naturally in the relationship in which Maurice stood to them, is a measure both of their master's own greatness and of the grace which his example and his teaching had nourished in them.

For this little group recognized, as did so few of Maurice's contemporaries, what manner of man he was. 'Among all the Churchmen of the nineteenth century', wrote Dr. Raven, nearly thirty years ago, 'it seems certain that we shall reckon him as incomparably the greatest, alike in life, in vision and in achievement.' If this is not certain yet, however, it may be partly because we are still too near to that century to establish such valuations, partly because estimates of this kind involve comparisons of the incomparable. Some may think that in a final assessment Maurice will stand with that one of his contemporaries who might seem in so many respects his antithesis; some may think that a synthesis of Newman and Maurice, impossible in human terms, may nevertheless be attainable in principle, and that if so attained, it would represent the highest which nineteenth-century theology and churchmanship could bequeath to succeeding ages. What is certain is that the stature of Maurice has increased in our time and will not henceforward diminish. Mr. Woodward says with justice that though he 'was as brilliant as he was sincere, he was too restless and spread his work over too many subjects'. This would be a fair criticism of a man who was seeking artistic excellence or scientific truth, but Maurice was after something very different from these. 'He was consumed', says Dr. S. C. Carpenter, 'with a passionate desire to follow and be led by the whole truth of God'; and he adds, 'his mind and soul were worthy of the great vocation'. It would be difficult to say more of any man. The essence of Maurice's teaching, and a clue to the revival of interest in it at the present time, is contained in another dictum of Dr. Carpenter: 'The increased willingness of modern Christians to recognize that it is not what we do but what God is doing that matters, I trace, in large measure, to the influence of Maurice.' And a younger theologian, Dr. A. M. Ramsey, finds his special importance to lie in the fact that 'while he fell foul of the advocates of the "isms" of his day—"churchism", "evangelicalism", "liberalism" alike—he is now seen to represent in a remarkable way the unity which they were missing'. 'He was able to be a pioneer precisely because he refused to succumb to the modernisms of his time.'

It is noticeable that those who find themselves most at home in parties commonly feel—and exhibit—a greater resentment towards those who do not belong to them than to their opponents who do. The period from 1835 to 1870 in which Maurice's life as a theologian and as an educator was passed was one in which party feeling ran exceptionally high in religious circles, and Maurice earned the animosity of men of every school primarily by not belonging to any of them. It would be untrue to say that this animosity was altogether unprovoked. 'My own nature', he said, 'is very prickly and disputatious'; and though he seldom or never attacked men for the positive beliefs they held, he was very wont to criticize them for failure to appreciate the truths held by others. His object in this was essentially eirenical; 'it is a hard case', he said once, 'to feel oneself at war with everyone when you wish to reconcile everyone'. But he wished to reconcile them by raising their controversies to a higher level—spiritual, moral and intellectual—than they were willing, or perhaps in some cases able, to attain. And men are seldom the more loved for attempting that.

Many of those who attacked Maurice did so sincerely, though often under misapprehensions, and misapprehensions which they did not take sufficient trouble to remove. Many more attacked him from motives the baseness of which was revealed by the complete unscrupulousness of the methods to which they resorted. Yet as one studies his life one is led to the conviction that these attacks are most frequently attributable to the fact that Maurice was trying to make men do what they are so reluctant to do—and Englishmen perhaps most of all—to look at things for themselves as in fact they were and not as it was convenient to imagine them to be. In short, he was trying to make men think, and think to a purpose; for though no one could have been by temperament less of a man of action, it was action that he looked for. And in nothing was he more admirable than in this —that he was never afraid to back up those whom he believed to be acting rightly on the inspiration which he had given them.

'To exclude the Divine Word and Will from any subject, however secular', says his disciple Llewelyn Davies, 'was as little possible for him as it would be to a naturalist to exclude gravitation from any class of physical phenomena.' Thus the affirmations about what the law of God required in the sphere of social justice, which came early in Maurice's career as a controversialist, were as essentially theological as were those that led to or arose out of the more spectacular disputations which followed later. And the clue to Maurice's attitude in all his theological struggles, with its weaknesses as well as its strength, is to be found in his conviction that the alignments in which the religion of his day had come to be involved, and which most of its exponents were content to accept without challenge and even without scrutiny, were essentially false ones. 'He saw', says Masterman, 'the good at cross purposes with the good, party attacking party, the Church bare and leafless in the frosty weather with no prospect of a second spring.' There can be no greater trial to such a man as Maurice was than the sense of frustration which comes from the realization that not the words only, but the very concepts which represent to him the most precious and fundamental realities are being used and understood by those of his own household in a sense different from or even opposed to that which he attaches to them. It is this experience which infuses Maurice's controversial methods with so much emotion, and at times gives them an almost rancorous tone. When he found the religious press of his day interpreting that Eternal Life which was for him the ever-present reality above all others, here and hereafter, merely as 'a very, very long time', and relying upon the idea of Hell as a threat to terrify the poor into social submission and moral conformity; when he found Mansel interpreting Revelation as a sort of heaven-sent dope for the disappointments attendant on man's inveterate curiosity, instead of as God's loving response to man's thirst after Him, 'as the hart panteth for the waterbrooks', Maurice was not merely rendered impatient, as any man may be who finds a cherished prejudice contradicted. Nor even was he simply dismayed and cast down, as one is who finds himself wounded in the house of his friends. He was tortured beyond endurance to discover that those who sincerely believed themselves to be calling upon God should be (as he felt) in reality calling upon the Devil, and in doing so be leaving the multitudes whom the Church was summoned to feed unsatisfied and astray in a wilderness of doubt and despair, or still worse perhaps, complacent in a prison of pride and self-sufficiency. Again and again in the violence with which Maurice hurls himself upon those who seem to him to be traducing the truths of God in the name of God, we hear an echo of Blake's frustrate defiance of his antagonist:

> *Both read the Bible day and night,*
> *But thou read'st black where I read white.*

In 1848 the bitterest of these experiences lay still in the future. But in the effort to affirm the theological basis for the claim that God's law must rule in economic relations no less than in any other sphere of human life, we find Maurice fighting, as always, for fundamental realities as he saw them, even at the risk of appearing to run counter to assumptions accepted by those who might have been expected to be his allies. 'The notion that wise and good men were set to work to make an improved society out of their own ideas was one which he repudiated with all his energy', says Llewelyn Davies, 'and he did not care what bewilderment the repudiation might cause.' He would not endure that men should ask, 'ought not human life *to be* founded on the principle of mutual help'. The question was, '*is* it not so founded?' Maurice is here contending for a basic and too often forgotten Christian truth, that God has acted before man is called upon to act, and that therefore His word is given to man first not in the imperative but in the indicative mood. The Kingdom of God, declared Maurice, is not to be thought of as an ultimate consequence of sanctified temporal effort; it has been planted by the great acts of God, alike of Creation and of Redemption, in the very nature of things as constituted by the Father, and reconstituted by the Son, and maintained by the Holy Spirit. Maurice is always returning to this point, and in a well-known letter to Ludlow, written in relation to a controversy occurring at the height of the movement's activity, he

proclaimed it as his mission 'to show that economy and politics
. . . must have a ground beneath themselves, that society is not to
be made anew by arrangements of ours, but is to be regenerated
by finding the law and ground of its order and harmony, the
only secret of its existence, in God.'

Ludlow, he feared, might think this 'an unpractical and un-
christian method'; to him it was the only one that made action
possible, 'and Christianity anything more than an artificial
religion for the use of believers'. And the paragraph concludes
with this characteristic sentence:

'The Kingdom of Heaven is to me the great existing reality
which is to renew the earth and make it a habitation for blessed
spirits instead of for demons.'

'The great existing reality': in this phrase is the core of all
Maurice's social teaching. 'When people told him that competition was the law of the Universe,' says Dr. Carpenter, 'he replied
not that it was an evil law which must be remedied, but that the
statement was a lie.' Am I wrong in thinking that in all this we
have a clue to the relevance which this Victorian theologian is
being found to have for our day in his assertion of what is implied in a Christian doctrine of Natural Law? At any rate I am
not alone in this speculation: it receives support from a somewhat
unexpected source. The socialist historian, Max Beer, himself no
Christian, quotes Maurice's dictum that 'God's order seems to
me more than ever the antagonist of man's systems. Christian
socialism is to my mind the assertion of God's order.' 'This', he
says, 'is a remarkable sentence; it translates a natural law doctrine into Christian terms.'

So regarded, the 'Christian Socialism' of 1850 is seen to be
something rather more significant than the effort of a handful
of benevolent clergy and barristers to instruct the working class
in 'the principle of association'. Nor is Maurice to be regarded
as a sort of nineteenth-century Wycliffe, the Morning Star of
a collectivist Reformation. Language can easily mislead those
who study the genealogy of social movements; indeed, it is too
seldom realized that one of the problems confronting those who
seek to gain a true historical perspective derives from the

changing significance of key words. Parliament was not the same thing in the sixteenth century as it was in the nineteenth century. Yet much of the historical writing of the latter period proceeded on the (largely unconscious) assumption that it was. Similarly Socialism in 1848 did not mean what most people take it to mean to-day, and Maurice, in deliberately adopting the term 'Christian Socialism' two years later, did not mean what the 'Society of Socialist Clergy and Ministers' would mean to-day by similarly describing its aims. It is not that the term was less likely to be unpopular then than it is now. Indeed it was likely to be a great deal more so; it is difficult for anyone born in this century to realize the sheer courage shown by Maurice and Kingsley in adopting such a description of themselves. It was not taken precipitately; for the first eighteen months the group was generally content to speak of 'the principle of association'; and Masterman, in his study of Maurice, says that 'the title was apparently adopted with a desire to offend the maximum number of persons on both sides'. But this is to under-rate, not indeed the courage of Maurice, but his intelligence. He gives us his reasons for deliberately taking the title and there is plenty of shrewdness in them.

'It is a great thing', he wrote to Ludlow in January 1850, 'not to leave people to poke out our object and proclaim it with infinite triumph. "Why, you are Socialists in disguise." " 'In disguise': not a bit of it. There it is staring you in the face upon the title page!" "You want to thrust in ever so much priestcraft under a good revolutionary name." "Well, did not we warn you of it? Did we not profess that our intended something was quite different from what your Owenish lecturers meant?" This is the fair play which English people like, and which will save us from a number of long prefaces, paraphrases, apologetical statements which waste time when one wants to be getting down to business.'
Maurice knew that there was a 'conflict which we must engage in sooner or later with the unsocial Christian and the un-Christian Socialists', and by adopting this designation he hoped to do something to spike the guns of both sets of enemies.

The Seven Years: 1848–1854

But what did Maurice mean by 'Socialism'? He certainly
meant something a good deal more concrete than that 'new
spirit in industry' which has done duty as a definition of Christian social principle at so many Rotary Club lunches. 'We did
not adopt the word Christian merely as a qualifying adjective',
he said once, and in the first of the *Tracts on Christian Socialism*
he declared roundly that 'the Socialism I speak of is that of
Owen, Fourier, Louis Blanc—of the Englishmen, Frenchmen,
Germans, who have fraternized with them or produced systems
of their own'. This no doubt sounded pretty alarming to the
respectable churchgoer of 1850. But what is the common feature
of these systems? Social historians might be a little puzzled to
define it, but there is one phrase in which they would be very
unlikely to define it and that is State 'ownership of the means
of production, distribution and exchange'. It is doubtful whether
Maurice ever read the *Communist Manifesto* originally drafted
by Marx and Engels for an obscure group of revolutionary
refugees at the end of 1847, but he would not have found much
about the State in it if he had. For Socialism in those days did
not signify a set of economic dispositions made on behalf of the
people, whether by the State or by anybody else. It meant that
the working class, or some association thereof, should undertake
something for themselves. That is what Maurice and Ludlow
were after, and it is not only what they liked to talk about; it is
what they set out with their working-class friends to initiate and
to promote. It is as far as they saw at all clearly, and if we can
perceive more easily now that 'association', as they envisaged it,
could never cover more than a part of the field, and that perhaps
an inevitably diminishing one, we can surely admire them for
acting on the convictions they had rather than waiting until
they had evolved an elaborate system which would be likely
to have no very close relation to those convictions. Maurice seems
to have seen no farther than a rather rudimentary sort of profit-
sharing where large-scale industry was concerned. True, he
thought that the association of the workers with an enterprise
would check the prevalent tendency to 'extravagant and ruinous
speculations'. 'If a healthy tone is restored to these occupations

87

by the unspeculative labourer taking the main interest in them, I must think that the benefit to morality will be very considerable.' In an age like our own, in which the plutocrat is more concerned in dodging risks than in incurring them, this reflection might not seem to be of great importance. It was much to the point in 1850, when the irresponsible hunt for profits was ruining both many a small investor and much of our loveliest countryside.

Time does not suffice to re-tell the story of the Trade Associations, nor is this necessary. It is a story which belongs rather to the history of Co-operation than to an outline of the development of Christian social ideas. The associations are important for our present purpose, however, for two reasons. In the first place, their establishment amidst so much difficulty and discouragement is evidence that the men round Maurice were not content to stop at the enunciation of principles. 'It is now', wrote Ludlow, in the fifth *Tract on Christian Socialism*, 'our business to show by what machinery the objects of Christian Socialism can, as we believe, be compassed; how working men can release themselves from the thraldom of individual labour under the competitive system; or at least how far they can at present by honest fellowship mitigate its evils.' Maurice, so often hesitant in action, was convinced that a practical experiment of this sort should be made. He wrote to Kingsley in January 1850:

'I do not determine that wages may not be a righteous mode of expressing that relation [of employers and employed]. But at present it is clear that the relation is destroyed, that the payment of wages is nothing but a deception. We may restore the whole state of things; we may bring in a new one. God will decide that: His voice has gone forth clearly bidding us come forward to fight against the present state of things; to call men to repentance first of all, but then also, as it seems to me, to give them an opportunity of showing their repentance and bringing forth fruits worthy of it. This is my notion of a Tailors' Association.'

It was natural that the group should start their experiments with tailoring. Attention had been called to the appalling conditions of sweating prevalent in this occupation by Henry Mayhew's articles in the *Morning Chronicle* in the previous year, an exposure which formed the basis for Kingsley's terrific onslaught on the Political Economy of Mammon in *Cheap Clothes and Nasty*, which Maurice had just read in manuscript, and which was published later this month, January 1850. A few weeks later still the Tailors' Working Association began its chequered career.

But the Trade Associations are significant, however, not only as evidence of a practical spirit among their promoters, but for the form which the experiment took. This was pre-eminently due to Ludlow, for whom the association of workers as producers had always a spiritual implication. 'Consumption', he said, 'is the merely human element in life; production is the divine. God is the Eternal Producer.' And more than forty years after the foundation of the first association he wrote, 'the condition of the wages-receiver is not to me an ideal one for the worker. It is a sort of washed-out slavery.' Thus twenty years before the emergence (or more truly the resurrection) of Guild Socialism, and in the very heyday of Fabian collectivism, Ludlow was proclaiming his unshaken faith 'that production should be carried on by the Trade Unions. That has been my ideal for the last forty years; ever since I thoroughly understood what a Trade Union was. That is what we old Christian Socialists preached to the Amalgamated Engineers of 1852.' This reference is a valuable reminder that some at least of the Christian Socialists did not confine their interest to small-scale production and self-governing workshops. The leaders of the best organized workers of the day, William Allan and William Newton of the newly formed A.S.E., were their enthusiastic associates, and before the great lock-out in the engineering industry in 1852 were preparing for an ambitious experiment in trade union control of a Liverpool ironworks. Indeed, it needs to be emphasized that the group round Maurice was no mere handful of dilettante gentlemen dabbling in matters of which they knew only by report. Before they attempted any practical experiments they had made close contacts with Owenite socialists like Lloyd Jones, who became in effect their organizing secretary, and

Chartist workmen like Walter Cooper, Joseph Milbank and Thomas Shorter. If Ludlow's inspiration, on its secular side, came from observations made in France rather than in England, he lost no time in making contacts with the co-operative movement in the north where similar experiments to his own were being set on foot by a group working for the 'Redemption of Labour' by 'setting the members to work both on the land and in self-governing workshops provided by their own capital'.

Despite the devoted efforts of Ludlow and of Vansittart Neale, who sank a fortune in the experiments, the Associations failed. Their extinction has sometimes been absurdly described as 'the failure of Christian Socialism', as if the validity of the religious challenge to an amoral plutocracy could be disproved by the incapacity of a handful of ill-educated workers to struggle against the enormous momentum of a society organized to elicit the energy and enterprise not of the many but of the few. It is rather curious, and significant perhaps of a certain bias, that so much stress has been laid upon this particular failure, for indeed all the efforts of working men to organize their own activity as producers had failed and continued to fail for decades. These failures were primarily due to causes more far-reaching and difficulties more obstinate than any lack of discipline, prudence and even honesty such as was natural enough in a class treated as the English proletariat had been for more than half a century. But these faults undoubtedly played their part in the matter, and it seems the more unreasonable, therefore, of so fair-minded a social historian as Mr. Cole to complain, as he does in his study of *A Century of Co-operation*, that 'the Christian Socialists aspired to convert the working classes to an impossibly high moral code, and to a theological approach to industrial problems which most working men were quite unprepared to accept'. No doubt Maurice and his associates earnestly desired, as such convinced Christians would naturally do, to persuade as many as would listen to them that it was the Faith which inspired them that alone offered a sufficient foundation for the establishment and maintenance of social justice.

The Seven Years: 1848–1854

No doubt their convictions, fortified as time went on by their experience, would lead them to emphasize the view that without integrity, industry and even on occasion self-sacrifice, men working on good principles in a society indifferent or hostile to these could not hope to make headway against those working upon evil ones. Even so inveterate an optimist and so strong an anti-Christian as Owen, came in his later life to the same conclusion. But to suggest that the associations failed mainly because their promoters demanded of their members an exalted virtue and a strict theological conformity is a travesty of the facts.

In what sense, then, if any, was the movement of 1848–1854 a failure? In some respects it obviously was not so. Concrete achievements, like the Industrial and Provident Societies Act of 1852, and the foundation of the Working Men's College, albeit this was all too soon diverted from its promoters' purposes, arose directly from the energies it generated. More important, however, were its long-term effects. Dean Stubbs, in his book on Kingsley, was perhaps claiming too much, both for Maurice and for the Church, when at the end of the nineteenth century he wrote, 'it was the doctrine of Maurice which for forty years kept the whole forward movement in the social and political life of the English people in union with God and identified with religion'. Yet the link between Church and people had been re-forged in these years, and at the very point where the connection had grown weakest, and it was never again broken. Ludlow, Neale and Hughes maintained to the end of their careers their connection with the workers' movements; Maurice himself continued to labour in the cause of their education; a slum priest, Septimus Hansard, carried the message into Bethnal Green; an Eton master, William Johnson, better known as the poet William Cory, became the teacher of two boys, contemporaries at the school in the early 'sixties, in whose hands the movement came to life again thirty years after 1854, through Stewart Headlam in the Guild of St. Matthew and Scott Holland in the Christian Social Union. Maurice's 'theocratic principle', that 'the Will of God should be recognized in all human affairs, public or private' must have seemed to his old associates through the 'sixties and 'seventies to be at best but a seed growing secretly, but grow it did, though little showed as yet above the surface.

Yet on a narrower, more immediate view, that the movement was a failure cannot be doubted. It was not the collapse of the workers' associations which really mattered, but the continued apathy, worldliness and sectarianism of the nation's church. To the great mass of the 'faithful' the Christian Socialists appeared as a handful of cranks and agitators led by a heretical eccentric. The religious public preferred to concern itself with the biological speculations aroused by the teachings of Darwin and the ritual prosecutions arising from what were thought to be the doctrines of Pusey. Moreover, industrial prosperity was setting in, and though the mass of the people did not enjoy very much of it, the worst scandals were over, and the ticklish question of social justice could safely be left in abeyance. 'The Church directly, and as an organized body', says an American historian, Mr. D. O. Wagner, of the period following 1854, 'had a distinctly minor part in the readjustment of society made necessary by the contemporaneous industrial changes . . . the control of Church affairs continued to be in the hands of a class, and of a class, moreover, which was little conversant with the special necessities of the new order. A long process of contact and education was needed before the requirements of the situation could be brought home to them.'

What is the central idea bequeathed to us by the movement which Maurice inspired? There is but a single contribution to our hymn books from the group which learnt what Maurice had to teach, and it is significant perhaps that this should have for its theme not justice nor pity, but truth. Tom Hughes in this hymn, too seldom sung, is calling upon God to lead men to repudiate the unrealities and evasions as a consequence of which His creation finds itself 'enslaved by sin and death'. It is a Maurician note that is struck here, and with the lines which follow this chapter may be not unfitly closed:

Set up Thy standard, Lord, that we
Who claim a heavenly birth

The Seven Years: 1848–1854

May march with Thee to smite the lies
That vex the groaning earth. . . .

Then God of truth, for whom we long—
Thou who wilt hear our prayer,
Do Thine own battle in our hearts
And slay the falsehood there.

Yea, come! then, tried as in the fire,
From every lie set free,
The perfect truth shall dwell in us,
And we shall live in Thee.

✠ IV ✠

SEED GROWING SECRETLY: 1854–1884

With the foundation of the Working Men's College in 1854, the 'Christian Socialist' movement, strictly so-called, is generally held to have come to an end. The statement is true so far as it goes, but it can easily be given a most misleading interpretation. To suggest that Maurice and his followers, dismayed and disillusioned by the failure of the Associations, put the whole matter of social righteousness out of their mind and never gave another thought to the subject, is to imply that their efforts made no impression and their teaching bore no fruit for a full quarter of a century. This would involve a state of things so inherently improbable that only the strongest evidence could render it credible. In fact, of course, there is no such evidence, and students of the subject may at first be puzzled to understand how such an impression has nevertheless been spread. Yet the explanation is simple enough. We are commonly accustomed to assess the significance and even (it may be suspected) the validity of ideas and truths by the extent to which organizations arise to formulate and contend for them. With the dissolution of the Council of Promoters of Working Class Associations the Christian Socialists lost the only organization to which their movement had given birth, though indeed its functions were rather practical than propagandist. Maurice's hatred of societies and 'systems' had not encouraged his followers to form what current jargon would describe as an 'ideological' organization, and after 1854 no body with a specific concern for 'Christian social' matters existed till Stewart Headlam founded his little parochial guild in Bethnal Green at the end of the 'seventies. Hence a student of the Christian Social Movement is tempted to regard the thirty years after 1854 as a sort of Desert of Gobi across which he must contrive to make his way somehow with what speed he can muster, with little hope of any interest in the landscape and with scarcely an oasis on the journey.

But organizations are not the only vehicle for a movement of ideas, and if we keep our eyes open as we travel from 1854 to 1884 we shall not find our journey unprofitable. In fact, of course, the intrepid caravan which set out so adventurously in 1848 did not give up its quest or lie down to die of despair in desert sands. Maurice never lost touch with his disciples of earlier days. In 1861 and 1862, under the impact of the disturbance caused on the one hand by the publication of *Essays and Reviews*, and on the other by the fashionable heresy of the moment, Auguste Comte's Positivism, the group drew together to publish a series of *Tracts for Priests and People*. Maurice, who contributed one of his most characteristic statements of political and social belief under the title of *Do Kings reign by the grace of God?*, was joined by both Hughes and Ludlow, and by Llewelyn Davies, who was perhaps the most influential of the more theological Mauricians and was to have much to say about the Church's relation to social problems in the coming years. The main purpose of the series was, however, apologetic and I have cited it primarily to show that the group which formed itself round Maurice in and after 1848 did not subsequently lose contact with him or with one another.

What was happening in these years, from the standpoint of our subject, was a twofold process, well summarized by Mr. G. C. Binyon in two phrases—Socializing Christianity and Christianizing Socialism. The latter task was undertaken, with slightly varying emphasis, by Neale, Hughes and Ludlow. Of Neale it has been said, with little, if any exaggeration, that the Co-operative movement is his monument, and Brentano described him, on his death in 1892, as 'a unique man . . . a hero and a saint'. He was less deeply committed than Ludlow to the principle of Producer's control and much less disposed to regard a conscious religious orthodoxy as necessary to safeguard the ethical character of co-operative principles and their application. We may prefer Ludlow's judgment in these matters and think it to have been verified by events, but we can never forget how much Neale gave, both of money and energy, to support the Associations while any possibility of their survival remained, or his subsequent lifelong service as Honorary Secretary of the Co-operative Union. The work of Hughes was more various; perhaps his most notable service to the working class was given on the Royal Commission on Trade Unions at the end of the 'sixties. Of Ludlow's great work on their behalf, which was especially valuable in the legal sphere, I have spoken already. More important perhaps than the practical services these men performed was the influence, right through these thirty years and beyond them, of their faith and witness as Christian laymen during a period in which the Church showed so slight an interest in the secular preoccupations of the mass of the English people.

Socializing Christianity was naturally the concern rather of theologians and priests. Here Maurice's influence was, of course, pre-eminent, but as the Golden Age of Victorian capitalism settled down upon the country in the 'sixties he became, unlike almost all his contemporaries, not less but more alarmed about the moral foundations of nineteenth-century civilization. That the principles upon which this civilization was based should appear, if only temporarily, to be succeeding inspired him to an almost apocalyptic vision of doom. It seems to me that Maurice in the 'sixties, in the metropolis of a triumphant commercialism, surrounded by a new race of confident scientists and optimistic Positivists on the one hand, and a new class of prosperous capitalists and their ever less discontented because more secure employees on the other, and yet able to see and proclaim how hollow and transient was the spectacle, is an even more significant figure than the 'Christian Socialist' of a dozen years earlier. Indeed, this role of Maurice irresistibly recalls that of another Londoner of those days. Maurice and Marx were sundered as far as two men could be in their philosophy of life, yet they were alike not only in their moral but in their intellectual repudiation of the claims implicit in the dominant principles of their age. Other men detected flaws in the capitalist system: Maurice and Marx, almost alone at that time (for Carlyle's jeremiads had their basis rather in emotion than in any process of reasoning) saw that capitalism contained within itself the seeds of its own decay. In 1867 the first volume of *Das Kapital* pronounced its doom. Three years later, almost within a year of his death, Maurice wrote to his son:

'It seems to me sometimes as if the slow disease of money-getting and money-worship, by which we have been so long tormented, must end in death, and though I do believe inwardly and heartily in a regenerative power for Societies as well as individuals, the signs of its active presence here are not yet manifest to me. Neither in Conservatism nor Liberalism as I find them here, can I see what is to make the dead bones stir and live.'

We must allow something for the influence of old age upon a temperament never disposed to take a sanguine view of current affairs, and no doubt a more confident note required to be sounded if the challenges of the immediate future were to be met. As Maurice fell silent other voices began to be heard which could be interpreted as in some sense 'socializing Christianity'. Already in 1864 Westcott, then a master at Harrow, who had been studying Comte, had declared that 'we claim then, by our Christian faith, that the sphere of religion be recognized as co-extensive with the utmost bounds of human thought and knowledge, while at the same time it is dominated by a moral purpose which springs from sympathy or love'.

Westcott, when he came to live in a less academic atmosphere, was to make more memorable pronouncements than this, but Mr. Binyon thinks that the essay in which this appears can be 'regarded as the starting point of an endeavour to formulate a Christian sociology'. But before the schoolmaster became in due course a Bishop, a lesser man had won for himself a justifiable pre-eminence as 'having created a new type of episcopal eminence'. James Fraser, the 'Citizen Bishop' of Manchester from 1870, 'the prince and leader in every movement of civic progress, civic elevation, civic righteousness', is to be found declaring at the end of the period covered by this lecture that 'what was wanted was not so much to Christianize our Socialism as to Socialize our Christianity'. The antithesis is not free from that superficiality which is the special temptation besetting the episcopate and one into which this bishop not infrequently fell. Fraser was no Maurice, and whatever he meant by this declaration it was something a good deal less than Maurice would have meant. But he was facing in these years, with a most exemplary courage and energy, practical challenges which theologians do not have to face, and he never allowed a social issue to be withdrawn from Christian scrutiny and treated as a 'reserved subject' for economists and politicians. 'A dignified neutrality is not my attitude on any question I think important', declared Fraser; and in acting in the spirit of this declaration he recurrently challenged not only the conventions of the Victorian episcopate but the self-sufficiency of an increasingly secularist civilization.

But not long after Fraser reached Manchester, Victorian capitalism was to sustain some heavy shocks to its complacency. The situation a quarter of a century before, at the opening of the 'fifties, was very different. Victorianism was emerging from the clouds and beginning its triumphant ascent to the sunny summit of 1870. Other analogies are suggested in a passage from Mr. G. M. Young's Romanes Lecture on Gladstone:

'The difference I have often thought between the England of the last Chartist demonstration in 1848 and the Great Exhibition of 1851, is like the difference in one's feelings at the beginning and end of a voyage in wartime through waters beset by enemy ships. It is like the opening of the city gates after a long wintry siege: *hiems transiit, imber recessit*. . . It was in that Maytime of youth recaptured that Gladstonian Liberalism was conceived. It was the only atmosphere in which it could have been conceived, an atmosphere composed in equal measure of progress, confidence and social union.'

If the 'social union' came slowly it was already promised by the new form of the workers' organizations. 1851 was the year not only of the Great Exhibition but of the 'new model' kindred-craft trade union, the Amalgamated Society of Engineers, pioneered by Ludlow's friends, William Newton and William Allan, though these men dreamed at first of using it for ends more inspiring than the brigading of wage-workers to bargain about their terms of livelihood. As for the confidence, that was there already—the achievements of industrial progress appeared to guarantee it. In such a conviction the poet Charles Mackay wrote about this time:

> *Blessings on Science, and her handmaid steam!*
> *They make Utopia only half a dream.*

The fact that the achievements of science and her handmaid were making large tracts of England's lovely countryside only half habitable was not held, by those prosperous enough to live outside them, to conflict with this Utopian vision. The new industrialists were quite prepared to 'forget six counties overhung with smoke'. Sir Henry Slesser reminds us in his *History of the Liberal Party* that 'Bright boasted that he would always oppose such Smoke Abatement Acts as interfered with trade'. Public opinion was easily mobilized against anything which threatened to do that. We shall never understand the violence of the antipathy with which the ideas of a Maurice and the projects of a Shaftesbury were met until we realize that Accumulation was the unquestioned and almost exclusive purpose, for at least two full decades from 1851, of every class in England below the landed gentry who had no need for it, and above the miserable hordes of slum dwellers who had no hope of it. Twenty years before this Maurice had put into the mouth of a character in his early novel *Eustace Conway* a declaration that the 'dense commercial strength which one encounters even in your religion is a more overpowering nightmare upon the soul than any bad influence I have felt elsewhere'. These are strong terms, but, as we have seen, the forty years that passed after they were penned would not have induced him to a more optimistic diagnosis.

The drive for Gain had persisted, unhampered by religion, and even, as we shall see, stimulated by it; though it is necessary to remember that the vast economic effort of Victorian England had a complementary inspiration in the zest and stimulus which the building up of a great productive mechanism tends to generate. The Russia of the twentieth century, with its passionate enthusiasms over river-dams, tractor factories and even tube railways, mobilizing slave labour by the million, and at a ruthless cost in human life and happiness, for the cutting of a White Sea Canal, presents a suggestive parallel to Victorian England, a parallel scarcely affected by the substitution of a social for an individualist idolatry.

For two decades, with only minor and transient checks from the mysterious but not as yet too merciless trade cycle, the enterprise succeeded. In a phrase peculiarly characteristic of the time, England appeared to be growing 'rich beyond the dreams of avarice', if indeed any limits could be set to such insatiable fantasies. All classes, save the most depressed, shared in the developing prosperity, but the exception is of some importance, since, as Mr. Woodward emphasizes, 'below the level of organized and protected labour a great body of sweated workers hardly known to the "decent poor" or even to the skilled artisans lived in misery or semi-starvation'. These classes were to attain a social consciousness by the end of the 'eighties; till then they were conveniently banished from the recollection of all but the devoted priests and sisters who began in the 'fifties to labour among them. Above that level matters steadily improved, until 'in 1870 most working-class families were absolutely as well or relatively better off by about 10 per cent than in 1850'. In the same year British imports and exports exceeded in value those of France, Germany and Italy combined. Two years later the maximum extension of British agricultural activity was attained. We have reached the climax of Victorianism. With Disraeli's extension of the franchise in 1867 Britain is on the way to becoming a democracy. As a result of Forster's Education Act of 1870, her people will at least cease to be illiterate. Even social reform, so long regarded as an unjustifiable extravagance, is about to become permissible. The Workshop of the World is 'on the top of the world'. Few foresaw the great trade depressions just ahead, or the threat they carried to Britain that the world might soon be on the top of her.

What part in all this had been played by that Faith which, despite the emergence of Darwinians, Secularists, Positivists, and 'honest doubters' of a more tentative description, was still the sheet anchor of the majority of the nation? Its role in Britain's industrial development was in fact no negative one. 'No one', says Mr. R. C. K. Ensor, 'will ever understand Victorian England who does not appreciate that among highly civilized, in contradistinction to more primitive, countries it was one of the most religious that the world has known.' The vigour and versatility of Victorianism is reflected in its religion, and even if we confine ourselves to the Church of England, it is impossible to do full justice to it in summary generalizations. We may be tempted to dwell predominantly upon the higher levels—the transition from the cloistered saintliness of the Tractarians to the slum-defying heroism of the 'Ritualists' in clergy-house and sisterhood; the impulse to a new standard of church life given in so many directions by Samuel Wilberforce; church-building as inspired by Pusey; education as reinforced by men so different as Maurice and Nathaniel Woodard; theology as revitalized by Westcott, Lightfoot and Hort. The catalogue could be much extended, to leave us in a perhaps rather too complacent haze of thanksgiving. But from the standpoint of our subject there is less to be grateful for. Indeed the religion most characteristic of mid-Victorian England is an only too Marxian reflection of its economic values. Its aim was primarily to make good, in this world and the next, and to do good principally with an eye upon that. Its spiritual like its industrial discipline was one of rewards and punishments—here again we have a clue to the hostility which the challenge of Maurice inspired among the pious, to whom Eternal Life was much more like a post-dated cheque than an 'ever-present reality'. Yet this outlook, however deficient spiritually, had moral consequences of some value— including economic value. As Mr. Ensor explains:

'If one asks how nineteenth-century English merchants earned the reputation of being the most honest in the world (a very real factor in the nineteenth-century primacy of English trade), the answer is: because hell and heaven seemed as certain to them as to-morrow's sunrise, and the Last Judgment as real as the week's balance sheet. This keen sense of moral accountancy had also much to do with the success of self-government in the political sphere.'

Moreover, as Mr. Arthur Bryant, in his *English Saga,* justly insists, Victorian hypocrisy has been much exaggerated.

'There was no make-believe in the genuine piety of the English middle-class home. Ocasionally tyrannical and more than frequently oppressive—for the English seldom did things by halves—it was none the less the central core of life for a great body of men and women who represented between them the major portion of the wealth, power and activity of the world. It gave them regularity of habit, a rule of sober conduct that made them invincible in their narrow achievement, and a certain intensity of purpose that lent dignity and even beauty to their otherwise monotonous and ugly lives.'

But such religion was not free from an economic valuation. The Sabbath, for example, was justified by Macaulay in the House of Commons on its merits as an industrial asset, for during it 'a process is going on quite as important to the wealth of nations as any process which is performed on more busy days. Man, the machine of machines . . . is repairing and winding up.' It is a moot point whether the Victorian Sunday did not do more harm than good to the Faith to which it was so curiously dedicated by the reaction which its taboos provoked in the defenceless young upon whom they were imposed. Yet if its Christian value was dubious, its Spartan influence may have been in some respects salutary; and Mr. Ensor considers that 'the habit of setting apart one rest day in the week for religion and serious thinking deepened the character of the nation'.

Assuredly the Victorians did not fail in seriousness, but their thoughts were given a new turn, or more truly a jolt, by the Evolution controversy which began to develop in the 'sixties.

This ill-considered and too emotional debate, in which many otherwise sensible and even profound persons said many far from sensible and only too superficial things, might seem at first sight to have little relevance for our subject. Yet its handling by the mass of church people, intelligent and unintelligent, is revealing. It was seen that the researches of Darwin and their fruits were being employed to raise in a revolutionary form the ultimately theological question, 'What is Man?' But it was far less often seen that whatever answers biologists might provisionally propose to the question were irrelevant to the issues with which religion was essentially concerned. As a result of this myopia churchmen plunged recklessly into a field in which they neither had nor were authorized to assume any particular competence, that of biology, while continuing to neglect the sphere of sociology in regard to which the Church, as guardian of the doctrine of man, has a primary responsibility. The truth entrusted to the Church concerns not man's physical descent but his human nature, with its spiritual and social needs. Theologians were only too ready to be specific about what happened in the garden of Eden, while remaining extremely hazy about what was happening under their very eyes in the garden of England. They allowed themselves to become entangled in scientific arguments about Adam when they ought to have been challenging the almost unquestioned economic 'science' which derived from Adam Smith. With the triumph of the Industrial Revolution, the real problems, both moral and material, concerning 'the survival of the fittest' related not to prehistoric but to contemporary man. The form in which scientific fatalism was to prove really dangerous had nothing to do with the Missing Link. But as the 'seventies were about to prove, it had a great deal to do with the Trade Cycle and its corollary, the missing market.

What is the explanation of the Church's extraordinary blindness at this time to the significance of the economic forces which were not only menacing the spiritual status of man, but actually corrupting Christianity itself into a sanction for and a stimulus to the materialism it should have been actively combating? No single explanation will suffice, for the causes were indeed diverse. In the first place, we must remember that the social tradition of the Church had been utterly lost. It flickered out two centuries before in Baxter's *Christian Directory*. The arid latitudinarianism and political sycophancy of eighteenth-century religion had provoked reactions certainly, both within Anglicanism and without, but their leaders had been concerned either with individual spirituality or with doctrinal orthodoxy, or sometimes with both, and had assumed that the fruits thereof in personal benevolence would be sufficient for the alleviation of human suffering. The sociological significance of the Industrial Revolution remained unperceived by the religious consciousness; even the Christian Socialists never brought their minds fully to bear upon the subject. The paradox that increasingly social techniques were increasingly being exploited to enhance the power and prestige, not, as was claimed, of 'the individual', but of a particular type of individual, energetic and enterprising perhaps, but predatory and insatiable too—this was a matter in regard to which the clergy were only too ready to accept the soothing rationalizations provided by philosophers and economists they were in no way equipped to criticize. It has to be realized, moreover, that the economic morality of the Establishment itself a century ago was far from high. A caste system of opulent, comfortable and needy was represented within the sacred ministry by bishops, incumbents of 'good' livings, and the wretched curates, for whom at this time '£80 seems a standard salary'. Dr. Lowther Clarke, who arrives at this figure from a study of *The Ecclesiastical Gazette* for 1849–50, finds that in its pages 'the sale of advowsons occupies much space. The details are frankly shocking. . . . There is no sign that advowsons are being bought to safeguard a particular version of Anglican teaching; all is unblushing commercialism.'

Mr. Christopher Hollis, in a penetrating essay on *The Meaning of Anthony Trollope*, traces the spiritless character of the Church in the mid-Victorian period to another cause:

'Under the assaults of Whiggery, of revolution and agnosticism, of aristocracy and democracy, Anglicanism had already lost its nerve. The Church allowed the tacit assumption that the problems of the world could be settled without any overt appeal to Christian principles, to go unchallenged. They could be settled, of course, only because men had in them a very fair quantity of general decency, and it was the private opinion of pious Christians that this decency was the product of generations of Christianity, that, had there been no Christianity, people would have been far less decent. But that was a private opinion. It would have been bad manners to insist upon it too loudly or frequently.'

Moreover, as Mr. Hollis goes on to point out, 'in addition to Christianity there was also progress'. Much of the faith of the age of Tennyson and Browning was, if not exactly a faith in man rather than in God, at least a faith that man was being providentially piloted into an expanding happiness and prosperity by God. By this all-too-humanist theism Churchmen, and the clergy not least, were much infected; they faintly trusted a considerably larger hope of humanity than their forefathers had done. This essentially sub-lunar optimism, meeting and blending with the persisting worldliness of the traditional Establishment, goes far to explain the atmosphere of Barchester and its clerical denizens, whose connection with a realm of supernatural revelation seems as tenuous as that of the priestly caste of paganism in the age of Augustus. Trollope was himself a Christian of an undenominational sort, but as Mr. Hollis remarks, 'there has never been another writer so dominated by the bland assumption concerning clergymen, not so much that they were insincere as that they were quite uninfluenced by their professed beliefs. . . . He did not dislike the Anglican clergy because they were priests. It never occurred to him for a single second that they were priests.' And Mr. Hollis goes on to point out that 'Trollope's conception of a likeable clergyman' was the prelate of whom a friend said 'that he had known the Bishop of Elmham intimately for a dozen years and had never heard from the Bishop's mouth—except when in the pulpit—a single word concerning religious teaching'. Such tactful restraint in princes of the Church is hardly likely to inspire a Christian challenge to the dominant forces of their age.

The vast majority of their clergy, of course, had not even begun to suspect that any such challenge was called for. It was assumed that in a Christian country such as England traditionally was, only those forces could represent a danger to religion which openly presumed to question it. And in the 'sixties, with the arrival of Comte, Huxley, Holyoake and soon (most defiantly) Bradlaugh, there were already enough of them to engage the anxieties of those churchmen who allowed their complacency to be disturbed by any such matters. The great majority were content to know that the famous leaders who fought their political battles for them, and occasionally turned round to rebuke impious Darwinians or disrespectful critics of the Established Church, were themselves conforming churchmen. Even Disraeli, in whom something less might perhaps have been forgiven, was such, though the quality of his attachment to Christianity was perhaps a little dubious. 'To Dizzy', says his most fascinating biographer, M. André Maurois, 'the Church of England was a great historic force which had to be respected and maintained, but the idea that the slightest importance could be attached to the letter of its doctrines did not even faintly occur to him.' But his lifelong rival was the man whom Troeltsch has described as 'the great modern representative of Christian politics', the man who in his youth had produced a book which has lately, and I think justifiably, been used by Dr. Alec Vidler as an ideal basis for 'a normative study in the relations of Church and State'. The first edition of Gladstone's book appeared in the same year as did *The Kingdom of Christ*, and the teaching contained or implicit in it had much in common with that of Maurice. Gladstone in his Preface perceived the necessity 'to plead earnestly for those great ethical laws under which we are socially constituted and which economical speculations and material interests have threatened altogether to subvert'. This determination he never abandoned, though his relative indifference to social as distinct from political issues prevented his perceiving some of the directions in which it should have carried him. But by the time Gladstone was called to enter upon political office he was confronted with the dilemma of remaining faithful to his 'normative' idea or of so far abandoning it as to permit himself to act in a situation to which it could no longer be applied. Gladstone was ambitious, though in no disreputable fashion; he believed, with as much justice as ever man did, that his vocation was to politics; and he determined to do what he could in the situation in which he found himself without pretending to consistency with the ideas he had earlier expressed. 'By shaking off his antique doctrine of Church and State, and the Church as the conscience of the State', says Mr. G. M. Young of the Gladstone of the 'fifties, 'he had released his energy, full powered and whole-hearted, for his real business of secular statesmanship.' This perhaps somewhat exaggerates what in fact occurred; but whatever be the truth in a rather complex matter, 'the great modern representative of Christian politics' never ceased to embody an ideal, however at times deficient, of Christian statesmanship.

It was Palmerston, however, a man with considerably less claim to—and perhaps little ambition for—the title of Christian statesman, who in this period took the first initiative in social legislation. When the Presbytery of Edinburgh appealed to him to deal with the cholera in 1853 by the pious expedient of proclaiming a National Fast, Palmerston pertinently replied that 'the Maker of the Universe has established certain laws of nature for the planet on which we live and the weal or woe of mankind depends upon the observance of these laws', adding that if the people continued indifferent to sanitary reform, 'the sources of contagion . . . allowed to remain, will infallibly breed pestilence and be fruitful in death, in spite of all the prayers and fastings of a united but inactive nation'. The Presbytery of Edinburgh was shocked by such a response to their appeal, but we can be sure that Kingsley was delighted. Even the pious Shaftesbury was so, and he declared that 'I have never known any Home Secretary equal to Palmerston for readiness to undertake every good work of kindness, humanity and social good, especially to the child and the working classes'.

The enduring friendship between the worldly, even cynical Whig statesman and the pious Tory reformer is one of the curiosities of history. It has been acutely pointed out by Miss Florence Higham, however, that Shaftesbury had in common with Palmerston 'an unquenchable interest in facts and a liking for the common man', and he had found little enough of either in that 'aquarium full of cold-blooded life', as in his later years he described the House of Lords. Shaftesbury's 'liking for the common man' was indeed genuine enough in its way, though it arose partly as a reaction from an incompatibility with the worldlings of his own class, and partly from a certain satisfaction he derived, however unconsciously, from the affectionate gratitude and admiration of the humble folk in whose interests he so unremittingly laboured. 'As he grew older', say the Hammonds, 'he edged away more and more into the little world where city missionaries and devoted workers thought of him only as a lord, a leader, a fine patron for the causes they served, an Olympian peak, somebody beyond the range of criticism.' Shaftesbury, as we can view him now, is not beyond that range. His religion was narrow to a degree; his temperament, which he never overcame, was so basically unco-operative as to make Christian fellowship in any true form impossible for him. 'It was not a simple matter', says Miss Constance Smith, 'for this proud, reserved and sensitive man to work on equal terms with anybody.' Indeed, the historian of the Christian social movement must account Shaftesbury not only as standing outside it, but as by religion, social philosophy and personal habit essentially opposed to the possibility of such a thing. Yet his life was not only one of the most selfless that a public man has ever lived, it was also one of the most effective. To quote Miss Constance Smith again: 'an awakened public conscience, if it is not to spend itself in futile emotion, must find a channel of expression. Shaftesbury taught it to speak with the voice of law.' 'I cannot bear to leave the world with all the misery in it', he said, at the end of a life which had probably done more to relieve that misery than any lived in the nineteenth century. The only virtues which he would claim for himself, in retrospect at the age of seventy, were 'feeling, perseverance and conviction'. Yet if we translate these into theological terms as Love,

Hope and Faith we see that they are just the virtues that the Christian can least of all afford to be without.

'The Evangelical framework of his faith', says Miss Higham, 'saddled Shaftesbury with a creed less enlightened than that which his own life proclaimed.' How far it was in fact this 'framework', and how far it was the peculiarities of his temperament, which prevented this devoted man from even beginning to envisage, through a lifetime spent in social rescue and amelioration, any Christian philosophy of society, is perhaps arguable. The Evangelical tradition never failed to produce its individual saints of 'social service'. One who was to become famous in more picturesque spheres, and was indeed already a notable figure, undertook in the half-dozen years from 1865 what an admirer has described as 'the pioneer effort which in the end made the public conscience aware that there is little righteousness in a nation which, possessed of so much wealth, can tolerate that Youth shall be blighted in an atmosphere of poison'. 'Chinese Gordon', as this brilliant soldier was then so widely known, was stationed in these years at Gravesend, in command of the defences of the Thames, but the Captain of Engineers did not sit down and wait for an enemy. He found one for himself, and set about to combat it in truly Scriptural fashion. The sordid surroundings of Thames-side were damaging the moral and physical life of its juvenile population. Gordon 'brought boys to live in his own house, cleaned, fed and clothed them. Then he gave them instruction in the Eternal Verities in language they could understand . . . he schooled them also to be useful and then found them jobs with opportunity.' In an age when Youth is courted with so much solicitude in clubs and community centres, it may be difficult to realize that eighty years ago it was not so but far otherwise. Charity in those days had often to begin at home if it were to begin at all, and the first Gordon Boys' Home was Gordon's own.

Social service of such a kind is service indeed. But however plainly it may imply a criticism of the assumptions of the society that creates so urgent a need for it, social service does nothing to formulate one. The necessity, the desirability, even the possibility of such a formulation was still almost universally denied, whether explicitly or tacitly, by Christian opinion. 'The years between 1854 and 1877', says Dr. Donald Wagner, 'witnessed an attempt on the part of socially-minded churchmen to cure the ills of society by voluntary action. Reform was to be accomplished by stimulating either the benevolent sentiments of the powerful or the disposition of the poor to help themselves. . . .'

But

'while Churchmen fashioned voluntaryism into a social philosophy which was a kind of emasculated *laissez-faire*, they often accommodated their actions to a much more lenient standard—the principle of opportunism. State action as a method of reform was virtuously waved aside when it presented itself in the shape of a theory, only to be welcomed as an expedient when all other means had failed.'

Nevertheless a genuine social concern was growing up and developing in these years, especially in those circles touched by Tractarian influences. The new note in fiction introduced by *Mary Barton* and *Alton Locke* was sustained by less eminent novelists, many of whom were women who found in this form of literary composition a means of expression for their ecclesiastical enthusiasms. In some cases the accent is merely one of benevolence towards the deserving and submissive poor. But in one instance, at any rate, the interest goes a good deal deeper than that. Charlotte Yonge was one of the most effective propagandists of Tractarian principles that the movement ever had, and Brother George Every, who has made an extensive and intensive study of her novels from the sociological point of view, declares that the developing social outlook of this school was at once reflected and elaborated as the long line of them continued, dropping their earnest messages of Christian duty and social responsibility into innumerable country rectories and pious homes of the professional classes. At first, as in *The Heir of Redclyffe*, the note is 'pure Young England', but as time goes on the scope grows wider. A story of 1857 includes 'an unsuccessful attempt to expose the moral evils of investment in South America'. In

1860 the problem is how to treat a gin distillery as a form of responsible property. In the next year the story is 'dominated by a strong smell of bad drains', and this theme recurs in later tales. In 1873 comes the famous *Pillars of the House*, where poverty compels the hero to exhibit his traditional standards of squire-archial responsibility in the editing of a local newspaper. Factory reform crops up in *My Young Alcides*. We are long past the days when 'Puseyism' could be dismissed as a purblind concern with ecclesiastical detail.

With Pusey himself, of course, it had never been that. No man had a stronger sense both of 'the untold sufferings and privations of our poor' and of the peril in which the wealthy stood from acceptance of the standards of a godless civilization. Though he was wont for the most part to couch his admonitions and indictments in personal rather than social terms, there is one sermon at least in which he makes what amounts to a sociological judgment. The theme is Almsgiving, and Pusey is calling his hearers to consider 'Why Dives lost his soul'.

'Doubtless Dives encouraged the manufacturers of Tyre and Sidon, and the weavers of Palestine, while he bound not up the sores of Lazarus. . . . If he were uncared for, it was that there were not enough Dives to give employment to the poor. Miserable, transparent, flimsy hypocrisy. Were the employment of the poor our end, would they be less employed in manufacturing comforts for themselves than in weaving luxuries for us? . . . A reckless, fraudful competition, whose aim is to cheapen every luxury and vanity in order that those at ease may spend on fresh accumulated luxuries and vanities what they withhold from the poor, lowers the price of things we crave for by cutting down the wages of the poor.'

We can agree with Dr. Peck that this passage 'shows beyond dispute that his mind was engaged upon the contrast between the Christian ethic and the economic processes', and that he here 'places his finger upon the fact that capitalist industrialism was taking too large a proportion of the product of industry from the workers'. But we may feel, too, that the sociological tendency of this denunciation, if it is not just an exception to prove the rule of Tractarian indifference to social issues as such, is at least rare enough to tempt us to concur in Mr. Binyon's verdict on the school as a whole that 'they opened a mine of precious ore, but never properly worked it'. They vindicated the Divine authority of the Church; they laboured too little to elucidate the Divine will for a disordered world.

Amidst the most obvious disorders, however, the spiritual descendants of Keble and Pusey worked with a heroism hardly matched until their time. The world knew these men as 'Ritualists', and with an easy superficiality their opponents condemned them for an indulgence in 'empty' ceremony and 'meaningless' formalism. Even the early Tractarians themselves, and notably Pusey, were apt to be suspicious of what they felt to be extravagances. What these critics, whether hostile or friendly, failed to see, however, was that the slum priests, while offering against the background of their hideous surroundings glory to God in such splendour and beauty as they could command, were also bringing sustenance to the starved souls of those to whom they ministered, and understanding to their minds in the only way in which this could reach them. W. G. Ward had made this very point already in that passage in his *Ideal of a Christian Church* in which he set himself to answer the question how an ideal Church would act if suddenly placed in charge of an apostate nation. 'How loving and considerate [would be] her tenderness to the poor sufferers' of such a godless society. Included in such consideration would be the restoration of religious ritual, since

'Religious ceremonial, in other cases but an accessory (though a most important one), becomes in these an absolute essential; for in what other way can religious truths be possibly impressed deeply on those whose minds are worn down by unceasing anxiety and care, and whose bodies are exhausted with severe and protracted toil?' The 'Ritualists' were teaching not only through the ear but through the eye—even in 'extreme' cases through the nose—an illiterate race of social outcasts who could learn only with difficulty by more intellectual means amidst the hideous and odoriferous squalor of such places as London

Docks and Miles Platting. The worship of God in which they joined was, by the violent contrast to all else in their lives, at once a vindication of the other-worldliness of their faith and an implicit condemnation of the filthy environment amid which the social sin of an acquisitive and complacent ruling class had condemned them to live. So regarded, the ritual, which mainly centred round the Presence of our Lord amid surroundings more hostile than those of his very Nativity itself, was not 'empty' but full of a profound significance; not 'meaningless' but clamouring for an interpretation even more far-reaching than most of those who practised it knew how to provide.

But there was, of course, much more in the marvellous flowering of devotion and sacrifice exhibited by the Catholic revival than ritualism. 'Puseyism' is indeed a much better title for it, as we realize when we remember the missionary effort which Pusey himself prescribed for it:

'The Church herself ought to debate upon remedies and should not leave to individual effort the work of the whole. We need missions among the poor of our towns, organized bodies of clergy living among them; licensed preachers in the streets and lanes of our cities; brotherhoods or guilds which should replace socialism; or sisterhoods of mercy. We need clergy to penetrate her mines, to emigrate with our emigrants, to shift with our shifting population, to grapple with our manufacturing system as the Apostles did with the slave system of the ancient world.'

The heroes who first responded to this call, though as determined to rescue bodies as they were to save souls, were a little inclined to envisage these salvations as having no organic relation with one another and needing no social philosophy to inform and to reinforce them. But among the later figures a more radical strain appeared. To Arthur Stanton 'all human flesh was lovable and venerable because Christ had worn the human form, and therefore the most depressed ought to be looked on and looked after as saintly brethren in obstructed embryo'. Robert Dolling had no objection to describing himself as a Christian Socialist, and when challenged by his bishop, asserted

H
113

that 'he agreed with, had preached and must continue to preach' all that had been proclaimed by a visitor to his parish who bore the then alarming name of Stewart Headlam.

But it was not only in towns that the clergy were confronted with poverty and social injustice. Their responsibility was in fact actually greater in the countryside, since here their influence was traditionally far more extensive, and if they made no effort to tell the town-dwellers what were the circumstances of the workers in rural England it was unlikely that anyone else would attempt to enlighten them. Some did indeed make the effort besides the author of *Yeast*. Sidney Godolphin Osborne, rector of Durweston in Dorset from 1841 to 1875 and a brother-in-law of Kingsley, 'a philanthropist of a militant and almost ferocious type', bombarded *The Times* with letters on the subject over a period of more than forty years. James Fraser, who before his elevation to the episcopate had been a country rector in the diocese of Salisbury, reported to a Parliamentary Commission that 'the majority of the cottages . . . are deficient in almost every requisite that should constitute a home for a Christian family in a civilized community'. ' "Vain", say the clergy, "are Churches and schools till the people are provided with better houses." This statement I believe to be simple truth.' The intrepid E. D. Girdlestone, as Mr. D. O. Wagner relates, began his fight for the rural workers in Devon in the 'sixties, organizing, against violent opposition, an intensive migration in a largely successful attempt to raise wages. British agriculture was then reaching the summit of its prosperity, but the rural workers had small share in it. At the climax of that prosperity there flared up in the west and the midlands the agitation which, under the leadership of Joseph Arch, led to the formation of the National Agricultural Labourers' Union. Arch had left the Church of England and become a Primitive Methodist after seeing the simple folk of his parish having to wait their turn at the communion rails until the Sacrament had been administered to the 'quality'; the experience had made a deep impression on him, and he gave his agitation an anti-Anglican twist; the journal he founded included 'Freedom from Priestcraft' among its objects. This attitude needlessly antagonized many of the clergy, and gave the more unsympathetic among them a convenient pretext for hostility to his movement. The extent of this hostility is difficult to assess. An Oxford undergraduate of the period declared in his latter days that:

'The only time in my life when I was very strongly driven to desert the Church was at the outbreak of the agitation against Joseph Arch. The attitude of the Church towards Arch's movement was lamentable; the clergy and the well-to-do laity were deaf towards the almost inconceivable record of injustice which the movement voiced.'

This verdict of Charles Gore nearly fifty years later is hardly borne out by other evidence. In 1873 the Church Congress, meeting at Bath in the midst of the agricultural dispute, spent one day of its deliberations discussing 'The Church's duty in regard to Strikes and Labour'. Naturally the rural agitation bulked large in the debate, and speaker after speaker, including nearly all the clerical ones, not only displayed his sympathy with the labourers, but often recorded action taken on their behalf. True, the Bishop of Oxford (Mackarness) who was the leading speaker, was cautious and platitudinous, treating the problem as solely one of personal morality calling for a stronger sense of obligation between the classes, noting in conclusion that 'the Church's training of the youth of the whole upper class has been deficient in that very important part of it which makes the rich humble and instructs the superior to be considerate and kind'. But when he said that the clergy had not, and could not have, the requisite knowledge to enable them to judge in such a question as the labourers' agitation had raised, he earned the rebuke of a later clerical speaker who 'ventured to say that if the clergy have *not* the requisite knowledge they *ought* to have it', and in reply to the Bishop's declaration that the clergy had not been invited to interfere, affirmed that 'the clergy in the country districts ought not to have waited for an invitation in a matter which concerned the welfare of the great majority of those who constitute their spiritual charge'. A fighting speech on behalf of the principles of trade unionism was made by Llewelyn Davies, who asked, 'is there any reason in heaven and earth why the strength of union should be denied to those who most need it? . . . Is it for us who learn and teach from the New Testament, to give sympathy and aid to the better-off in keeping the worse out of power?' He made a telling point when he reminded the Congress that the Secretary of the Church Defence Institution was later to address the gathering, and asked, 'how do you think it must strike the labourers when they find that Bishops and clergy consider the man who is paid to agitate in defence of their wealth and privileges worthy of honour, but hold up to scorn those who try to get the poor man's wages raised from 10s. or 12s. to 15s. a week because—there being nothing else to say against them—they are paid agitators?' Girdlestone, now a Canon of Bristol, struck a deeper note. 'When I think', he said, 'of that last great day, when we must all meet together, rich and poor, learned and unlearned, master and servant, pastor and flock, for my own part I feel, and feel it terribly, that the man whom I shall fear most to meet on that great day is the labourer.'

He had less cause to fear this than most of his brethren. For the clergy, though not seldom sympathetic, were vacillating. They were the victims of economic shibboleths they had not been trained to probe or even to question, and of maxims restricting the Church to a purely 'spiritual' mission which should have revealed to them how sadly the lack of a truly Christian sociology hindered her members from arriving at a Christian judgment in concrete situations. This was the more serious in that the economic situation was changing abruptly for the worse in a quite unexpected manner. No doubt when Matthew Arnold wrote to Frederick Temple in 1869, 'the times, in spite of all that people say, are good, and will be better', he was not thinking primarily, if at all, of economic conditions. Yet he might have said the same if he had been, for no one then suspected that Britain's prosperity, on the basis of which Disraeli's government embarked upon its programme of social reform in the middle 'seventies, was about to sustain its gravest crisis since the 'forties. The American Civil War of the 'sixties, and the wars precedent to the establishment of the new German Empire, postponed the economic development of this country's greatest potential competitors, but by 1875 their competition began to be seriously felt. The old unquestioned predominance of the workshop of the world had come to an end; the countries to which she had been exporting her capital, her machinery and her skilled workers began to muscle in on her racket. That no one seems to have foreseen this inevitable consequence of a predominantly export economy only made its lessons the more difficult to learn; even to-day we can hardly be said to have learnt them. The industrial slump which hit Lancashire so hard in 1878, causing the benevolent Bishop Fraser so much moral distress and intellectual perplexity, was accompanied by an equally intense and far more prolonged agricultural depression, due to the novel competition of prairie-grown wheat. From this blow our countryside never recovered. Germany and France imposed tariffs to save their farmers; Disraeli as premier, despite his bitter opposition to the repeal of the Corn Laws thirty years before, made no effort to follow their example, nor did public opinion prompt him to do so. A reason for this, suggested by Mr. Ensor, is interesting. 'Country-dwellers', he says, 'were supposed to make the best soldiers. The continent wished to preserve them for conscripts; but, England not having conscription, did not care what became of them.' Whether a tariff would in fact have saved Britain's agriculture is doubtless arguable; that the nation as a whole did not consider the effort to save it worth while is undeniable, and is indicative of the degree to which the iron (and by this time the steel also) had entered into her soul. Blood she was content to leave to Bismarck.

The slump lasted from 1875 for a full fourteen years, with only a brief interval round 1881. In these years were born both the social conscience and the social protest, in stimulating each of which the spokesmen of the Church played no mean part. Where Maurice and Ludlow had largely failed, Samuel Barnett and Arnold Toynbee on the one hand, Stewart Headlam and Scott Holland on the other, did in a measure succeed. They arrested the attention of the Church and organized a challenge in her name. Toynbee Hall, projected at a meeting held in the rooms of a Balliol undergraduate, one Cosmo Gordon Lang, was founded in 1884. In the same year the socialist movement in England may be said to have begun with the foundation of the Fabian society and the acceptance of a somewhat diluted Marxism by Hyndman's Democratic Federation, founded three years before. Headlam's Guild of St. Matthew adopted a socialist basis in the same year. The story of these movements, so far as it concerns our subject, belongs to the period covered by the next lecture, but their roots are to be found in the 'seventies. In 1873 Barnett came to Whitechapel as vicar of St. Jude's, a parish described by his bishop as 'the worst in my diocese'. He at once set himself, as he afterwards put it, to 'open channels between eternal sources and everyday needs'. His understanding of the latter was perhaps stronger than his hold upon the former, but the scope and the influence of the work which he did was remarkable indeed. It has been described, not untruly, as 'the most constructive of all Christian social efforts in the nineteenth century'. Mr. Ronald Preston, the author of this eulogy, goes on to affirm that Barnett 'had too optimistic a view of the results of removing bad environmental influence'. It is an error to which those who see around them such conditions as then prevailed in East London are not unnaturally prone. It led to the settlement movement which, whatever its benefits to the poor whom it devotedly sought to 'raise', was a liberal education for the imported undergraduates, who thus learnt about the masses by living amongst rather than by reading about them. The moving spirit here was Toynbee, that 'radiant and beautiful figure', as Scott Holland called him, who 'gave himself from the political economy of the schools to the democracy of the streets' and whose influence in his short life was immense, not only on practice but on theory. 'In 1873', wrote a contemporary, 'the *laissez-faire* theory still held the field. . . . But within ten years the few men who still held the old doctrines in their extreme rigidity had come to be regarded as curiosities.' Lord Elton, who quotes this passage in his *England Arise!* holds Toynbee to have been largely responsible for the change.

'You have to forgive us', said Toynbee, addressing the poorer classes, 'for we have wronged you; we have sinned against you grievously—not knowingly always, but still we have sinned, and let us confess it.' But there were some, in the Church as well as out of it, who thought that something more than confession and forgiveness were needed; it was time, they held, for amendment, and personal service was not enough. It was in this spirit that in the year of Toynbee's premature death a famous and successful member of the professional classes made a striking gesture. William Morris affirmed himself a socialist, and early in 1883 joined Hyndman's Federation. Morris has been made the subject of an essay in a volume treating of 'Christian Social Reformers of the Nineteenth Century', but quite unjustifiably so, for he had no belief in supernatural truth of any kind. 'The aim of Socialism', he said in 1884, 'should be the founding of a religion.' But his significance for our subject is that he came into the socialist movement to recall to men just such truths as had, sociologically speaking, inspired the social practice of the ages of Faith. He challenged not only the distribution of wealth under capitalism, but the purpose of that economic activity which had become for his century an end in itself, and the modes by which the masses were compelled to engage in it. Industrialism, he declared, was 'keeping many thousands making *nothing* with terrible and inhuman toil'; if work was ever again to be pleasant and honourable the worker 'must have a voice, and a voice worth listening to, in the whole affair'. Morris is the greatest name in British Socialism; but his appearance there is really fortuitous. It was not politics, says Lord Elton, 'that was turning this man into a revolutionary: it was the Middle Ages.'

In 1877 Harrison Riley, the son of a Methodist local preacher, published half a dozen numbers of an obscure journal in Sheffield to preach Socialism as a contemporary embodiment of primitive Christianity, commenting that 'all true socialists feel that they have little time to waste either on theology or anti-theology'. In the same year a combative curate in Bethnal Green, Stewart Headlam, founded a Communicants' guild which should occupy itself with both, its first declared object being 'to get rid, by every possible means, of the existing prejudices, especially on the part of Secularists, against the Church, her sacraments and doctrines, and to endeavour to "justify God to the people".' The last phrase is Kingsley's; he had died four years before it was added on to the foregoing words in 1879, and there is no doubt that Headlam used it in a conscious effort to revive the impulse of Christian Socialism. This he was destined to do in significant fashion, for he blended with the message of Maurice, under whom he had sat at Cambridge, the Catholic heritage restored by the Tractarians. The seed growing secretly through so many years was now at last to thrust its shoots above the surface. Many had been the sowers, for the influences converging upon men of sensitive conscience and alert mind in 1884 were diverse, and not all were to prove so salutary as was then widely supposed. Ten years later the eponymous hero of these Lectures, who was to be a leader in much that was to follow, summed up the situation in the middle 'eighties in a passage with which, whatever may be thought of its syncretic deficiencies, I may fitly conclude.

'From every side windows were flung open, barriers were thrown down, we were ready for a call, and it came. From over the sea we began to be aware of a Social Philosophy which, however materialistic some of its tendencies might have become, has had alliance with the spiritual Hegelianism with which we had been touched. It took its scientific shape in the hands of Karl Marx, but it also floated across to us, in dreams and visions, using our own Christian language, and involving the unity of the Social Body and the law of love, and the solidarity of Humanity. It read out the significance of citizenship in terms that were spiritual and Christian. It challenged us to say why we were not bringing our creed into action as the true secret of all social well-being. Were we not engaged in asserting the pre-eminent value of the community over the individual by our faith in the Church? Were we not preaching the sanctity of human nature here on earth by our belief in the Sacraments? If we brought this creed to bear on Society, would it not show itself in the form of Christian Socialism, as Maurice and Kings-

ley had understood it in the 'fifties? We woke up to Maurice.
His influence, which had lain, as it were, alongside the Oxford
Movement, now passed within it. . . . We had been shown by the
Tractarians, the depth and intensity of significance to be dis-
closed by faith in the Incarnation. Now we added to this a fuller
estimate of the far-reaching extension of its meaning and the
scope of its activities. Christian doctrine showed itself as the very
heart of a Social Gospel!'

How faded now sounds that fifty-year-old phrase; yet how
vital for us to-day the reality of which it speaks.

'THE BANNER OF CHRIST IN THE HANDS OF THE SOCIALISTS': 1844–1914

In the spring of 1883 *The Rock*, a journal published in the interests of the extreme Protestant party in the Church of England, saw fit to call attention to the activities of a certain H. C. Shuttleworth, then a Minor Canon of St. Paul's. This gentleman, it appeared, though not he alone, incarnated 'an alliance utterly inexplicable, between the Ritualists and the Revolutionists'. From a union so unholy the most dire results were naturally to be expected. 'If insurrection should break out in England', declared *The Rock*, 'it will be due, and largely indeed, to the clerical and other firebrands, Mr. Shuttleworth and his friends, who are seeking to propagate what they call Christian Socialism.' Since the friends of Mr. Shuttleworth here stigmatized were the hundred or so members of the Guild of St. Matthew which he had lately joined, it may be thought that the influence of this still rather obscure association was being somewhat over-estimated. The truth was that the respectable classes in Church and State for which *The Rock* spoke were showing some signs at this time of losing their nerve. The omens were not propitious. Prosperity, whose fleeting reappearance in 1881 had been hailed with so much relief, had abruptly vanished again; a strange new word had emerged for the first time in common parlance, and men spoke now of 'the unemployed', and were soon to talk of 'unemployment' as of a phenomenon integral to the social order and now, on a greater or lesser scale, to be permanently expected. Moreover 'the unemployed' did

not any longer remain in their barren homes, waiting patiently
for the trade cycle to revolve; they had taken to coming into the
streets, and would even a year or so later display themselves in
the churches of the metropolis. It was bad enough when a
Bethnal Green curate espoused the cause of these people, and
continued to do so when, partly perhaps as a consequence, he
found himself unemployed. But when a Minor Canon aspired to
the role of a minor prophet it was time for the Chapter to do
something about the matter. It was decided, says Shuttleworth's
biographer, that 'to offer him one of the Chapter's livings was the
easiest and most decent way of evicting the unruly member',
and the Minor Canon became in November, 1883, the Rector of
St. Nicholas Cole Abbey. The almost immediate result was to
transform a museum-piece of seventeenth-century architecture
into a packed and pulsating church. Shuttleworth, who had
many of the gifts of a popular orator (Mr. Shaw has confirmed
the rumour that he was one of the models for 'Morell' in
Candida), was given the chance of a lifetime, and most handsomely he took it. Scott Holland records that when he went to
St. Paul's a year later 'they all spoke a little sadly of his "dreadful Socialism" as if he had "gone wrong", but of course this only
amused me'. No doubt it also amused the 'clerical and other
firebrands' of the Guild of St. Matthew, who were indeed easily
amused.

The Guild, now more or less explicitly a socialist society, was
to enter upon its most influential period in the tumultuous years
that were to follow, years of ferment in which its leaders were
temperamentally at home. The very fluidity of the situation
suited them, for it enabled them to impose their own interpretation upon social events without restraint from secular dogmas.
Since the social and economic orthodoxy of the Left had not yet
crystallized, those who prophesied in the name of Christian
orthodoxy had the better chance to do so without danger of
compromising the supernatural doctrines which they professed.
For the great rival Authority had yet to secure acknowledgement as such. Karl Marx died in London in 1883, ending his life
as unostentatiously, almost one might say as secretly, as he had

for so many years lived it, and as his great expositor was for a few years to live his no less influential life in the same city a quarter of a century later. Perhaps no more people knew Marx, as he toiled away in the British Museum at the three volumes of *Das Kapital*, than were to know Lenin here afterwards; scarcely anyone in England but H. M. Hyndman had as yet read a word he had written. But Capitalism was at this moment revealing in practice those inherent contradictions which Marx had already exposed in principle. Men could with ever increasing capacity produce, but they could not with corresponding facility contrive to buy. And the frustrations and frictions thus engendered were building up among perhaps the most temperamentally peace-loving population in Europe a movement of resistance. In William Morris it had found a voice, and one a good deal more alluring than that which had issued from the reading-room of the British Museum. With Morris the idea of Revolution returned not as a dialectical theory but as a personal challenge. In April, 1884, he wrote that:

> *the day is drawing nigh*
> *When the Cause shall call upon us, some to live and some to die.*

'Things are hotting up', Hyndman was fond of telling his audiences. And by the winter of 1885–86 they were. Vast meetings, with Stewart Headlam prominent at them, fought for and won the right of free speech in the open air of the East End. Inflammatory speeches in Trafalgar Square a few months later led to a procession through the West End, whose members stoned the windows of fashionable clubs, looted Piccadilly shops, and terrified the governing classes into subscribing £60,000 for the relief of these alarming 'unemployed' within a space of ten days. The next winter brought clashes with the military round the Houses of Parliament, and 'the day was drawing nigh' when happily not 'some' but only one, a young workman by name Alfred Linnell, was called upon by the Cause to die, if not at the hands of the police, at least at the feet of their horses. The funeral procession, from Bow Street, down the Strand and past St. Paul's to the cemetery in Whitechapel, attracted vast crowds, and at the head of it marched the officiating minister, Stewart Headlam.

It was the year of the Queen's first Jubilee, a celebration in which a spontaneous patriotism and a no less spontaneous bitterness born of destitution struggled for mastery, often no doubt in the same individual. But there was a new note in the national celebrations, deeply resented by many, but indicative, ironically enough, of that new factor in Britain's economic situation which was about to rescue her people from their gravest strains. The 'imperialism' which was so decoratively represented in the royal procession, and more practically exemplified by the first Colonial Conference, was, by the expanding markets to which it led, to relieve industrial tensions and put an end for thirty years to revolutionary policies. A great victory over poverty had still to be won, but the first battles of the new campaign were fought in a spirit of expectation rather than of frustrate despair. The Dock Strike of 1889 was, as Mr. Ensor points out, a 'prosperity strike', a strike of 'workers with low standards revolting against their continuance in the face of swelling and obtrusive prosperity'. The long depression is over and we are on the threshold of a new time, in which a plutocracy grown confident and even exuberant will be challenged by a socialism claiming to be constructive and evolutionary.

But the challenge was made on too narrow a front, and its influence upon those who allied themselves with it in the name of Christ and His Church tended to be in some degree narrowing also. It is not difficult now to see how this came about. To be wise after the event is at once the prerogative and the snare of the historian. It is a snare because it may induce him in all too facile a manner to assume that what he can see in his day could just as easily have been seen by those who had to grapple with the situation which he has only to appraise. In fact, of course, moral challenges and social problems do not present themselves to the men of any given generation conveniently and unmistakably arrayed in due precedence and accurate perspective. Those whose subsequent function it is to assess the wisdom and the faithfulness with which their forefathers have confronted such challenges and problems are easily tempted to forget the difficulties and limitations imposed upon would-be reformers, and Christian reformers not least. It has to be remembered, in the first place, that short-term issues are apt to clamour so loudly for attention that one of two consequences commonly results. To one type of man the immediate duty appears so pressing that he is inclined to dismiss long-term issues and fundamental solutions from his mind with a good conscience, or even without any realization that his conscience requires to be consulted in the matter. To an opposite type of man nothing but fundamental solutions—or preferably a single all-embracing 'solution'—make any appeal, and 'revolutionary' views come to be accepted rather from impatience with the inadequacy of palliative measures than from any profound conviction that nothing less will suffice to affect the situation. But beyond this, in the second place, the reformer is confronted with the difficulty which arises from the limited amount of attention which he can hope to secure at any given time from the public mind—and even from his own. The danger of which he is often—if only sub-consciously—aware is that if he sets too much store upon seeing the social life of his time steadily and seeing it whole he may find himself inhibited, whether psychologically or practically, from doing anything about it. And the result too often is that he either concentrates all his interest upon a practical issue in one corner of the field, or looks round for a panacea which he can induce himself to hope will solve—or at least vastly relieve— every social problem indiscriminately and simultaneously.

It is in the light of these considerations that we should do well to look at the reform movements between 1884 and 1914. It is not difficult to see now, what it was too disturbing and incon-venient to acknowledge then, that the evils, injustices and heresies which were afflicting society were extremely diverse, and incapable of being comprehended in a single formula. There was the question of industrialism's social and economic purpose, which Carlyle had talked about for so long in general and William Morris was now talking about so vigorously in particular. There was the problem, akin to that, of industrial technique and its specific exemplification in mass production, which Kingsley had approached already and about which Ruskin continued to be so disturbingly earnest. There was the starvation of agriculture, which few or none yet perceived might one day threaten the starvation of England. There was the problem of money-power in its relation both to economic realities and to political sovereignty, a problem to which Thomas Attwood had called the attention of the Chartists nearly fifty years before, but to which no one in England had, in fact, paid any attention since. There was the question of man's self-government at his work which so much exercised the early Co-operators, but which had now become buried out of sight beneath the accumulating piles of groceries in the distributive stores, until at the moment that Ludlow died his lifelong challenge was resurrected in a new form by the protagonists of national guilds. There was the question of in what spheres, if indeed in any, and by what methods, men might ever again hope to own their own means of livelihood; if that can be said to have been at this time any longer a question at all, Capitalism having degraded ownership into share-holding and Socialism having equated it with sin.

But for a quarter of a century after 1884 it was almost impossible to get any serious attention for a discussion of any of these problems. Men's social activities might be aimless, their work soul (and body) destroying; their countryside falling slowly into decay; their monetary system increasingly a distortion and a usurpation; their daily lives, in an age enthusiastic for democracy, a servitude of postulated passivity, based on the 'permanent hypothesis' of the wage-system. Yet for the vast majority of reformers and revolutionaries alike, all these were academic issues, if they were even recognized as issues at all. Society, these men agreed, was the victim of a great moral evil—economic inequality, manifesting itself in a widespread social evil—poverty. Both could be cured, an increasing number were coming to think, by the application of a new social and economic principle—Socialism, which it was not very easy—but happily not at all necessary—to define. Socialism was to be welcomed, in addition, as a great moral force, essentially Christian if you liked to think it so, with Keir Hardie; fundamentally anti-Christian if you preferred it that way, with Robert Blatchford. Those disposed to argue about such differences were commonly adjured to sit down and stop rocking the boat, for we were all going the same way home, terrestrially speaking at any rate. Church socialists who might still be dubious on the matter were warned against evasion of their moral responsibilities in an age in which God, rebuffed by the Pharisees of ecclesiastical orthodoxy, was bidding those who had ears to hear to turn to the Gentiles of the Labour movement. Let Christians have the vision to see and the courage to proclaim 'the banner of Christ in the hands of the Socialists'.

Naturally there were church people not especially timid, avaricious or 'reactionary', who did not find the matter so simple as all that. And indeed it would be unjust to Thomas Hancock, who in 1887 preached the sermon with the title I have taken for this Lecture, and to the younger men in the Guild of St. Matthew whom he inspired, to suppose that they ever thought that it was. The widespread, if often tacit, assumption of most of those who were soon to follow that noble idealist Keir Hardie into the I.L.P., was either that the doctrinal aspect of Christianity was a matter of indifference, or that religion was essentially a private affair which could be indulged in without reference to political opinions. Nothing could be more flatly opposed to the theology of Hancock and Headlam and to the whole standpoint of the G.S.M. than such assumptions; indeed, the Guild might almost be said to have been founded to contravert them. The subsequent development of the G.S.M. into a more or less socialist society, even though its socialism tended to reflect the particular opinions of its Warden rather than those of any of the competing schools of Hyndman, Webb and Hardie, is apt to obscure the fact that its primary purpose was apologetic. When Headlam first banded together his followers 'to justify God to the people', he was thinking chiefly of the need to vindicate the Faith against the Secularist lecturers who were under-

mining it among those in East London to whom he was commissioned to minister. Many of these, like their leader Bradlaugh, were violent opponents of Socialism, and it was a part—
and be it said an entirely legitimate part—of Headlam's vindication of the Faith to establish its integral connection with the
cause of social justice and the rescue of the people from the evils
and miseries by which their daily lives were maimed. It is
indeed vital to an understanding of all that Headlam was and
stood for to realize that social justice for him was not an isolated
concern in which he happened to have a particular interest.
His zeal for it was part of a challenge which he felt called upon
by God to make, against all obstacles, on behalf of a total
interpretation of human life and human society as he saw them,
in the light of the Gospels and the Sacraments. This interpretation may have been in some respects less authentic and less well
proportioned than he honestly believed it to be; his passion for
the ballet and his championship of its performers may have owed
more to the character of his particular interests than he realized;
it may have been less necessary than he regarded it to embark
upon an elaborate discussion with a bishop in his palace about
the length of a dancer's skirts and the colour of her tights. But
however idiosyncratic Headlam's opinions may have seemed to
others, and however reckless or quixotic some of his challenges
to the respectable may have appeared, they were not undertaken merely in a spirit of bravado. He saw the complacency,
the callousness and the mere dullness which, as he thought,
characterized the church life of his time, as standing in the way
of the full vitality and selfless energy which an understanding of
Catholic truth involved for those who professed to accept it.
The vindication of social justice was demanded as a part of the
challenge thus implied, and with the heightening of the social
tension in the latter half of the 'eighties it became, quite
naturally, a major part. But it was still only a part of a wider
thing, which for want of a more satisfactory term we may call
Christian Humanism, and much as Headlam suffered for his
opinions, it was not for his socialist opinions that he suffered
most. He was turned out of his first curacy as a result of Bishop

Jackson's dissatisfaction with his supposedly too Maurician views on Eternal Punishment. He was banished from his beloved Bethnal Green for a lecture in which he advised the mothers of dull young girls to send them to the Gaiety Theatre, where they might learn better from actresses 'so full of life and mirth'. He lost his third curacy for friendly gestures towards his great antagonist Bradlaugh; and it was only from a fourth that he 'got the sack for being political' from a not too intolerant vicar. The chance of a fifth was ruined by his appearance at a meeting in Hyde Park to demand the abolition of the House of Lords. 'Both in doctrine and discipline', said the prospective rector, 'he goes beyond the bounds of the most lenient interpretation.' A Victorian incumbent might perhaps be pardoned for thinking so.

For this was an age in which priests who told congregations what they were reluctant to hear had often not only to sacrifice all hope of a benefice but to lose the chance of any employment whatsoever. Such was for a number of years the fate of Thomas Hancock. He was a somewhat older man than Headlam, who extolled him as 'a masterly theologian and authority on Church history', as to whom 'it was nothing less than a scandal that a man of his powers should ever have lacked a charge or appointment'. Hancock was perhaps the most truly prophetic figure in the Church of England between the death of Maurice and the advent of Charles Gore, and he lived up to his own conviction that 'no word of rebuke has a just claim to be called a prophetic word unless it is uttered against the Catholic Church'. Judgment, he felt, must begin at the House of God, and Christ would come as a thief in the night, even to that House, when it was profaning His message. 'If the English nation', he asked, 'often suspects us as possible foes, as probable agents of English deterioration rather than of English culture, is it not because we have been so eager to show ourselves upon the side of interests and classes, rather than upon the side of the "flesh and blood", which is summed up in the Son of Man? Is it not because we clergy have preferred rather to hold the brief of Mammon than to bear witness to the Man who is ready to be revealed as the housebreaker of every house of His which Mammon is using as its own?'

This extract is from a sermon preached in 1874, when challenges of this sort were extremely rare, and it is not perhaps surprising that Hancock should have left St. Stephen's, Lewisham, the following year and found no incumbent willing to employ him. Sermons which he delivered while at St. Stephen's were collected in a volume entitled *Christ and the People*, published in 1875, and their prophetic power and penetrating exegesis are such as to make the reader appreciate the truth of Mr. Binyon's declaration that Hancock 'was, at that time, the theologian of the Christian Socialist Movement', and one who 'well understood the "proportion of faith" '. There is something about these sermons, their sense of urgency, their zeal for the cause of the common man, their strong roots in the Faith and the scriptures, which recall another and much more popular preacher, who was to kindle men's hearts and challenge their complacencies fifty years after Hancock began his ministry at Lewisham. Hancock never achieved the wide recognition which was to sustain but never to spoil Studdert Kennedy, but in 1883 he was given an unexpected opportunity and a new congregation, members of which were little likely to get up and stalk out of the church as heretofore, even at the most daring challenges. When H. C. Shuttleworth was appointed to St. Nicholas Cole Abbey, he immediately instituted Hancock to a lectureship there, perhaps realizing that the older man's more solid gifts in the field of theology and exegesis would complement his own qualities as a popular preacher. 'He had given my youth back again to me', said Hancock later, 'and re-opened the doors of the House of the Lord to one of His ejected priests.' By this time, of course, Hancock was an ally of Headlam, whose sympathy, as he had declared the year before, had 'uplifted me at a most despondent period', and a leader in the Guild of St. Matthew. His sermons were to become an important feature of *The Church Reformer* which Headlam took over in 1884, and transformed into the most vital journal the Church's social movement has ever possessed. There is, not unnaturally, a new note of hope and confidence in his preaching after this, since Hancock is no longer a voice crying in the wilderness, but an interpreter of the spiritual significance of a movement on the march. Very literally so, indeed, for Hancock's most forceful, if not his most profound, sermons were preached in the years of the great labour processions already described. To these disturbing events Hancock supplied a theological interpretation. If the unemployed appeared as vultures it was 'the carcase of a corrupt and putrid civilization' which had gathered them together. 'If we English people, like the people of Jerusalem, refuse to be gathered together by the Son of Man—united rich to poor, educated to ignorant, as one family of equal brothers and sisters in Him—our day of judgment, the end of the world, the consummation of our age, cannot be long delayed.' Similarly when the unemployed began to march in organized parades to the churches, and most notably to St. Paul's Cathedral, as a means of calling attention to their grievances, Hancock found this highly significant, and it was in this connection that he preached that most famous of all his sermons which I have taken as the title for this lecture:

'The non-churchgoing "masses" have taken to churchgoing. We have seen what journalists of Mammon and Caste call an "invasion of the Churches" by the poor Socialists. We have seen nothing else like it in our generation. "This is the Lord's doing and it is marvellous in our eyes. . . ."

'You see that they carry banners with mottoes upon them. Who is *the author* of those texts which express the social faith of this huge multitude? From what teachers have they borrowed the dogmas which they call upon all the city to read and respect, to observe and to obey? On whose authority are these innumerable crowds of the poor and rough doing this unwonted thing? They, or a great many of them, call themselves "Socialists". Let us read what is on their banners; let us discover *who* is the ultimate dogmatist of this multitudinous sect. . . .

'Oh, come all ye faithful! Look again and again at these inscriptions. Recognize while you have time, what they are: see, clergy and laity, out of whose mouth the cries of "the mob" have come. They are the words of *your* Master. They are the laws of the Eternal Father. They are the lessons which he taught us by His Son. They are the new commandments which you and I were pledged at our baptism to keep. "Feed *My* lambs." "My house is a house of prayer, but ye (capitalists and landlords) have made it a den of thieves!" "*I* was an hungered, and ye gave *Me* no meat, naked and ye clothed *Me* not." It is a small matter to what sect or party this great "multitude" fancies it belongs, or by what denomination it pleases to call itself. You can see to *whom* they have felt obliged to go in order to find the fullest expression of their faith. . . .

'The undogmatic "socialism" of the desolate and oppressed, when it speaks freely out of its own heart and conscience, falls back upon the words with which the crucified and ascended Head of Humanity has provided His brothers and sisters. It reminds Christians that they are living in rebellion against Christ. It does not articulately name itself "Christian Socialism". No: but it declares inarticulately that the thing which economists, politicians, scholars—in hatred or in love—call "Socialism" is itself "Christian".'

I have quoted this passage at length because whatever reservations we may have about its contentions sixty years later—and I suppose it is inevitable that most of us now *should* have some such reservations—it is a particularly illuminating exposition of the outlook of the G.S.M. at that time. The primary concern of these men was to force upon the imagination of the Church the realities, the sufferings and the challenges of their age. As John Oakley, who could hardly be counted an extremist and later became Dean of Manchester, wrote to Headlam, 'there is no doubt that we are, many of us, engaged in a stand-up fight not with individuals or even with authority as authority, but with the dominant class and with the characteristic sentiment of the class which have hitherto ruled the Church of England'. These words were, in fact, written in relation to Headlam's Church and Stage Guild, and the parallel which the main purpose of this body provided with the object of the G.S.M. is suggestive. Headlam declared that 'there was one thing we always re-

pudiated as a Guild, and that was having any idea of under-
taking a mission to the dramatic profession. Such a notion would
have seemed to us an impertinence. Rather, we used to say,
should there be a mission among the clergy to teach them a
right understanding of the stage and the players, and to preach
to some of them a broader charity.' Headlam could hardly, of
course, have said, or desired to say, that the preaching of the
Faith to the working classes could ever be in itself an impertinence, but he himself would have felt it to be so unless he was at
the same time preaching to the comfortable classes their duty
towards the hungry and the outcast, as the unemployed of that
day so truly were. The Guild of St. Matthew was perhaps
primarily 'a mission among the clergy to teach them a right
understanding' of work and the worker, and to exhort them in
this instance less to charity than to justice.

It is the duty of the prophet who speaks in the name of the
Lord to speak of the situation by which the Church is at that
moment challenged. Hancock, preaching on 'The Worship of
Mammon' in 1885, found it necessary to remind his hearers that
'in London, the richest city in the world, one person out of nine
dies in a workhouse'. It is not to be wondered at if the hunger
and destitution of those days, when 'social services' were for all
practical purposes non-existent, sometimes moved men to extract more from a text than it could properly bear or drove them
into inflammatory denunciations. H. H. Champion, the aristocratic leader of the unemployed, and editor of a journal called
The Christian Socialist, cried out in 1887 that 'if the whole proper-
tied class had but one throat he would cut it without a single
thought if by so doing he could redress the injustice of our social
system'. It is reassuring and perhaps a little surprising to find that
the expression of this sentiment did not prevent his being invited
in that same year to address the Church Congress, which he did
in considerably milder terms, exhorting his hearers 'to find in
their common worship at the Cross of Christ an overmastering
impulse to unite in bringing about a speedy but powerful
solution of the social problem'.

The shock tactics of the G.S.M. were not without success.

'The Banner of Christ in the Hands of the Socialists'

As Bernard Shaw declared of this period ten years later, in the Preface to his *Pleasant Plays*, 'religion was alive again, coming back upon men, even clergymen, with such power that not the Church of England itself could keep it out'. And whatever illusions it may have encouraged or itself have cherished, about the spiritual hungers and natural virtues of 'humanity', which Hancock was perhaps rather too fond of contrasting with the Pharisaism of Bishops and the Mammonism of churchgoers, it was essentially a dogmatic and doctrinal religion which was thus coming back. As James Adderley, soon to become a stalwart of the movement, justly pointed out later:

'Headlam based his gospel on theology. There were old doctrines to be re-stated and properly understood in view of the new learning if the Church was to take its proper share in social reform. . . . It did not interest him to further political reforms as such. What did interest him was to make Christians orthodox and to persuade them to recognize the implications of their religion. . . . Baptism was the entry into the greatest democratic society in the world. The Mass was the weekly meeting of a society of rebels against a Mammon-worshipping world order. Let the working men of England claim their rights as Christ's members and do their duty as Christ's soldiers and the present order would crumble.'

Not only was Headlam himself interested in theology, he firmly believed that everybody else was. In a Fabian lecture on the movement of Maurice and Kingsley, given as late as 1907, he declared that it was precisely because they were above anything else theologians that they were in touch with the great mass of the people, 'for theology is the one science in which everyone is enormously interested'.

Whether or not this is true, the G.S.M. can hardly be said to have proved it so. It never showed the slightest sign of becoming a popular society or of attracting the interest of the working classes. Ideal as 'shock troops' of the Church in what appeared to be a revolutionary situation, it was already by 1889 revealing certain limitations, not all of them connected with the idiosyncrasies of its Warden. 'Our day of judgment, the end of the

135

world, the consummation of our age', which Hancock declared
in 1886 could not be long delayed if the English people failed
to achieve a valid social union, was in fact obviously being delayed three years later by the prosaic factor of returning 'prosperity'. Economic imperialism was beginning to pay dividends
—and wages. There was still plenty of talk of Socialism, but it
was a different sort of talk, calling, as it seemed to many, for a
different sort of interpretation from the Church. There were
forward-looking churchmen who felt as strongly as Headlam the
futility of a mere religiosity, which *pace* his declaration that 'the
common people have always known that theology is important',
was in fact the form in which the masses liked best to clothe their
transcendental aspirations, which were soon to take an institutional shape in 'Labour Churches' that became less and less
theological in spirit as time went on. But such churchmen felt,
too, that the doctrines of the Church could not be set forth with
authority, or in the long run with effectiveness, while they were
employed so predominantly to establish the validity of humanitarian and sociological contentions. They felt again that enough
had been done to shock the susceptibilities of the average churchgoer, and that the number who would be attracted by such
methods was inevitably few. What was necessary now was less
the forcible conversion of the man in the street than the peaceful
persuasion of the man in the pew. These considerations, in-
fluentially held, led to the genesis in 1889 of the Christian Social
Union.

The contrasting and yet complementary character of G.S.M.
and C.S.U. are strikingly illustrated by the characters and
careers of their chief protagonists. Stewart Duckworth Headlam
and Henry Scott Holland had been born almost within a fortnight of one another. Both were educated at Eton and sat under
the same tutor, William Johnson, who was a disciple of Maurice;
to him, says Headlam, 'my mind at Eton was indebted for most
of its broadening'. Holland's biography records at some length
Johnson's influence on a considerably more promising pupil.
Despite this common influence, nothing seems to have brought
them together, either at Eton or afterwards. The biographers

of neither man make any reference whatever to the other, save that Mr. Bettany records that Holland was (significantly) wont to refer to the leaders of the G.S.M. as 'Headlong and Shuttle-cock'. The two men, though they shared in the passion for social justice, and had each in their own way a vast vitality, could hardly have been more different, alike in their temperaments and in their destinies. Headlam not only stood for the people's cause, but he was at home among them; he was the 'Pied Piper of Bethnal Green', followed everywhere by crowds of children as he trod its streets. He was what is often called a 'born rebel', with the audacity and something of the perversity of the type. He not only accepted conflicts with authority, he enjoyed them; he did not merely tolerate unconventional and flamboyant people, he actually preferred them. He was not concerned to grapple with the more profound issues emerging in his time; he had acquired his stock of ideas early in life and was not much disposed either to add to them or to modify them. 'There was no uprooting possible of the ideas he had once accepted', says his biographer, and Archbishop Davidson, who showed him more friendship than most members of the episcopate, spoke of him, not unfairly, as going straight ahead 'with blinkers on'. It was very different with Holland. Though a person of strong indi-viduality and with a bubbling humour—'a man with a natural surge of laughter within him' said that sympathetic spirit Chesterton, 'so that his broad mouth seemed always to be shut down on it in a grimace of restraint'—Holland spontaneous and unconventional as he was, was yet a don among dons, and his interests were primarily academic. He had never known failure; he never had to face violent hostility. What he did face, with unfailing energy and unwavering faith, were the great intellectual challenges of his time. While Headlam strove to vindicate the outcast and to defy their oppressors, Holland sought to interpret the signs of the times and to win men to his own understanding of what that interpretation required.

The tasks were indeed complementary. Can it be said that the roles of G.S.M. and C.S.U. were so? In effect this was largely the case, though their leaders hardly saw them as such. The men round Headlam tended to regard the men round Holland as academic escapists, 'ever learning', as Charles Marson put it with characteristic mordancy, 'but never coming to a knowledge of the truth'. 'Here's a glaring social evil; let's read a paper about it', was an epigram at the expense of C.S.U. popular in G.S.M. circles. It has more point, however, against John Carter, the indefatigable study organizer of the Oxford branch, than against such fearless souls as Holland and Gore, who for twenty years and more did all they knew to spur the middle-class churchgoers into zeal for social righteousness. The C.S.U. leaders, for their part, were apt to feel that the Guild's determination to *épater* the ecclesiastical bourgeois in season and out of season had become a form of reckless indulgence which made their own task of awakening the conscientious but cautious churchman unnecessarily difficult. Men like Holland and Gore and E. S. Talbot had no fear of authority and not an atom of sycophancy in face of it; but they knew what authority meant, they appreciated alike its responsibilities and its possibilities, and they were resolved to win it for their cause, so far as this could be done without surrender of principle. If they could not do all that demanded to be done, they could at least, through the C.S.U., do that which they were so brilliantly equipped to do, 'claim for the Christian Law the ultimate authority to rule social practice', and gradually build up theological scholarship and episcopal authority behind the claim. Between 1889 and 1913, out of 53 episcopal appointments, 16 went to members of the C.S.U. There was a fundamental divergence of outlook between men content to work patiently for such a result, and men like Hancock and Headlam who considered themselves (with some justice) as every bit as much the subject of victimization at the hands of established authority as did their working-class friends who lost their jobs for fidelity to trade unionism. On the one side we see the intellectual aristocracy of Christ Church and Balliol; on the other the Robin Hoods and Friar Tucks, no longer of Sherwood but of Bohemia. As my friend, Canon Widdrington, who knew both camps well in the 'nineties, has written to me:

'The Banner of Christ in the Hands of the Socialists'

'The leaders of the C.S.U. were unable to free themselves from the accidents of their education. They had been dons and they were never able to shake off the traditions of the universities, though Holland came very near to doing so. When I urge that the divergence of C.S.U. and G.S.M. was a matter of clashing temperaments, I do so because, for example, it passes my imagination to see Gore or even Holland at one of Headlam's Sunday night "At Homes", surrounded by budding poets, painters, writers, actors and ladies of the ballet. Yet I have seen that pious priest, Fr. Hogg of St. Albans, Holborn, apparently quite at his ease there.'

1889 was an appropriate moment for such a new departure as was represented by the formation of the C.S.U. It was a day of new things, and new men. It was the year in which Britain's establishment in the new imperial markets had decisively banished the most obstinate trade depression since the 'forties. It was the year in which the success of the Dock Strike set the New Unionism of the unskilled workers upon an unshakable foundation and brought a revolutionary influx into the official councils of Labour, to react upon the old-established artisans, and at the same time be in a measure tamed by the impact. It was the year of *Fabian Essays*, the classic formulation of the English school of evolutionary Socialism, which was not to be effectively challenged for more than twenty years. We are on the threshold of a new decade, no longer tumultuous with threats of revolution, but noisy and confident in a manner altogether its own. The keynote of the period from the first Jubilee to the first defeats in South Africa is ebullience. A social historian, Mr. Wingfield-Stratford, has characterized it as the Roaring 'Nineties. In the 'eighties an alternative form of amoralism had arisen to challenge that most characteristic of Victorianism; the cult of the useless competed with the idolatry of the useful; art for art's sake with work for work's sake. The green carnation, like the red flag, was a defiance of the utilitarian standards of the bourgeois, and a protest against the devitalized sort of morality that appeared to go with them. When Oscar Wilde preoccupied himself with 'the soul of man under Socialism' it was with the professed desire for a state of things in which one could 'avoid the sordid necessity of living for others'. The significance of William Morris, the greatest all-round artist of his time, lies in the equal rejection of aesthetic man and economic man which was involved in his demand for integral man, and for art and for work to be embraced for life's sake and not for their own. He did not win his battle, but he did not altogether lose it; aestheticism collapsed with Wilde, for whom Headlam so quixotically went bail; economic theory developed traces of humanism under the influence of Marshall, and the rigours of economic practice were alleviated by the introduction of the eight-hour day. If ebullience can be seen as struggling with decadence in the early 'nineties, it was ebullience which won. It even established itself in a sphere where we might hardly have expected to find it. The Puritan strain in nineteenth-century religion did not expire with the Methodist revival or the Clapham Sect. The Tractarians were strong ascetics; Pusey doubted whether it was ever right for a priest to smile, except at a child. Nor when attention began to be concentrated on Greek theology was there at first any perceptible difference of outlook. Maurice had reacted against his Calvinist upbringing, but he continued to call himself, with some justice, a 'hard Puritan'. The gentle Westcott said much the same of himself, and Llewelyn Davies speaks of 'the extreme seriousness of his disposition and of his life'. He abjured smoking, gave up all alcoholic drinks in middle age so as the better to preach what had oddly become known as Temperance, and felt such qualms about driving in a carriage that he tried to shrink away out of sight behind rugs and panels. Charles Gore, when a schoolboy of fifteen at Harrow, had been much impressed by a sermon of Westcott's on 'The Disciplined Life', preached in 1868, and he preserved much of this tradition into a later period, though in seeking a community life Gore was obeying not only his convictions but his temperament. By the 'nineties, however, Gore was in this respect something of an anachronism among religious leaders. The renewed stress upon the doctrine of the Incarnation, blending with and in a manner hallowing the relaxed tensions of a society now beginning to expend those savings which had been the reward of an abstinence lasting for the best part of a century, was giving rise to a new emphasis in Christian evangelism and apologetic. Its note was one of thanksgiving; its message one of consecration. Headlam gloried in the title of 'anti-Puritan', and integrated a philosophy of ballet dancing into his theology. Scott Holland's writings continually re-echo the General Thanksgiving in their delighted gratitude for 'our creation, preservation, and all the blessings of this life'. Recalling Westcott's dictum that 'the Creation came before the Fall', he was wont to exhort perplexed audiences to ejaculate in joyous thankfulness, 'I am'. Chesterton's early writings, full of a challenge, not only to the moral nihilism of the aesthetes, but to a still deeper scepticism as to the reality of life which he had overcome in himself, are a series of triumphant shouts of thanksgiving for God's gift to him of opportunity to share in the human adventure. The sardonic frivolities of Charles Marson, the genial ironies of James Adderley and the prophetic audacities of Conrad Noel, are aspects of the same exuberance. Plain living and high thinking had given way to plain speaking and high spirits. To those of a later day who have seen the liquidation of human idealism, and something dangerously near to a collapse of Christian morals, the mood of the whole period from 1890 to 1914 is something a little mysterious and more than a little disreputable. Even its theology, dismissed as 'a snug Incarnationalism', is something of a scandal to a generation of Neo-Thomists and Neo-Calvinists. That we should be thankful for the Grace sufficient to enable us to walk without despair through a vale of tears—that is only proper. But that Christians should once have been grateful merely for the opportunity of experiencing the journey and enjoying the scenery is apt to seem to the contemporary orphans of so many storms, if not a little shocking, at least distinctly odd.

Such puzzlement in our generation is understandable enough. Yet we should be superficial indeed if we were to suppose that all this vitality had not had its roots in a profound spiritual energy and in truly dedicated lives. The Christian Social Union was but one of the three upshots of that recurrent summer gathering which its members called in characteristic fun the 'Holy Party'; the other two were *Lux Mundi* and the Community of the Resurrection. Such things as these, whatever judgment may be passed on them, are hardly the outcome of mere ecclesiastical high spirits. Indeed, the phrase 'holy party', though the group dropped it later, was a happy description of the assembly which in a few short meetings gave rise to so much. It had the spontaneity and the conviviality of a successful party, but it had the earnest energy and true dedication that holiness demands. Dr. Prestige, in his biography, records that Gore, whom they called their 'pope', would fall down on his knees and raise clenched fists to heaven to plead with his colleagues for recognition of a point that was precious to him. And their projects hung together. Gore infused the social zeal which sprang from his 'permanently troubled conscience' into his community, so that by the time the Church Socialist League arose to embrace responsibilities from which the C.S.U., whether rightly or wrongly, shrank, many of its most effective propagandists were Mirfield priests. As for *Lux Mundi*, this represented, says Dr. S. C. Carpenter, 'the union of two strains, that which came through Church from Newman, and that which came from Coleridge and Maurice through Westcott and Hort', but the confluence was welcomed with more enthusiasm by those who swam in the latter stream than by those who refreshed themselves from the former. The intention of its authors was not controversial but rather constructive and evangelistic; 'we needed', said Gore, 'as the Church has often needed, to bring that with which we are ourselves identified into relation to the claims, intellectual and practical, made upon us from outside.' The book, says Ruth Kenyon, 'was in fact the foundation of a new apologetic in which Catholic thought no longer stood on the defensive against the thought of the age, but incorporated it and made it a vehicle for its own doctrine. The guiding principle was found in the Johannine doctrine of the Incarnate *Logos*, the Word entering to redeem the world of which He was already the Creator—a world which included the historically developing social order. . . . Evolution was accepted as the work of the *Logos* through

Whom all things were made.' It will be evident from this summary that the outlook of *Lux Mundi* is as much sundered from the most characteristic 'orthodoxies' of contemporary theology as it was from the Tractarian orthodoxy of its own day, though not altogether, perhaps not mainly, for the same reason. It is, of course, easy for the criticism of one period to perceive that an earlier school of thought has 'the limitations of its time'; it is not so easy to believe that one's own viewpoint may be similarly affected by historical contingencies. We are not here directly concerned with theology, however, but with sociology, and the sociology of *Lux Mundi* is scarcely at all explicit; it remained to be worked out by those of its authors, Holland, Talbot, Gore and W. J. H. Campion, who were interested in these matters. Perhaps the strongest 'social' note in the volume is struck not in Campion's essay on 'Christian Politics' or Ottley's on 'Christian Ethics' (though the latter does stress their essentially social character) but in a short Appendix on 'Some Aspects of Christian Duty', by Professor Ingram. In this he declares that 'the most significant fact of our time is perhaps the process of transition from (so-called) political to ethical economics. To reason rightly on social problems we must ever have regard to personality. . . . Our problem is how to supersede the technical and legal relation by the personal.' There is an equivocal character about this declaration, however. Clearly the writer meant well. But did he mean much? Men might have asked the same question of the C.S.U.

When I say that there is an equivocal character about the statement of the social problem as primarily one of establishing a true relation between men as personalities, I mean that it leaves unsettled, or even overlooks altogether, two issues in regard to which an authentically Christian attitude to society cannot afford to remain in uncertainty. One is the extent to which the relations of men to one another constitute the essential subject-matter of sociology; the other is the degree to which improvement in the ethical level of human relations can be relied upon to affect, or even to dispose of, social problems. The very existence of the former issue was shrouded from every school of the Christian social movement in the nineteenth century from a failure to realize that man has a relation and an obligation not only to God and to his neighbour, but also to the surroundings, and especially to the organic creation, within which God has set him. Perhaps only Kingsley came near to an understanding of this, unless we are to include such figures as Hawker of Morwenstow and Barnes, the parson poet of Dorset, who can hardly be said to fall within our subject. In regard to this issue the statement I am considering is indeed not so much equivocal as inadequate, but upon the other perhaps even the C.S.U. leaders, and certainly the majority of its members, never cleared their minds. Some were apt to think that the Church's social duty was fulfilled if her children did their best in the social relationships in which they found themselves, after duly informing themselves of what justice and charity required of them. Others, and this is certainly true of most of the leaders, saw the matter in a wider and, we must surely say, in a truer perspective. They saw that relationships could be invalid in themselves, that no amount of conscientiousness could alter the essential falsity of the situation in which a fatalistic acceptance of an acquisitive economic theory had placed the agents of the industrial process *vis-à-vis* those who hired them as 'hands', to speak only of one aspect of the plutocratic economy. A categorical declaration in this sense was made by the President of the C.S.U. within a year of its formation. Westcott, though universally revered, was widely regarded as a 'moderate', a restraining influence on the reforming zeal of his younger colleagues. But it was Westcott's famous address to the Church Congress of 1890, with its surprisingly warm references to the spirit and ideals of Socialism, which contained, amid some rather cloudy generalizations, this clear-cut and revolutionary judgment:

'Wage labour, though it appears to be an inevitable step in the evolution of society, is as little fitted to represent finally or adequately the connection of man with man in the production of wealth as in earlier times slavery or serfdom.'

No wonder that the deliverance in which this sentence occurred was reprinted and eagerly distributed not only by the C.S.U. but by the G.S.M.

But the C.S.U. never found what could alone give it unity and conviction—a Christian sociology, based on an authentic doctrine of man and society, and the social traditions of the Church. It was assuredly not lax in its theology where creeds and sacraments were concerned. Gore, his great collaborator, is fully justified in saying of Holland that 'his whole soul beat in tune with the great theology of the creeds', and by his exposition of this he never failed to illuminate and inspire his hearers. Nor, on the other hand, was the Union content to be merely theoretical. It struggled manfully and intelligently with the symptoms of social disease, such glaring abuses of its time as sweating, lead poisoning, dangerous trades. But it failed most conspicuously to do the very thing it had explicitly set out to do. As Mr. Binyon dryly observes, it 'had claimed for the Christian Law the ultimate authority to rule social practice; but it had omitted to explain what the Christian Law was.' It failed to assess the characteristic activities of its time from the standpoint of purpose; it was too prone to inquire into the motives from which men acted rather than into the validity, even the feasibility, of what they were attempting, perhaps with the best intentions, to do. Hence the perpetual tension within the Union, not between those who were emphasizing religious demands and those who were stressing social obligations—that is a healthy tension from which a valid and balanced outlook and policy can result—but a tension between what Holland called the 'partly cracky, partly fervid set' and the 'silent and unforward Respectables'. He felt the futility and the falsity of this confrontation without seeing how it could be overcome. 'I have been and am oppressively anxious over the Social Union', he wrote to Talbot in 1894. 'The problems are deepening fast and we do not know where we are.'

By the side of Holland stood his ever loyal and admiring friend, a man strikingly different in temperament and outlook, though bound to him in so close and so continuous a collaboration. Holland was in many ways in tune with the liberal aspira-

K   145

tions of his time; he had learnt his Hegelianism at the feet of
T. H. Green; the course which 'social progress' was taking was
one of which he in general approved and could happily strive
to accelerate; in a democratic state, he argued, what was called
'grandmotherly legislation' only meant that 'every man was his
own grandmother'. Gore's outlook was in essence very different
from this, much more so indeed than he seems himself to have
appreciated. Progress, he declared in effect, was bound to be
delusive unless it was preceded by penitence, and especially by
the overt penitence of the Church for her complacent conniv-
ance at the organized avarice of commercialism. There is a
characteristic cry on page 210 of his Bampton Lectures on *The
Incarnation of the Son of God* (1891):

'What I am complaining of, what I want you to complain of,
with a persistence and a conviction which shall make our complaint fruitful of reform, is—not that commercial and social
selfishness exist in the world, or even that it appears to dominate
society; but that its profound antagonism to the spirit of Christ
is not recognized, that there is not amongst us anything that
can be called an adequate conception of what Christian
morality means.'

Seventeen years later, addressing the Pan-Anglican Congress, he
struck the same note, and went further:

'Penitence must lead to reparation while there is yet time,
ere the well-merited judgments of God take all weapons of social
influence out of our hands. . . . We must identify ourselves with
the great impeachment of the present industrial system.'

But though Gore did go on to say that 'we must identify ourselves, because we are Christians with the positive ethical ideal
of socialistic thought', he did not understand such an identification as involving a merging of Christian social effort with the
secular protest or the programmes that arose out of it. His most
characteristic thought ran on different lines, his primary concern being ever with the recovery of the idea of the Church as
above all else 'The Way', a visible symbol of the life of man as the
Creator meant it to be lived. The utter failure, as he saw it, of
the 'established' church to reach after this ideal, or even to

understand it, was at the bottom of that ecclesiastical radicalism which led him, when a diocesan bishop, to cry out, 'I hate the Church of England', and to stigmatize it as 'an ingeniously devised instrumentality for defeating the objects which it is supposed to promote'. Of all figures of comparable moral and intellectual stature during his lifetime, Gore was perhaps the most fundamentally in revolt against the aims and assumptions of English society, and if he did not appear so it was because he was less inclined than the more 'cracky and fervid' revolutionaries to pin his faith to the secular prescriptions then most in vogue. Gore was a good deal more suspicious of the collectivist trend than was Holland or were the majority of the more 'forward' spirits in the C.S.U. 'I may confess myself' he said once, 'among those who would jealously set limits to the paternal supervision of the democratic state.'

To one with such an outlook neither the expansive imperialism nor the businesslike collectivism of the 'nineties could afford much comfort. To a much older man the contrast with the Hungry 'Forties was almost too much of an encouragement. To the early deliberations of the C.S.U. there came 'a bent figure' with 'a nobility in the prophetic head which', said Holland, 'made the rest of us look very cheap. . . . The fire gleamed still in his eyes, so that they shone with the passionate light which is only to be seen in men who have known Maurice.' Ludlow's message was one of consolation; forty years ago matters both in Church and State had been far worse. Younger men and women, however, were arising with a message of challenge; it was high time, they said, that things became far better. The new figures, both in G.S.M. and C.S.U. (and many belonged to both) are far too numerous to be recorded here, but some stand out. Among the women were Gertrude Tuckwell and Constance Smith on the reforming side, and amidst those accounted more revolutionary a young woman with the 'strange magnetic influence of the born orator', whose 'eyes sought justice everywhere'. Enid Stacy was a product of the vigorous Bristol group of Christian Socialists started by E. D. Girdlestone in 1883. When only twenty-four she led a strike of working girls in that

city and showed powers of leadership and of oratory which soon
made her one of the best known socialist propagandists in the
country. Dying at thirty-five in 1903, she left behind her two
who were to be prominent in many phases of the movement
down to our own day, Paul, her brother, and Percy Widdrington, whose first wife she had become in 1897. Among the
younger men were the scholarly Percy Dearmer; the witty
James Adderley, whose life was passed both 'in slums and
society', as his autobiography records but a good deal more in
the former than in the latter; and two men, born in the same
year, 1860, but of contrasting gifts and characteristics, Charles
Marson and Lewis Donaldson. Marson, with his flashing wit,
his defiance of every form of ecclesiastical convention and his
utter devotion to the poor, made an impression upon many of
his contemporaries the power of which it is impossible to
exaggerate. 'I cannot remember', says Paul Stacy, in his preface
to the 1930 edition of Marson's *God's Co-operative Society*, 'any
casual five minutes' conversation with him that would have been
called ordinary; everything he said either informed, arrested,
pleased or amused . . . he let light in all round.' Perhaps his
greatest service to the movement was to recall its members to
the social teaching of the Bible and of the Fathers, a task carried
farther by a younger contemporary, Conrad Noel, who had
something of his defiant brilliance and personal magnetism.
Transplanted from the Soho which he loved, Marson brought
to a Somerset village the same devotion to and insight into the
needs and feelings of the poor, pioneering the revival of their
folksong and foreshadowing in his ministry a new alliance between Church and countryside. Donaldson also had worked as
a curate in Soho, and elsewhere in London, but it was with his
arrival in Leicester as vicar of St. Mark's in 1897 that his period
of greatest influence began. His most striking action, a gesture
reminiscent of Headlam himself, was to put himself at the head
of the march to London of two hundred representatives of the
local unemployed. By doing so he turned the march into a pil-
grimage, challenged the attention, and often won the sympathy,
of the churchmen in the towns and villages through which the

procession passed, and reinforced the claim of his fellow-citizens that their plight was no local misfortune but part of the social and economic failure of a nation.

The unemployed of 1905 were symptomatic of a new turn in the nation's affairs. Complacency had been shaken by the South African defeats; 'we have had no end of a lesson', Kipling told his countrymen, but it remained to be seen whether it would 'do us no end of good'. The economic benefits of imperialism were showing signs of exhaustion; real wages were falling, unemployment (against which there was still no social insurance) was rising. New social programmes appeared; Joseph Chamberlain demanded a breach with Free Trade; Liberalism rose to the challenge with a vigour which was to carry it back to a last long lease of power, with a new Labour Party for ally. But after 1910 the mood changed. Evolutionary philosophies of progress came up for review; a radical revaluation began in every sphere of activity and thought, from theology to sociology. Men were still confident that life held no problems to which they could not find the answer, but they no longer trusted to see that answer unfolded for them in the progressive development of events. Scrutiny, discrimination and revision were demanded and were forthcoming. Eschatology and Syndicalism, votes for women and freedom for Ireland—there was a tremendous lot to think about and to argue about; everything seemed to be beginning afresh. Scarcely anyone suspected, even dimly, that a phase of European civilization was at no new beginning, but coming abruptly to its end.

By these rapidly changing moods the Church's social movement, with too insubstantial foundations in its own soil, was inevitably caught and rocked. The General Election of 1906 kindled a fervour of reforming zeal and disinterested social hope such as this island had never perhaps witnessed before and has certainly never seen since. The new 'Socialism', ethical, altruist, owing 'little to Karl Marx but much to the Bible', wrote Canon Widdrington, who lived and laboured in the heart of that enthusiasm, when recalling it some twenty years later, 'was bringing back hope and courage into the drab lives of the

people, creating a type of character which was indubitably
Christian and a fellowship which put the fellowship of our
churches to shame'. It was but natural that priests in the industrial areas should often be ready to meet and mingle with a
movement to which the best among their people were giving so
much and which was giving so much new hope and energy to
them. Many of these priests no doubt needed no more than their
everyday experience, alike as pastors and as citizens, to win
them to the cause but those who required more profound
theological and sociological sanctions did not find them lacking.
In particular Dr. F. W. Bussell's massive and wide-ranging
Bampton Lectures on *Christian Theology and Social Progress*, while
in no specific sense 'socialist' in tendency, did lead to the conclusion that there was a 'Needful Alliance of the Gospel and
"Democracy".' Bussell detected 'some ground of apprehension
that religion's efficacy and intimate connection with the social
life of humanity may suffer, that the forces which seem to
threaten what we have termed the democratic ideal may resent
its interference; and that faith may follow the anchoritic tendency of the various movements of reform, by surrendering
some department of human life to an alien power, by limiting
its empire, like stoicism, to some inward citadel and by retreat-
ing into a purely subjective state—out of all strict relation to
things as they are.' But Bussell's anxiety on this score derived
precisely from his absorption with the value of the personal,
which he found 'everywhere denied'. 'It is my aim', he wrote in
his preface, 'to show how general welfare is bound up with the
faith and hopes of Christian belief; and again, how the general
welfare can only rightly be secured by justice to the particular,
by respecting the units which make up the whole.' This emphasis
remained in the minds of those who pondered this weighty contribution to apologetic (for such it primarily was) when it
appeared in book form in 1907, and was recalled a few years
later when doubts began to be mooted whether the 'evolution'
of socialistic reform, on which so many hopes had been founded,
was not carrying the masses forward into a 'servile state'.

But it was with no such fears that the Church Socialist League was founded in 1906. The mood was one of almost unbounded confidence. At last, it was felt, a unifying principle had been found, and a slogan was coined by Lewis Donaldson to express this conviction: 'Christianity is the religion of which Socialism is the practice.' Headlam himself would hardly have gone as far as this, and indeed the G.S.M., almost moribund by this time, was suspected, owing to its warden's Liberal leanings, of a deficiency of collectivist zeal. As for the C.S.U., even its leaders were beginning to despair of arousing it to a degree of energy appropriate to the mood of the moment. 'Our great effort to give the C.S.U. a new lease of life has failed', wrote Gore to Holland in this year; 'I seem more and more to feel as if the C.S.U. had done its bit and had better (not dry up but) acquiesce in being academic and leave the Socialists to make a fresh start.' This they were only too ready to do, and an effort made by Percy Widdrington, at the foundation meeting of the C.S.L., to secure the inclusion in its Basis of the revival and the restatement of a Christian sociology as an integral part of its task, was defeated as savouring of an intellectualism inappropriate to the democratic aspirations of the League. 'The fact was', says Canon Widdrington, writing twenty years later, 'that the exercise of the critical faculty was not the strong point of the conference. We were caught in the wave of enthusiasm which was sweeping the country and were inclined to make a too facile identification of Christianity with Socialism. Many of those present seemed to hold that Socialism provided us with a ready-made sociology, and that it was a waste of time to attempt to create our own.'

They were not alone in so thinking. There were many churchmen who, while they might suspect the C.S.L. leaders of a certain recklessness in identifying themselves so closely as they did with a rising political movement, yet welcomed the socialist ideology with an equal fervour. A young Fellow of Queen's College, Oxford, by name William Temple, wrote in *The Economic Review* that 'the alternative stands before us—Socialism or Heresy; we are involved in one or the other.' No middle ground appeared to him to be tenable. This was in 1908, the year of the great Pan-Anglican Congress, at which the relations of Christianity and Socialism were a burning issue, but there was little doubt in which direction the greater enthusiasm was to be found. Lewis Donaldson spoke of 'the splendid Socialism of the Congress', and quoted the slogan he had coined for the C.S.L. Amid the eager protagonists rose a bent and bearded figure to speak his *Nunc dimittis*. Ludlow was eighty-seven. He protested against 'any narrowing of the large word Socialism, which stood for the faith which brought men together in one common force—the faith of Frederick Maurice'. He believed, he added, that the true Christian Socialism was the faith of all present.

He was over-optimistic, as is often the habit of the aged. Socialism, however large a word, could not be large enough for that. *The Church Times* was particularly critical, and in a leading article on August 14th on the Albert Hall meetings containing some not unjustifiable warnings against the danger of identifying the Church's mission with the promotion of a merely material welfare, concluded with a truly astonishing attack upon the working classes. 'Their greed, their self-indulgence, their dislike of obedience, call for stern rebuke. By administering such reproof in the spirit of love much more than by adulation or by pulpit-babblings about the tyranny of capital will the Church be furthering the "welfare" of the poor.' The whole article shows the mood of bitter antagonism to the aspirations of the masses against which the C.S.L. leaders had to contend within the Church, and which no doubt provoked them at times into incautious utterances. But there was much that was truly scriptural in the fiery speeches with which the League's first organizer, Conrad Noel, was carrying its message round the country; much that was truly pastoral in the ministries of such priests as Donaldson at Leicester, Gobat at Darlington and Widdrington at Coventry. The championship of the new unemployed, the Trafalgar Square demonstrations, the great procession to Lambeth during the Mining dispute in 1912, with George Lansbury bearing a scarlet cross at the head, and the presentation of the protest at the Palace, recalled the heroic episodes of the G.S.M. in its early days a quarter of a century before. But the drama was acted against a more hopeful background; the men of the C.S.L. felt that the tide was with them. So did others, less deeply committed politically. 'Socialism', wrote Scott Holland in 1911, 'in emphasizing the moral significance of the State, has got hold of the real trend of things, under which we are all mentally and rationally moving.'

But in fact 'the moral significance of the State' was a matter which was just at this moment coming up for reconsideration. A new 'pluralism' was emerging in political theory, and John Neville Figgis, perhaps the greatest member of Gore's Community of the Resurrection, was making a striking contribution to it.

'The State (he wrote, in his influential study of *Churches in the Modern State*) did not create the family, nor did it create the churches, nor even in any real sense can it be said to have created the club or the trades union, nor, in the Middle Ages, the guild or the religious order, hardly even the universities; they have all risen out of the natural associative instinct of mankind, and should all be treated by the supreme authority as having a life original and guaranteed.'

This element in Figgis's teaching as a political theorist provided a link with the industrial movement of the workers, which was by 1911 in strong reaction against the political passivity and bureaucratic reformism of Labour's official leaders. The National Guilds, projected by S. G. Hobson and A. R. Orage in *The New Age* as the workers' only 'way out of the wage system', came in for eager examination by members of the C.S.L. The challenge, says Canon Widdrington, 'made us reconsider many ideas which we had too readily accepted, and turned our minds back to the social traditions of the Church'.

But Figgis's influence as a religious teacher was perhaps even more important than his work as a political theorist, and here he combined a true Christian humanism with an emphasis upon the Church as 'the Fellowship of the Mystery', a separate society set over against the world order. In this he provided a check to the too optimistic humanitarianism by which the C.S.L. had become somewhat infected through its intimate contacts with democratic movements. 'Too many Christian Socialists', wrote a C.S.L. leader, Egerton Swann, in the League's monthly journal, just before the 1914 war, 'think of the Kingdom of God as merely a human society in which perfect justice rules and whose members are bound together by perfect human love. It is simply the apotheosis of humanitarianism. . . . God for them remains quite in the background.'

It is clear that the readiness to associate democratic idealism with the theology of the Kingdom, which in one form or another was the guiding principle of the various groups whose activities I have been considering in this lecture, was due for radical challenge. The impulse behind it was spontaneous and sincere; it arose from a salutary consciousness of implication in social sin and a generous sympathy for the poor in the wrongs and sufferings inflicted upon them. But it disastrously obscured certain essential issues. Is it the mission of the Church to infuse human ideals with spiritual fervour, or is it not for her rather to define the purposes to which a world responsible to its Creator should direct its energies? Has she or has she not unique resources, not only in her Faith but in her best traditions, for doing this? What has been and will be the effect upon man of conformity to the characteristic trends of a secularized economics and a materialistic industrialism? For thirty years the Church's social movement, despite much opposition and inertia among church people, had been trying to work with the grain of secular idealism, in a society the stability and advancing prosperity of which were scarcely doubted, even by those most critical of its shortcomings. For a century the Church of England had again and again appeared to be failing the people of England, and had been threatened with collapse under the irresistible pressure of Progress; but in the event it was Progress and not the Church which collapsed. 1914 revealed a truth of which Chesterton was to write a few years later: 'The Church is dying as usual; but the modern world is dead; and cannot be raised save in the fashion of Lazarus.'

❧ VI ☙

'NOT TO BUILD BUT TO DIG': 1914–1946

In 1914 Scott Holland was still editing *The Commonwealth*, which he had taken over some seventeen years earlier. Its August number had no word to say about the Serajevo murders or the international crisis which followed them. It announced, however, that an International Congress of Social Christianity would be held at the end of September in Bâle, when papers would be read on 'Christianity and Universal Peace'. In all this Holland's journal is typical of the Liberal-Labour outlook by which his political sympathies were coloured, an outlook which still dominated the Christian social movement. Holland, like the rest of this school, had always denounced those who declared that a war was inevitable. Three weeks after its outbreak he wrote in a letter:

'I will not allow that all the weary idiots have been right. My one comfort now is to remember that I never insisted on war as inevitable, never shouted Armaments . . . it is just this which I denounce in the Germans. By talking like this they have made war inevitable. Our folk who did it are open to the same damning charge.'

But a fortnight later he was writing to Neville Talbot that Prussianism 'is the last word in iniquity. I could not have believed that man could be so diabolical.' It is a recurrent handicap of good men that they cannot bring themselves to face in advance situations which predicate a kind or a degree of evil in others of which they would be incapable themselves.

Christian men do well to protest against resignation to war or any other man-made catastrophe as inevitable. The war of 1914 was not unavoidable; some historians are disposed to think that it was, in fact, very nearly avoided. But there were two errors in regard to the matter into which Holland, along with almost everyone else among the social idealists of his day, allowed himself to be betrayed. The first was that in rejecting war as inevitable, one should come to regard it as unthinkable. Or if this is to put the matter too strongly, one must at least say that the idealist was apt to assume that one should, in effect, act as if war could best be avoided by not thinking about it. And the other error derived from this: to regard war as a hideous and illogical interruption of the development of industrial civilization, rather than as an all too natural outcome of it, which is only by the most elaborate effort to be forestalled while the moral and economic assumptions of that civilization remain unrepudiated and largely unrealized. The complete failure of Christian idealists before 1914 to envisage the probability of war and to face its implications is a measure of the inadequacy alike of their theology and of their sociology. It is but fair to remember, however, that it is a great deal easier to see this now than it was then. Those of us who survive from the world of 1914 have lived through more than thirty years of recurrent crisis. With this situation, indeed, a specific 'theology of crisis' has now been evolved, with whatever disproportion of emphasis, to grapple. We have twice seen not only the horrors of war but the frustrations of 'after-the-war'; we have seen that the extremity of peril can give to a nation a unity and a purpose for which, without that stimulus, it seems to grope in vain; we have even seen reason to suspect that war, so far from being an interruption to the working of our economic system, is a goal towards which it blindly works, and that these are apparently the only terms on which it can continue to work at all. 'Crisis' for us recalls not only 1914, 1918 and 1940, but 1926 and 1931. We are hardly likely now to be deceived by the impression created by a book which was found very persuasive in progressive circles before 1914, that war was a 'great illusion' because it could no longer be made to pay, a calculation dubious in itself and only too characteristic of the commercialist philosophy of life from which it proceeded. A far greater illusion was that long fostered by the orthodox economists, as a result of which men assumed that a world increasingly unified by purely economic ambitions would be a world increasingly united for peace. In fact, of course, war was the logical upshot of an expansion inspired by a combination of nationalist ambition, organized avarice, and a frustration which drove the industrialized 'Powers' into world markets to compensate themselves for failure to dispose of a sufficiency of goods to their own nationals. Holland himself had come to see something of this when in a pamphlet he wrote for the National Mission two years before his death he declared that 'a limitless desire for riches, for power, for pleasure, has run like a flame through the Nations . . . and the result is that all Europe is at war'. The operative word here is 'limitless', but Holland saw the evil too exclusively as an ethical one. He did not see war clearly enough in the light in which Dr. Demant was twenty years later to describe it, as 'the most blatant expression of the tragic nature of man', as much the abhorred consequence of mistaken social aims as the upshot of wilful sin. For, as Dr. Demant points out, the situations which bellicose adventurers exploit develop out of 'the desires of peoples for certain valid satisfactions. War comes as the last tragic resort by which they . . . definitely seek the fulfilment of satisfactions they know no less terrible way of obtaining, or [is] the emotional release of psychic and social tensions brought about by frustration.'

It is more important for our present purpose, therefore, to see 1914 as marking the beginning of a new era in European history than to discuss the controversies to which the war gave rise within the Christian social movement at the time. For in this new catastrophic phase we see at once the culmination of economic insatiableness, the 'limitless desire' of which Holland spoke, and what Peter Drucker has called 'the end of Economic Man'. By this he means an era characterized by the harnessing of economic means to non-economic ends, as for example in the erection of 'full employment' into a value in itself, and 'the attempt to substitute non-economic for economic satisfactions, rewards and considerations as the basis for the rank, function and position of the individual in industrial society'. This latter objective, not necessarily ignoble in itself, only emerges with the development of Fascism after 1920, but this development was itself a consequence of the breakdown which war had first revealed, and was an attempt to create a new order to replace that of which the outbreak of war had signified the bankruptcy. In effect, of course, it only produced a new idolatry more devastating than the old. Moloch supplanted Mammon; what will follow upon his overthrow has yet to be revealed. We live still in the phase initiated in August, 1914.

The Church, you may say, did not understand all this in 1914; she did not see that we in western Europe had come, as Nicholas Berdyaev was to say some ten years later, to 'the end of our time', or, to adapt to our present theme another of his phrases, that 'war is what peace rots away into'. Certainly the Church did not perceive these things; reviving in so many directions in the nineteenth century, she had assuredly not revived her prophetic function, or learnt to discern the signs of the times. No one of the stature of Maurice had arisen since his day to sustain the prophetic note at the level on which he sounded it. 'Be not conformed to this world', said St. Paul to the Romans, 'but be ye transformed by the renewing of your mind that ye may prove what is the good and acceptable and perfect will of God.' That transformation had still to take place within the Church of England so far as the great trends of contemporary history were concerned; it simply had not occurred to the vast majority of teachers or taught within her fellowship that any such interpretation was called for from her. But under the impact of a war to face which men had been even less prepared spiritually than materially, there are to be discerned the first stirrings of what was to become that quest for the autochthonous which I take to be the characteristic mark of the period with which I am dealing in this lecture. To suggest, as is still sometimes done, that organized religion abandoned itself blindly in 1914 and after to a glorification of war and of the nation's share in it is a gross travesty of the facts. It would never have been

allowed to do so, for there were many who, under the shock
and strain of war, were venting their grievances against civilization upon 'the churches' which had failed to keep it in order,
and even upon a God Who seemed to have let them down.
Why did God allow the war? Why was Christianity powerless to
avert or to restrain it? The pacifist denounced the Church for a
spiritless surrender to nationalism; the patriot was prone to
regard her as existing primarily to stoke up enthusiasm for the
combat and commend the national cause. The Church was
thrown on to the defensive and forced to re-examine a good
many aspects of her apologetic. But the situation was one not
only of difficulty but of opportunity. 'The war and war conditions', said Archbishop Davidson, 'are, in God's mercy helping
us to the breaking down of ingrained or instinctive prejudices.'
The outcome of all this was the projection for 1916 of a 'National
Mission of Repentance and Hope'.

The National Mission was widely accounted afterwards to
have been on the whole a failure. It is a little difficult to know
by what standards it could have proved itself a success; judged
by the aims which they necessarily set before themselves all
missions must be in some measure a failure, and the wider the
scale of the effort, the more disparate will ideal and achievement appear. Moreover, to found a national mission, to a
people convinced of the righteousness of its cause and suffering
for its conviction, upon a call to repentance is to court misunderstanding, essential as such a call may be. A bishop in the
recent war recorded that his priests were unanimous that this
demand was the one thing their congregations would not
stand! Judgment in 1916 certainly began at the house of God.
'We are face to face with failure', said Dr. Greig, then Arch-
deacon of Worcester, 'in that the Church does not effectually
or effectively represent the nation, either with the ideals of
worship, righteousness or fellowship. It is this which calls for the
National Mission. There has been an unworthy surrender to a
compromise with the world; it is we who have failed, and not
religion.' This was a much less familiar confession from church
dignitaries thirty years ago than it has since become; but still

less familiar and even more important was the interpretation which the sponsors of the Mission put upon the word 'national' which they had attached to it. 'There is a real difference', it was officially declared, 'between a converted nation and a nation of converted individuals. All the citizens of a nation might be individually converted, and yet public life be conducted on principles other than Christian.' The implications of this statement were perhaps even larger than was realized by those who made it, and they were eagerly seized upon by the spokesmen of the unofficial social movements within the Church. For the statement conceded a main point for which they had been contending for decades—that the social order was in the intention of God a spiritual reality and an essential sphere of grace, with purposes which required to be understood and laws which needed to be obeyed. And since this was so, social righteousness could never be assumed to arise automatically out of the consecrated intentions of individuals.

If the National Mission thus represented in principle a turning point in the development of the movement which these lectures have been discussing, it did so even more signally in practice. Till then the little societies whose activities we have been studying were not only minority movements, as such bodies are always likely to be; they appeared, whether revolutionary or reformist in tone, as eccentric to the essential purpose of the Church, involving at worst a grave distortion of religion and at best a more or less legitimate hobby for specialists. And they in their turn suffered, both in spirit and in numbers, from what was at its most favourable a somewhat chilling tolerance. For all the stir they made, G.S.M., C.S.U. and C.S.L. always remained very small societies. The Guild never numbered more than 400; the Union, for all its moderation, had only 6,000 members when at its height in 1910; the League about the same time boasted 1,200. When one considers not only the number of practising church people at this period, but the wide and excited interest in social issues which characterized the years before the 1914 war, these figures appear almost microscopic. And the members of those bodies, feeling themselves to be regarded as eccentrics or even as outlaws, with little or no authorization from official sources for the message they had to proclaim, often allowed themselves to be driven into a posture of opposition to their ecclesiastical superiors which was good neither for them nor for the Church to which they belonged. To such of these as were not temperamentally incapable of a more co-operative attitude, the National Mission offered an opportunity of reconciliation and the chance to work constructively for social justice within the established framework of Anglicanism. No one saw this more clearly than the man who was by this time the strongest influence in the Church Socialist League. 'The time for criticism is past. The day of action has come', wrote Percy Widdrington in April, 1916; 'it has been our misfortune to find ourselves in constant opposition to the authorities in the Church, and we have been out of sympathy with our fellow churchmen. We have been driven for our fellowship outside rather than inside the Church. We have almost become "aliens" to our mother's children. Such a state of things is to be deplored. It has been to some of us spiritually disastrous. Thank God the day of better things has come.' Happily a discerning bishop knew how to employ the co-operative enthusiasm of a great propagandist, and the vicar of St. Peter's, Coventry, became his diocesan missioner, with beneficial results for the diocese of Worcester in which Coventry then was, and for the movement of which Widdrington was to emerge as a leader in the post-war years.

The Mission was followed by the setting up of five Committees which reported in 1918. The last of these reports to appear was that on 'Christianity and Industrial Problems', which was published at an auspicious moment in the month following the Armistice. Such 'reports' are commonly invested with a good deal more importance at the moment of their issue than history is disposed to accord them. I have felt myself justified in these lectures in omitting any reference to the great majority of these documents, the products of heterogeneous and largely fortuitous groups of persons, assembled for their allegedly representative character, who are often forced to take refuge in generalizations to conceal the differences they are unable to resolve. But the once famous 'Fifth Report' has more importance than most of its forerunners and successors, partly on account of its inherent merits, and partly because of the exceptionally energetic propaganda devoted to making its conclusions known. These conclusions indeed were regarded by more forward-looking spirits as hardly worthy of the radical analysis which had preceded them; they were, said a reviewer in the *Church Socialist*, 'utterly inadequate' and 'such as might be drawn by any body of worthy progressives . . . but the Report, apart from its conclusions, furnishes us with an admirable instrument of propaganda'. The Report was in fact described by one of its sternest critics, Dr. Hensley Henson, then Bishop of Durham, as a capitulation of the Church to the C.S.L., though the League had in fact only two representatives on the Committee, which was an exceptionally strong one. If Dr. Henson had said C.S.U. instead of C.S.L. it might have been more difficult to contradict him, for the Chairman was Bishop Talbot of Winchester, a leader in the Union since its earliest days, and Dr. Gore, Dr. Kempthorne (then Bishop of Lichfield) and Miss Constance Smith were amongst its members. Others included A. L. Smith (then Master of Balliol), the present Bishop of Chichester, and Mr. R. H. Tawney, who was credibly rumoured to have written a major part of the Report. Speaking generally, the Report is an excellent exposition of the best thought of what I could call the penultimate phase of the Christian social movement, the phase previous to that 'quest for the autochthonous' of which I have spoken as characterizing our present period, the first signs of which were to appear a few years after 1918. In a notable sentence which recalls Westcott's famous dictum of 1890, the Report prophesies that

'a future age will probably look upon some features of our industrial system with something of the same feelings that are aroused in us when we survey the nineteen centuries which it has taken to make a professedly Christian world apply Christian principles to the case of slavery'.

It was natural that the Committee should show itself to be

affected by the Guild Socialist propaganda which was at its height at this time, as it did in deploring

'an organization of industry which treats the workers as hands rather than as persons, and which deprives them of the control which they may reasonably claim to exercise over the conditions under which they earn their livelihood'.

This comment might be regarded as an implication of what the Committee had demanded on the previous page, 'not merely the improvement of individuals, but a fundamental change in the spirit of the system itself'. But it is noteworthy that the Report says 'the spirit of the system' and not 'the system', which left it to be inferred by those who liked to make the deduction, that 'the system', however this might be defined, would work out to satisfactory results if it were operated with nobler motives. Others of more radical disposition could argue that a fundamental change in the spirit of a system must manifest itself in a modification of the operations of that system. There was unlimited scope here for argument between the Christian Rotarian who preferred the former interpretation and the Christian Socialist who preferred the latter, the one laying his stress on motive, the other on organization. But both alike tended to leave unexamined the character and the purposes of Britain's industrial system as they found it, the validity of its role in the world's economy, the limitations imposed upon its achievement by Finance, and the effect of its techniques upon those involved in its mass-production. We are still at a stage when Christian reformers of every school tended to regard industrial problems as lying entirely within the sphere of the relations of men to one another, whether within the existing system or in another one.

The Fifth Report was accepted with substantial agreement by a Committee of the Lambeth Conference in 1920. But before this it had become the charter of an organization which was to obtain a greater degree of episcopal patronage than any Christian social body had yet enjoyed. The Industrial Christian Fellowship came into being as a timely fusion of an evangelistic agency (the Navvy Mission) which lacked a social message and a 'socially-minded' organization (the C.S.U.) which had never achieved any successful contact with the working class. The death of Scott Holland in March, 1918 seemed to signalize the end of the organization in and for which he had laboured so abundantly, and the C.S.U. leaders who remained were quick to recognize the fact. A new initiative was required and new men came forward to supply it. They were, for the most part, men who had served overseas as chaplains with the citizen armies, endured their hardships, shared their soul-searching experiences, and gained thereby an insight into their needs of body, soul and spirit such as they could have attained by no less exacting means. The I.C.F. was built up and carried forward by these men, and pre-eminently by one of them. Geoffrey Studdert Kennedy, it has been well said, 'was in the true line of succession of Stanton, Dolling and Wainwright', one of those completely selfless lovers of God and man, impetuous and often it may be injudicious, but ready to burn their lives away without hesitation if the truth that is in them can but be spoken and the souls they yearn to rescue can but be reached and restored. The Church of England has known several such men in the last quarter of a century; they have their critics, as Kennedy did, and often deserve such criticism and may profit by it, but they do what only such as they can do, and the early death which is commonly the price of so much vitality may represent the only terms on which their vocation can be fulfilled. Kennedy died at forty-six in 1929. Three years before, a writer in the *Church Times* said of him:

'No words can convey, to anybody who has not heard him, the impression of the amazing personality of this priest . . . tender and fierce, humorous and very serious, with keen and very tired eyes, a man working himself to death for God and his poor.'

Kennedy himself once defined a priest as 'one who bears upon himself the burden of the sins and sorrows of his people'. From this burden he never shrank, and to it he added the strain imposed by a restless and hungry mind, never satisfied with the formulation of a truth until he could express it in a way that could make it spring into life, first for himself and then for those to whom he strove to communicate it. The Christ he struggled to proclaim truly 'made all things new'—including Christianity, or rather he made it seem new to those who heard him.

Though Kennedy was before all else an evangelist, he ever desired and sought to carry his message right through into the social issues of his time. But as Archbishop Temple said of him, 'the urging impulse was not in his thought but in his heart; it was the passion of sympathy with the victims of our present injustice.' It is not easy to extract from his sermons and writings any very specific social teaching. It is significant that Mr. P. T. R. Kirk, who shared so intimately in Kennedy's I.C.F. work, in contributing an essay to his memorial volume, can give a graphic picture of Kennedy's personality and tell us much that is illuminating about his methods, but has nothing whatever to say about the content of his social message. Kennedy was not a trained social thinker; he trusted too much perhaps to unco-ordinated notions and intuitions; and some of his favourite ideas, as for example that industrialism ought to be regarded as 'sacramental' in character, begged some difficult questions and led to very dubious conclusions. Yet there was much in his teaching about that sacrament of the Altar, which was always so especially precious to him, that carried with it the most salutary warnings to those who, finding their Lord in the sanctuary, were all too ready to leave Him there. As for instance this passage:

'Right at the heart of the Christian devotional life there has always been the Breaking of Bread, and when that Sacrament is divorced from the dream of a Christian social order, it is deprived of its true significance. If we cut off that Bread which is His Body from all connection with our daily bread, and the means whereby we earn it; if we declare that He is present in the Bread of the sanctuary, but absent from the bread of the street—we deny the truth of the Incarnation. . . . It is this presence of Christ in common bread and His concern with the way we earn it that the world denies emphatically. They are quite willing, the men of the world, to allow that we may find Him by an act of faith in that Bread upon the altar, so long as we do not drag Him in to the bread of the common street.

Nobody worries about Christ so long as He can be kept shut up in churches; He is quite safe there, but there is always trouble if you try to let Him out.'

The I.C.F., with its great open-air 'Crusades', its missioners at the street corners and in the factories, and its educational work through correspondence class and study circle, was manifesting in the post-war years, more effectively than had ever been done before, the concern of the nation's Church at once for the spiritual and the social condition of the masses of the nation. Its 'platform' was the Fifth Report; but there were some in the Church's social movement who had always found that platform a trifle wobbly and were beginning to suspect that its foundations were not well and truly laid. The internal crises of propagandist bodies are not as a rule a matter of enduring historical interest, but the process of self-criticism and exploration through which the Church Socialist League passed between 1913 and 1923 had implications and repercussions which affected, then or subsequently, far more than its own small membership. Doubts about the validity and sufficiency of the League's basis had begun to spread before the war. These doubts had both a sociological and a theological origin. The C.S.L. had been founded at a moment when the Collectivism which was a blend of *Fabian Essays* and *Merrie England*, the bureaucratism of Webb and the idealism of Hardie, had established itself as a virtually unchallengeable interpretation of the Socialist idea. It was not the Socialism of Frederick Maurice or of William Morris, of Stewart Headlam or of H. M. Hyndman, but it had been taken over by the pioneers of the C.S.L. with little or no scrutiny because it was 'in the air', and because its earnest ethicalism concealed from all but a few both the flimsy character of its social philosophy and the antilibertarian tendencies of its more systematic exponents. But after 1911, as I have explained, it did begin to be challenged, and on grounds which made an instant appeal to the more alert minds in the C.S.L., for whom personal liberty and corporate responsibility were matters too closely bound up with a Christian doctrine of man to be slurred over without protest if it could be shown that they were in fact at issue. The National

'Not to Build but to Dig': 1914–1946

Guild propaganda involved such fundamental criticisms of the collectivist position that it represented something more like an attack on Socialism from a new angle than a mere revision of it. Its claim that there was no other way out of the wage system (which Westcott had not hesitated to rank with slavery and serfdom) than by the development of the workers' unions into responsible guilds, recalled in the first place that 'principle of association' preached by the earliest Christian Socialists, and secondly, and perhaps even more significantly, the industrial organs of a civilization which sprang directly out of a Catholic interpretation of life. But while the Guild Socialists claimed to stand on the left of the Labour movement, the catastrophic achievements of a militant Marxism in eastern Europe were suggesting that the word 'revolutionary', which Church socialists had been accustomed to employ with a somewhat light-hearted vagueness, would require in future to be used more circumspectly. Hardly anyone in Britain had taken dialectical materialism and the dictatorship of the proletariat seriously before 1917; but the emergence of Bolshevism, with its open defiance not only of the claims of supernatural religion but of many of the moral values of the culture which had grown up under the auspices of Christianity, created a changed situation for the Christian who had been wont to demand, in all too familiar terms, 'a new social order'. Here in Russia, defiant, militant, and alike by hypothesis and by the Muscovite tradition, indefinitely expansible, was indeed a new social order. Christian critics of their own country's social order who rejected the Marxian claims were led to suspect that the most hopeful clues to freedom and justice might be found not in the present but in the past. Perhaps, they began to reflect, it would be better for the heirs of a Christian civilization to talk rather less about a new social order until they had thought a good deal more about an old one.

But though sociological issues led thus to a reconsideration of religious sources, the root problems of which the C.S.L. leaders were being made aware were theological. Percy Widdrington had always been anxious that the League's function as a religious society should be properly understood; he was in particular alarmed by the tendency to regard the Kingdom of God either as a mere synonym for the Church or as a sort of earthly paradise to be ushered in by socialistic legislation. He was insistent on the prophetic responsibility of the Church to make judgments in the light of her own unique sanctions, and was fond of quoting a dictum of Bussell's that 'the Church must criticize from its own point of view or be false to its mission'. Widdrington had grown up in the Guild of St. Matthew, which had strong roots in Maurician theology; and in the post-war situation, with the reaction against immanentism in theology, with the growing doubts about the validity of that evolutionary collectivism with which Christian social thinkers had tended all too unreservedly to ally themselves, and with the challenge of Marxist materialism as at once an interpretation of history and a philosophy of life, he felt that a radical re-examination of the title deeds of the Church's social movement was necessary. It was a time, he might have said with Maurice, 'not to build but to dig, to show that economy and politics . . . must have a ground beneath themselves'. He sought for that ground where Maurice had sought for it, in the conception of the Kingdom of Christ as 'the regulative social ideal', though 'ideal' was hardly the right word to express what was in the mind of the group which he inspired, which might have done well to recall Maurice's own phrase—'ever-present reality'. The conception led the thoughts of his group—and of wider interdenominational groups which it largely inspired—backwards, but also forwards, since here was truly a case of *reculer pour mieux sauter*. It led backwards, first to the Gospels themselves for the recovery of the idea of the Kingdom as something essentially constitutive of human order, and secondarily to medieval Christendom, in which, amid all the social limitations of feudalism and the spiritual evils of ecclesiasticism, there was nevertheless a conscious and not unsuccessful effort to incarnate a Christian interpretation of life in the institutions of society. But the conception led forwards too, for it raised the question expressed by the title of a significant pamphlet by one of the C.S.L. leaders, *Is there a Catholic sociology?*

'Not to Build but to Dig': 1914–1946

The writer, Egerton Swann, answered the question in the affirmative, finding its three pillars to be distributed property, the Just Price, and a guild organization of industry. This, claimed Mr. Swann, is 'purely *the Church's own programme*; and it is perfectly distinctive. It does not involve the Church taking over ready-made opinions from the Labour movement or from any secular philosophy like modern Socialism. . . . The position sketched out cuts clean across all existing cleavages. It would leave the Church in an attitude of sovereign independence, and might require it to defy alike the Labour movement and the plutocracy.' This pamphlet was published in November, 1922. In the same month appeared a more ambitious publication, which arrived however, if less explicitly, at much the same sociological conclusions. *The Return of Christendom* was the product of several years' work by the group round Widdrington and represented an elaborate, if not wholly satisfactory, exploration of the philosophical, theological and sociological foundations for a reformulation of Catholic social teaching. In this volume what I have called 'the quest for the autochthonous' becomes for the first time explicit, and the impulse which it signalized is not yet exhausted.

The group from which this effort proceeded was Catholic in its inspiration, yet its members were attached either somewhat loosely or not at all to the organized Anglo-Catholic movement which was then promoting ambitious Congresses and an energetic propaganda throughout the country. Headlam's fusion of Maurician theology with Catholic sacramentalism had, for understandable reasons, met with but little welcome or understanding in the Anglo-Catholic movement, which despite the heroic work of its slum priests, had never wakened to the implications and the responsibilities of its heritage of social teaching. But at the 1923 Anglo-Catholic Congress a revered figure struck a challenging note. 'It is folly, it is madness', cried Bishop Weston of Zanzibar to the pious churchfolk in the Albert Hall, 'to suppose that you can worship Jesus in the Sacrament and Jesus on the Throne of Glory when you are sweating Him in the bodies and souls of His children.' His immediate call was to corporal works of mercy, and the call did not go without response; but there were some among the leaders at the Congress who felt that the matter should not stop there. They turned for aid to Percy Widdrington and his newly-constituted League of the Kingdom of God, and the most notable result of the cooperation thus initiated was the launching in 1925 of an enterprise which has been sustained down to our own day. The founders of the Anglo-Catholic Summer School of Sociology were Father Reginald Tribe of Kelham, George David Rosenthal of St. Agatha's, Birmingham, and Percy Widdrington, who was by this time a country priest in Essex; thus community life, a city pastorate and a rural ministry contributed their several experiences to the initiation of the task now set on foot. But I must here take the opportunity to mention also the name of Ruth Kenyon who from the beginning performed for the School a work of illumination exceeded by none. Her services of mind and heart had been given to the Christian social movement with the complete selflessness characteristic of her for twenty years before this, but henceforward they became of even greater value than previously. Here was a woman equipped both to dig and to build, and one who, whether at a Summer School study circle or on a Town Council committee, both pre-eminently understood and expounded the truths of Christian sociology and exemplified the qualities of Christian citizenship.

While these developments had been going forward in Anglo-Catholic circles, a more spectacular enterprise had been carried through upon a wider stage. The conference on Christian Politics, Economics and Citizenship known as COPEC, elaborately prepared for and ambitiously presented, was interdenominational in character and does not strictly fall within my subject. Yet it must be noticed, if only because so large a share in it was taken by Anglican leaders and especially by two of them. True, Bishop Gore only appeared as a speaker at the conference once, but the occasion was a memorable one for the tremendous ovation he received. Gore was at this time universally regarded as something more than a leader of the Christian social movement in any ordinary sense; rather was he venerated as a prophet who had spoken out boldly for the cause in days when to do so demanded a courage and an insight no longer needed, yet had never since fallen behind in an understanding of what the situation required. The bishop was speaking in the city of his most successful pastorate, a city in which his statue already stood in grateful acknowledgement alike of his civic and of his diocesan services; he was speaking, moreover, to what was the upshot of an interdenominational effort which, unswerving Catholic though he was, he had for over a dozen years done as much as any man to foster. He called, as he always did, for deeds to follow upon words; the conference, he declared, 'would be judged by its practical work, and for that he trembled. . . . We needed tremendous courage to ask ourselves frankly whether we were really prepared to accept these fundamental principles and to apply them, whatever the effect upon our party politics.' It was obvious that Gore was uplifted by the inspiring spectacle which the great gathering presented, but it was obvious too that he was not altogether happy about the intellectual foundation upon which it rested. Three years later, at the age of seventy-five, he addressed himself to the task of clarification by a consideration of the Church's social mission in the light of her historical development. The Halley Stewart Lectures on *Christ and Society* represent Gore's final effort to formulate a basis for one of the main tasks to which he had devoted so large a measure of his prophetic energy, and they begin with 'a demand for so thorough a reformation as to amount to a revolution'. The historical analysis is the strongest element in the lectures, and the most suggestive lessons are taught in the course of it; but when Gore came to consider the Church's contemporary task, while he was not hesitant in offering suggestions of his own, he was quite clear about 'the need to make a fresh start on a freshly laid intellectual basis and with a new plan of campaign'. But it is hardly surprising to find that Gore had not, in fact, very much help to give in this direction. He had fought the good fight for the recognition of social justice as a vital concern of the Church for a full forty years, and the leadership would now have to pass to other hands.

Copec itself had made it clear where that leadership would lie for the next two decades. To say that its presiding genius was William Temple is not in this case to employ a cliché but to give an exact description of the facts. There were other chairmen to share his labours, but it was the Bishop of Manchester who held the whole gathering together, who knew uniquely how to express the best of its mind, and who in doing so showed that especial genius for presidency which revealed itself increasingly as among the greatest of his gifts. How far this was at Birmingham primarily an achievement of personality it is not now easy to determine. The sense of his power and his primacy was strongly felt at Copec and lingers clearly in the memory more than twenty years afterwards. Yet when the deliverances which made and confirmed that impression at the time are re-read in the volume of the Conference 'Proceedings', it is not easy to find any insights which challenge the attention by their originality or any phrases which arrest us to-day by their prophetic suggestion. The Bishop called for a 'real repentance— that is a change of outlook such that we cease to look at life as men tend to look at it, and learn to look at it as God sees it'. This was to re-state in a more theological form the declaration made by Lucy Gardner, Copec's secretary and strongest driving force, that 'we want to establish a norm of Christian thought and action for the further working out of a Christian order'. The ambition was noble, but the question was whether the necessary theological, metaphysical and sociological formulation had been provided or even envisaged, and the answer which Copec suggested to many who attended it was not reassuring. The conference in fact represented rather the climax of a phase of social idealism than the initiation of a new phase of Christian realism. Indeed the Bishop himself had not yet wholly emancipated himself from certain influences of that earlier phase, and so his finest qualities had still to be released for leadership in the later one.

Two years after Gore had told the Copec Conference that it would need 'tremendous courage to ask ourselves frankly whether we were really prepared to accept these fundamental principles', a social crisis developed in which one of those principles was clearly involved. Whether or not the claim for a 'Living Wage' is in fact the most authentic formulation of a Christian social principle is at least arguable, but it had been adopted as such in a report to Convocation as long before as 1907 and more or less explicitly affirmed by the Lambeth Conference in 1920. The 'Fifth Report' with which the bishops at Lambeth declared themselves to be in substantial agreement, had defined a Living Wage in generous terms. 'The first charge upon every industry', it affirmed, 'should be the payment of a sufficient wage to enable the worker to maintain himself and his family in health and honour, with such a margin of leisure as will permit reasonable recreation and the development of mind and spirit.' It is perhaps significant that this claim should have been formulated during the industrial expansion induced by a war economy; the occasion recalls the terms of a telegram said to have been despatched by a profiteer during the short-lived period of post-war 'prosperity' to his wife on the Riviera: 'Business booming, spare no expense.' But after 1920 business was not booming; as Mr. Bevin was to declare twenty-five years later in the House of Commons, 'the Government of the day, without a word to industry, without mentioning it to a trade union official in the country, without knowing what was really happening, deflated the currency by 40 per cent', and Mr. Bevin, when he asked Mr. Montagu Norman in the crisis of 1926 why he had done it, got the reply, 'if a man is working and living on £3 or £4 a week he causes so many imports and upsets the exchanges and the gold situation cannot operate'. Now the bishops, in adopting what they believed to be the 'principle' of the Living Wage, were not assuming it as axiomatic that the 'gold situation' should 'operate'; it is very unlikely that the postulated requirements of this mysterious metal entered any more into their calculations at this time than it did into those of ninety-five per cent of the population, which was serenely unconscious of the influence of monetary policy upon social affairs. Because the demand for a Living Wage involved no overt attack upon the wage system and the established relationship of employer and employed, it looked like a 'moderate' demand. But, in fact, it raised issues the importance and even the nature of which were seemingly never appreciated by the authorities of the Church when they advanced it. When they were told by the Federation of British Industries, in February 1921, by which date the first effects of deflation were being felt, that 'the real and ultimate test must always be what industry can bear', and that 'it may be necessary . . . for the workers to be prepared to accept a money wage which may, till trade revives, give them a lower standard of living . . . even than their pre-war standard', Church leaders had no reply to make, and received the challenge in silence. It was of no avail for the C.S.L. to declare, as it did in a manifesto addressed to their lordships, that 'if the principle enunciated by various Church authorities was a Christian one in the first instance, it cannot become less so when it is found to involve profounder changes than some of its propounders perhaps realized'. The bishops had no more idea than the rest of the great mass of social idealists what such 'profounder changes' might be, since they knew little or nothing of the financial factors which had transformed the situation on which had been based their cherished 'principle'. It was all very bewildering, and it could only be hoped that trade would soon 'revive' again and permit moral demands to operate with the approval of orthodox economics.

Trade did not thus energetically revive. But the workers' organizations, defeated in 1921, did do so, and with them the resolution of their members not to 'accept a money wage which might give them a lower standard of living even than their pre-war standard'. Nowhere was this resolution stronger than among the miners, and the consequence was that nine days' wonder of proletarian solidarity, the so-called 'General Strike' of 1926. We are only concerned here with that demonstration, the revolutionary implications of which were at least as alarming to most of its ostensible leaders as they were to the community in general, so far as the situation which it precipitated affected the Church. That, in fact, the Church did react strongly and independently to the challenge of the situation is attributable partly to the efficacy of seven years' intensive propaganda by the

Christian sociological agencies, but partly also to the notable stand made by the leader of the Anglican communion. Archbishop Davidson was not by temperament or by habit the sort of prelate likely to welcome so audacious a gesture as that which the Strike represented. Indeed he spoke in the House of Lords of 'its unwisdom and its mischievousness', and found it 'simply shocking that it should be possible at this time of day in our country for a set of men who are a kind of oligarchy' to challenge the Government in this way. But he responded to appeals made to him by religious leaders within the Church of England and outside it to promote the quest for a way of reconciliation, and himself sponsored a set of proposals intended to serve as the basis for a resumption of negotiations. But the Government had determined upon the unconditional surrender of the men, and was in no mood to encourage a Primate to address the public in a sense different from that of the Premier. The Archbishop's proposals were excluded from the Government's newspaper and at first refused for broadcasting, and the spiritual leader of the Established Church was referred to in Parliament as 'an irresponsible agency'. The Archbishop and the religious leaders acting with him did not accept these rebuffs with resignation, but on the contrary resorted to every device of publicity open to them to proclaim their proposals to the nation. While these proposals involved no specific endorsement of the workers' claims, and were not such as the miners were ready to accept at that time, the persistence of Church leaders in their independent stand at a moment when emotions ran high and the greater part of the middle class was in no mood to listen to any considerations of the strikers' case, made a great impression on wide circles of the working classes. Here was evidence of two things of which organized religion, in its more official aspects at any rate, had been thought incapable since the Industrial Revolution—sympathy for the claims of a proletariat in revolt, and independence in face of the great ones of the earth. Men of historical minds recalled Laud and Latimer, Thomas of Canterbury and Hugh of Lincoln, and simple folk, for the first time for centuries, cheered an Archbishop in the streets.

With the end of the Strike a committee of religious leaders, including ten bishops headed by Bishop Kempthorne of Lichfield, the Chairman of the I.C.F., fought a dogged rearguard action on behalf at once of their principle of the Living Wage and of the miners, threatened with destitution for lack of such a standard. But while the struggle was tenacious, the basis of fact and principle on which it was conducted was inadequate. The bishops had no real answer to the claim of the owners, backed by the Government, that the living standards of the operatives must come down, because they did not know how to challenge the assumptions upon which that claim was made. They had always, at any rate implicitly, accepted the wage system as a 'permanent hypothesis', thus forcing themselves to demand as a 'living wage' what could perhaps only be technically implemented over an indefinite period as a living income; now the question arose whether they were tacitly to accept the financial system also. It would probably have made no immediate practical difference if the religious leaders had, on clear and sufficient grounds, explicitly repudiated both these upshots of a plutocratic secularism; but it would have immensely clarified and fortified the generous sentiment on social matters which had spread so widely in Christian circles if they had qualified themselves to reinforce their moral leadership by an intellectual one. As a little book on *The Miners' Distress and the Coal Problem*, published at the end of 1929, declared, 'only when the Christian community has brought its ethical demands face to face with the complicated series of economic factors will it be able confidently to assert that the industrial problem, of which this is so acute an example, is not due to any economic laws which must be considered as laws of nature'.

The author of the book was V. A. Demant, the newly appointed Director of Research of the Christian Social Council; his name was then almost unknown, but it was not long to remain so. Demant emerged at the opening of the 'thirties as a new voice in the Christian social movement, demanding that it should advance 'from Ethics to Sociology', from aspiration after what ought to be to proclamation of what essentially is. In

'Not to Build but to Dig': 1914–1946

July 1930 *The New Age*, a secular journal espousing revolutionary principles of finance, published a 'Lambeth Conference Number' in which no fewer than five Christian sociologists took upon themselves to advise their lordships on the need for a radical reconsideration of the basis of Christian social teaching in the modern world. The article by Mr. Demant struck a particularly fresh and challenging note, and may almost be said to have initiated an outlook upon the whole subject which has won an increasing acceptance in the Christian social movement right down to our own day.

'The dilemma of industrialism (he wrote) makes it more and more difficult to face squarely the direct moral issues of personal, business and political life. In its religious aspect the problem is how far the theories of men are mistaken for (or imposed as representing) laws of Nature. Religion is concerned with "rightness" in the whole of life. . . . The witness of the modern church to social health has been largely ineffective because religion has been confined, after the manner of the Pelagians, to questions in which *directly* moral issues are raised. But religion is as much concerned with truth as with goodness. . . . While the resolving of such a contradiction between industry and economic theory [as financial orthodoxy has introduced] is a technical and not a moral task, its existence is an ethical and social issue of the first magnitude. You cannot moralize a contradiction. But if you are ignorant that a social situation involves contradictory policies you are looking for wrong ethical *motives* to account for the [resulting] disasters—and you will mistake for these the moral perversions and poisoned relationships that spring from the strains imposed by the social dilemma. Your moral principles will then be looked upon as unreal, and the Church despised as a meddler adding one more link to the chain of difficulties.' Christian critics might reject, as many did, the particular economic thesis in relation to which these considerations were adduced; they could hardly, unless too unintelligent to comprehend them, resist the validity of the contentions themselves. Henceforward the movement for an autochthonous Christian social policy pioneered by Widdrington, and strongly aided by

M

contributions made, from different angles, by R. H. Tawney and Egerton Swann, allied itself with the demand for an authentically religious (as distinct from a merely moralistic) judgment formulated by Demant, and the basis for a Catholic sociology was securely laid. A willing and energetic band of labourers set to work upon the superstructure, and their activities, in what is now known as the Christendom Group, are not yet at an end.

We have inevitably in these Lectures been concerned with the Church's social movement rather as an organ of prophecy than as an agency for social service. But it would be at once unjust and misleading to suggest that its activities were at any time theoretical only and had no results in inspiring social action, whether of a 'neutral' character or specifically undertaken in the Church's name. But 'social service', which had been so pre-eminently inspired by Christianity, had passed into a new phase with the increasing extension of the State-controlled social services, raising problems in regard to the scope of voluntaryism and the spirit in which Christian work in this field could be done which have not even yet perhaps been clearly envisaged. The great age of the Christian 'Settlements' was over; they were beginning to be metamorphosed into the youth club and the community centre. But the spirit of *Caritas*, an exasperated zeal for persons born of a vision of men and women as God would have them be, which had burnt so fervently in the Anglo-Catholic movement in the days of Stanton and Dolling and Headlam, flamed up again in the nineteen-twenties and found outlets for its energy in directions where personal contact would always count for more than impersonal administration. Examples of this were manifested in the work of the Fellowship of St. Christopher for homeless boys and that of the Society of St. Francis for tramps and workless wayfarers. But the most striking gesture was the pioneering work of the Christian Housing Associations in rousing the conscience at once of the Church and the nation to the appalling conditions amid which large sections of the population were required to lead what it was a travesty to describe as home life. Here a shining figure emerges from a crowd of earnest wellwishers and welldoers. Basil Jellicoe was described by William Temple as 'one of Christ's most precious gifts to the Church of our generation'. The archbishop's warm heart led him sometimes to be almost too generous in his tributes, but the description is in this case no exaggeration. As a young man of twenty-two in the sordid wilderness of Somers Town Jellicoe saw a vision of the Church summoned to 'build the old wastes and raise up the former desolations', and within a space of ten years men and women all over England, from Newcastle to Penzance, were banded together, as churchfolk explicitly, to do this very thing, often as a direct consequence of his inspiration and his initiative. Jellicoe's faith removed mountains of slum property, and he never had a moment's doubt as to the Christian validity of the task begun in 1924 in the St. Pancras Housing Association. 'Over-crowding and poverty', he declared in forthright terms, 'are being used by the Devil to steal from the children of God the health and happiness which are their right; and so the Church must fight for these things, confident in the presence of the Living God.' No one could be more confident of that presence than this man was; it carried him forward into enterprises which only he could have successfully set on foot and which did not always survive the withdrawal of what it is for once no cliché to describe as his magnetic personality. Such men as he was have commonly the defects of their qualities; they attempt too much, they expect too much, they often demand too much, and suffer bitterly from frustration and disappointment in consequence. Jellicoe had a burning passion for setting the world to rights in God's way and the passion gave power to his utterance, but what he said was not always equal in depth to what he felt, and he was too much tempted—and perhaps by his admirers encouraged—to assume that he had gone some way to solving a problem by coining a challenging phrase about it. As he grew older, however, he came to see that church social action needed to be buttressed and clarified by a Christian sociology; he attached himself to the group round Widdrington, and through a notable year set himself to inspire the undergraduates of Oxford to a perception of the challenge which the breakdown of the world, as manifested by the economic crisis, was presenting to the Church. The moment was a propitious one for such an effort; by 1933 things were going so badly for civilization that purely aesthetic interests no longer sufficed to satisfy the livelier spirits among the younger generation. Even the more irresponsible among them 'lacked', says one who was at Oxford at the time, 'the essential blend of destructive violence and soulless apathy which marked the jaunts and jollities of the late 'twenties. In 1931 something had happened. There'd been a crisis: the country had opened one eye.' Basil Jellicoe and Miles Sargent contrived at this time to induce a group of Oxford undergraduates and ordinands to open both, as a result of which there occurred a salutary reinforcement of the Church's social movement, the effect of which is still strongly felt. But Jellicoe's course was almost run. Like Studdert Kennedy, whom he so greatly admired, yet strangely never met, he had packed into a short life far more than most men achieve in a long one, and as Temple well says of him, his death in 1935 'belongs to that nature and that life'. He was only thirty-six when he died; 'Jellicoe', says his biographer, Kenneth Ingram, 'was much more genuinely a Franciscan than an ecclesiastic.' There was indeed something of Francis himself about this man, assuredly one of the saints of church social action.

By the time that Jellicoe died the mood characteristic of him, hopeful and high-hearted, but a shade too facile and irresponsible at times, was ceasing to measure up to the menace looming over European civilization. 1935 was the year of the invasion of Abyssinia; the 'clash of ideologies' had ceased to be purely ideological. The 'Right-Left' dichotomy, that characteristic crystallization of secularist heresy, now cast its deforming shadow over Christian social thinking. There was a 'Christian Right' which hailed Mussolini as a defender of the Faith, accepted Hitler as a bulwark against Bolshevism even while he was overthrowing almost all that Communism threatened, and acclaimed Franco with enthusiasm as the leader of the 'Last Crusade'. There was also—and much more conspicuously—a Christian Left. It is interesting to observe that at the very moment when the Church Socialist League developed such doubts about the validity of its basis as to induce it to abandon any explicit faith in Socialism, a pronounced sympathy for the idea was spreading amongst wide circles of the clergy. When in 1924 a socialist politician took office for the first time as British Prime Minister, an address of congratulation to him was signed by many hundreds of Anglican priests. How far Ramsay MacDonald fulfilled the confidence thus reposed in him, either then or half a dozen years later, is perhaps dubious, but there were some among the earlier Church socialists at any rate who are unlikely to have had very much of this. Included among such was surely that most intensely individual of socialists, Conrad Noel, who had been since 1910 the famous—or as his enemies preferred to say, notorious—'Red Vicar' of Thaxted. It cannot be questioned that in virtue alike of the vigour and fertility of his mind and the force of his personality, Noel was for two full decades the real leader of the political and ideological Left in the Church of England. The 'Battle of the Flags' at Thaxted church in the early 'twenties, whatever may be thought of the validity of the issues or the wisdom of entering on such a conflict, was the sort of tussle that only such a man as Noel could have inspired and so long sustained. The struggle involved acceptance of an interpretation of the moral significance of the Russian Revolution which the 'Red Vicar' then most conscientiously held, but later, perhaps even more conscientiously, began to doubt. When minority movements become majority enthusiasms those whose *métier* it is to champion the underdog, regardless of its breed, are apt to become embarrassed, and later developments, both at the Kremlin and among those who supported it, caused a split in Noel's esoteric 'Catholic Crusade' and tended to divert his interest from political affairs. Whatever his faults or limitations, Noel was always a dogmatic Christian and never a sectarian thinker, and enthusiasm for Moscow, even in Christian circles, was tending to harden into the blind fanaticism characteristic of a sect. Noel had found it easier to be a friend—albeit ever a candid friend—of the Soviet Union than to be a slavish friend of its official 'Friends', and as the Christian Left developed more and more into a quasi-ethical cult its leadership naturally passed into other hands.

Apart, however, from what most church people felt to be aberrations, the growing social consciousness in church circles, which became still more marked after the bankruptcy of economic secularism, was plainly revealed by the crisis of 1931, was marked, and it was on the whole the sign of a genuine spiritual and intellectual awakening. The old complacency was dying, and the Church was no longer to be counted on as a supporter either of economic orthodoxy or of social conformity.

In November, 1936, the Albert Hall was packed to the doors by an eager gathering of churchfolk who, under the leadership of Archbishop Temple, solemnly pledged themselves to combat malnutrition, bad housing and unemployment, and 'to take every possible action that may secure for our fellows their birthright as the children of one Father'. But it was not so clear as many desired and perhaps believed it to be what forms such action should take. For the totalitarian threat revealed to those who could discern the signs of the times that the old alignments and the assumptions on which they were founded no longer corresponded to basic realities. As the Church Union Summer School's syllabus declared in 1937:

'The whole position to-day is a vastly changed one. In the nineteenth century the mere fact of identifying the Church with any social, i.e. anti-individualist, trend was a salutary gesture. It emphasized an aspect of life which both society and religion had perilously neglected. But this is not so to-day. A movement is no longer *ipso facto* to be welcomed because it is called a social movement. On the contrary, among those claiming that name are precisely the characteristically dangerous tendencies of our time. They are not genuinely social at all, for a true Socialism must respect the person, as well as society. They imply a collectivism which has become demonic.'

Two years later the demonic collectivism of Nazi Germany broke its bounds and the four horsemen of the Apocalypse set out upon the most destructive and the most extensive of all their rides, a foray which is not yet concluded. Under the shadow of that huge catastrophe we still live. Its monstrous manifestations, from the gas chambers of Auschwitz to the atomic devastation of Hiroshima, and its enormous tragedies, from the vast migrations of forced labour to the slow death of hundreds of thousands from famine, darken the whole of our sky. In this darkness we cannot assess the meaning or divine the promise of our time, for we can scarcely see anything but the enormous moral and material nihilism which looms right ahead of us. But at the opening of the war it was not so; the end of the frigid and frozen 'peace' of the 'thirties came almost as a release, and men looked to the war to deliver them from the old world and give them a new one after it. A fortnight before the German break-through in the Low Countries in 1940 a little group of churchmen, with the approval of the Archbishop who was their unchallenged leader in this field, met to plan an ambitious conference on 'the life of the Church and the order of society'. Thus, on the eve of a disaster which nearly destroyed the framework of civilization altogether, was born the project that became so widely known by the single word 'Malvern'. Despite the menace of that historic summer, the plan, though its execution was postponed, was never abandoned. In January, 1941, perhaps the most powerful, albeit informal, representation of the Church of England ever assembled to consider such a subject gathered at the foot of Langland's hills to debate issues which a hundred years before hardly one churchman in a thousand would have allowed to fall within the scope of Christian thinking at all.

The importance of the Malvern Conference has doubtless been exaggerated, more especially by those who were not present at it, or even living in the country in which it was held. It is reported, I cannot say with how much truth, that a book appeared in the United States entitled *From Pentecost to Malvern*, suggesting a climax of Christian development such as even the most enthusiastic of propagandists of the Malvern findings would hardly have desired to claim as implicit in them. As a conference, indeed, Malvern was regarded by many of those present as a failure. The 'platform' did not, for the most part, succeed in establishing contact with the gathering as a whole; the speakers were not understood. Blame for this failure has been variously distributed. It was asserted on the one hand that those who read papers lapsed into unintelligible jargon and indulged in an unjustifiable obscurity. It was argued in reply that if an assembly embodying so much authority and eminence was unfamiliar with the terms in which the profound issues raised were necessarily stated, or even unaware of the existence of the issues themselves, then its members had no right to be at such a conference at all and the sooner they qualified themselves for attendance at such discussions the better. No doubt there were faults on both sides. The purpose of the conference had not perhaps been envisaged with sufficient clearness. The drafting of the syllabus had been primarily, and the preparation of the papers to be read to the gathering in large part, entrusted to members of what had come by this time to be widely known as the 'Christendom Group', which now emerged as the strongest nucleus of Christian sociological thinking. A talent for popularization has never been included among the gifts of this coterie. Its members returned from the conference to bemoan not that they were opposed or defeated, but that they were misrepresented and misunderstood. Some of them at any rate were prepared to consider that this might have been not only their misfortune but in some measure their fault.

Such deficiencies in clarity could certainly not have been urged against the outstanding man who presided over the conference. Never were the brilliant gifts of William Temple more strikingly displayed than at Malvern, and that the influence of the gathering and its 'findings' was to prove so great was pre-eminently due not only to his unique authority but to his characteristic qualities. Some might perhaps have objected, or at least suspected, that the 'findings' which the conference discovered to be so acceptable when he offered them to it, were in fact found not by the assembly but by its chairman. Such an objection would have been superficial. Temple's understanding of the issues at stake in such discussions as those which took place at Malvern was so complete that he often knew better than the protagonists of the various views expressed what was most true and most important in what they were striving to express. It was a primary source of his strength—as also of the weakness into which his exceptional generosity of mind occasionally led him—that he was ever anxious, before all, to elicit and to restate the positive truth which any man or group of men had to affirm. His genius was in this best sense synthetic; 'it was the settled philosophical habit of his mind', says Dr. Peck, 'ever to seek reconciliation between apparently opposed ideas', and this he achieved at Malvern without descending into trite generalization or dishonest compromise. The only point upon which Temple's interpretation of the mind of the conference was questioned, and after a vigorous debate revised, was in regard to the question of industrial ownership. Though as expressed in challenging fashion by Sir Richard Acland this issue caused some excitement at the time, the resulting resolution said no more than that 'the maintenance of that part of the structure of our society, by which the ultimate ownership of the principal industrial resources of the community can be vested in the hands of private owners', may be such a stumbling-block 'as would make it harder for men to live Christian lives'. From such an opinion perhaps few Christians at any time would dissent, and none did so on this occasion, though amid the emotions of the moment some at Malvern preferred to abstain from endorsing it. This much-advertised verdict was acclaimed in many quarters, at home and abroad, as involving acceptance of a full-blooded Socialism, and so interpreted gave a totally misleading impression of the mind of the conference, besides diverting attention from some less platitudinous and more inherently important judgments included in its findings.

These findings are on record and cannot be further analysed here; some of the issues which they raise will emerge for discussion in my final lecture. But it is interesting to note Temple's declaration that the conference 'fulfilled my own hopes in a very high degree', and still more interesting to know what were in his view the three main differences of 'Malvern' from the Copec conference over which he had presided seventeen years earlier.

In the first place, he tells us, Malvern was 'far more theological. There was a more pervasive belief that the evils of society arise from our desertion of an ascertainable order for society which springs from and coheres with Christian faith in God as Creator, Redeemer and Sanctifier.' Secondly, 'Malvern was more concerned than such conferences have usually been with the function of the Church itself and the need for drastic reform in the financial and administrative system of the Church of England if its voice is to be heard in connection with social and economic questions'. Thirdly, 'the main problem now is not concerned with the conditions of employed labour but with security of employment or at least of status. . . . Our discussion led us to suggest that the remedy must be sought in a new appreciation of the true relations between finance, production, distribution and consumption and adjustments of our economic system in the light of this; we further considered that a reform of the monetary system might be indispensable; and that the rights of labour as compared with those of capital called for redress.'

Not many months after his leadership at Malvern Temple was called to a greater sphere of leadership in the Church of England; less than three years after it he was dead. The blow was everywhere felt to be a heavy one indeed. Not only within the Church were men looking to him for a spiritual initiative against the immense forces of discouragement and difficulty which it was already plain would face us all in the post-war years. For such a leadership not only his massive mind, and his notable courage, but the remarkable union of energy and serenity which he embodied had come to be taken for granted as indispensable. 'His valiant attempts to reach a statement of Christian social doctrine', says Dr. Peck, 'will doubtless prove to have been amongst the most significant intellectual labours of our epoch.' But his contribution in this field was not intellectual only. He was never afraid to make the sort of protest or gesture of which a less courageous or a less imaginative man would not have been capable. Temple will surely be ranked among the greatest in that splendid succession of figures descending from Maurice and

Ludlow, whose bequests to us we have in these Lectures been considering. His thinking will be a primary source for us in pondering the lessons of the last hundred years and preparing to confront what the twentieth century has still to demand from us.

❦ VII ❦

THE LESSONS OF A CENTURY

Any lessons that may, as I hope, emerge from this lecture will be for the most part implicit rather than explicit. But there are two such lessons surely which cannot fail to impress themselves upon us as we reflect upon the story which we have traced from the day when we found the youthful Ludlow standing on that doorstep in Queen's Square. We can learn in the recollection of so much faith and courage and devotion and perseverance to be humble and we can remember to be grateful. I confess that these are the first emotions which flood my heart and mind. We must all feel these things surely, whether we think of the organized groups led by their great triumvirates: Maurice, Kingsley and Ludlow; Hancock, Headlam and Shuttleworth; Westcott, Scott Holland and Gore; or of the more isolated figures, Ward with his noble 'Ideal'; Fraser finding a new role for the episcopal office in a great 'conurbation'; the flashing wit and magnetic personality of Charles Marson; Conrad Noel with his prophetic fire; George Lansbury with his glowing humanity, as faithful to his Church as he was devoted to his people. And behind them the multitude no man can number of slum priests and social workers, travelling organizers and branch secretaries, whose inconspicuous labours made the opportunities for the great figures, and without whose sustained energies under every sort of discouragement the movement could not have 'moved' at all. Even in the most secular sense, piety would surely require that we should salute those who have gone before, who struggled against misunderstandings, misrepresentations and downright hostility of which we have experienced little or nothing, and in conditions such as are seldom encountered nowadays. Teachers like Maurice ejected from their posts; priests like Headlam deprived of their cures; men of the deepest spirituality accused by worldlings of secularizing their faith and by prosperous bourgeois of preaching a merely materialist salvation—they endured all this, and we have entered into their labours. When we are tempted to think that we live in an age of unprecedented difficulty for the full presentation of the Faith: when there seems no answer to the world's problems and no end to our own: when even those of us who sincerely seek the rescue of society in the name of Christ feel ourselves more divided than we ought to be and more baffled than we like to admit, even to ourselves, let us look back and remember that better men than we faced and overcame similar difficulties because they loved God, because they loved the victims of an inhuman industrialism, and—no less important—because they loved one another. For in the last analysis it is the divine love which 'moves the sun and all the other stars' which can alone move our human movements to any fruitful end.

We give thanks then for those who have gone before us. Can we give thanks too for the upshot of their activities as reflected in the development of our social order in the last hundred years? How far indeed has this development responded to their efforts; how far can it be seen as fulfilling their hopes?

Social Progress is among the most elusive of human conceptions. If the 'Christian Socialists' of a century ago could see what has been achieved in the field of industrial and sanitary reform since their day, they would be amazed that so enormous an advance could have been made. We have seen that so much as fifty years ago the aged Ludlow thought that 'the change had been something perfectly marvellous'; and he was thinking not only of the inroads made upon poverty and misery, but of the growth of the social conscience which had made these things possible. What would he say now to the imposing structure of 'the social services', supplemented as they are by the ever more elaborate and efficient network of voluntary 'social service'?

Perhaps indeed Ludlow might have some questions to ask us about all this. He might want to know why it is that such a complex and costly apparatus should be necessary to enable people to assure themselves of elementary satisfactions which those in a position to do so have normally preferred to secure for themselves. He might in particular inquire what has happened to that desire of the workers, so widespread a century ago, to direct their own working lives; why co-operators no longer desire to co-operate, and why, now that Socialism appears to have arrived, there no longer seem to be any guild socialists and certainly no sign of guilds. Kingsley, vastly impressed as he would be by the progress in sanitation, would perhaps be distressed to see the needs of the countryside still so little understood and so tardily met. Maurice would doubtless be gratified to see the extent to which Christian sociology is now rooted in theology, though disappointed perhaps that no such 'theological reformation' as he looked for has developed to purge and renew the mind of a Church of England having more slender links with the great mass of the nation to-day than even his unsanguine nature could have led him to foresee. But the desperate poverty, the appalling sweating, the 'human soot' which inhabited the ghastly new towns, and the helpless peasantry at the mercy of their squires, with the nation's Church smug and blind and callous while such things went on—all that at least has gone. Social progress, hard as it may be to define, is a reality, and the contribution to it of dedicated lives and illuminated minds, made through the medium of the Church, is a fact of history. In these years of discouragement and danger we do well to remind ourselves of these things and thank God for them, and for those who in His name did so much to bring them to pass.

For this is a moment in human history when 'progress' seems to have no more encouragement to offer us. The wind has changed; it blows now full in our faces and from a frigid quarter. Or, to alter the metaphor, the major currents of industrial civilization, if they continue in the direction in which their course looks to be set, and we are borne along with them, will converge to whirl our seemingly helpless societies to destruction. For the truth would appear to be, not that social progress has been an illusion, though some manifestations of it may be dubious enough, but that it has been taking place within a cultural situation which, in this century at any rate, has become more menacing with every decade. Were we to congratulate ourselves too warmly on our social amelioration we might resemble a man who in rejoicing over the healing of serious wounds omitted to notice that he was, in fact, dying of consumption. For our real problems have ceased to be social problems in the familiar sense of the word; they have become vast cosmic issues; and even where a way out of these issues has been discovered or is discoverable, the question remains of how mankind is to be induced to take it. Four of such problems appear as particularly intractable, and a prolonged failure to solve them liable to be, in one way or another, lethal in its effects. The most obvious of them is the international problem in 'the era of atomic energy'. If terror of the consequences of making war restrains the 'powers' from it for a time, it will do nothing to teach them how to make peace; and the devastating results of getting one's blow in first with an atomic bomb may sooner or later tempt a nation sufficiently avid of world power, or sufficiently fearful of the future, to chance the experiment. But if we do not know how to avoid the enormous peril of war we do not seem to know much better how to forestall the less spectacular menace of famine. The problems here are many and grave: the spread of soil erosion; the artificial stimulation and consequent exhaustion of the land and the deterioration of its products; least regarded, but perhaps most serious of all, the increasing difficulty of manning the agricultural process in face of the superior rewards offered by industrial production and the artificial prestige of 'white collar' occupations. A third problem is to find a monetary mechanism to distribute whatever it may be that a nation decides to grow or to make. Despite the considerable amount of attention which has been given to this subject, our industrial societies seem no nearer to achieving a solution of the problem than they were when the failure to find one defeated so many social hopes and ruined so many individual lives in 1921 and 1931. Slump, it seems, must still follow boom as does night the day. And finally, we face that great psychological failure of our culture, a failure so deep that its existence is still almost wholly concealed in the subconsciousness of men, the absence of any hope of finding a normal satisfaction in the processes of their daily work. This takes the heart out of human activity and sets up innumerable frictions in the social order, to relieve which we are still restlessly seeking the most irrelevant alleviations.

Now these great issues are related to the ends which men set before themselves; they are therefore religious problems in a sense deeper than were those problems of human suffering, or even of human injustice, in the more direct sense of the term, with which the earlier Christian reformers set themselves to cope. What is Man? In what sense is his society a valid and necessary mode of life for his accomplishment of God's will? What is his obligation to the natural resources which his ingenuity enables him to exploit? What are the basic psychological needs of his nature in work and play? These are the sort of questions with which a living Church has now to deal, and theology must take hands with anthropology and sociology and psychology if answers are to be found for them.

Can we be satisfied that sufficient efforts to find these answers are being made? The situation in this respect is not altogether reassuring. The latest generation of the faithful does not seem to be displaying any conspicuous interest in the subject, and certainly not upon the scale which its importance demands. This is, however, quite understandable, nor is the tendency altogether one to be regretted. For the fact is not primarily, though it may be partly, to be attributed to the enormous discouragements of the contemporary situation and the complexity of the new factors by which it is being transformed. No doubt when an enterprise shows no early prospect of paying dividends it becomes dangerously easy to persuade oneself that one has neither need nor even right to embark upon it. But I do not think that it is the formidable nature of the task of relating theology to our social predicaments which too often deters the best minds among our younger men from sparing their attention for it. I think it is rather a doubt, however vaguely felt, as to its authenticity as a sphere of Christian energy. Under the impact of the 'theology of crisis' and the challenge of a Neo-Calvinism the force of which has been felt every bit as much among the best men of Catholic mind in the Church of England as it has in more evangelical circles, the very word 'social' has become an object of suspicion to those who have recognized the gravity of Karl Barth's strictures upon a religion of 'Christianity and . . .'. Realization of the spurious or inadequate character of what was so unhappily described as the 'social Gospel' has disposed many (though not of course the zealots of the Left) to avoid such dangerous ground. They have apprehended that a social concern pleaded in the name of religion implies only too often a flight from the other-worldliness of an authentic Christianity. This attitude is, as I say, understandable, but if it is persisted in the results will be deplorable. I hope it is not impertinent to ask whether what was undoubtedly begun as an effort after a renewed fidelity may not in its turn pass into an escapism not unlike that which it was first sought to avoid.

The discussion alike of theology and philosophy in the more technical sense is outside the scope of this course of lectures—and of this lecturer. I have not the competence, even if I had the time, to discuss such questions as 'the extent to which the Christian can fuse teleological with eschatological conceptions', or the reconciliation of the Biblical view of Man and of history with the concept of Natural Law as developed within the Christian tradition, though I have no difficulty in perceiving their vital relevance to our subject. I have no doubt that our sociology still needs to become, what Maurice always strove to secure that it should be—more fundamentally theological. That, however, is not really the point at issue, which is rather in what sense, if any, theology should be expected, nay rather required, to furnish a sociological illumination and a social incentive. I can appreciate the reasons which have led to a reaction against the theology of the Incarnation characteristic of Westcott and the *Lux Mundi* school, even though I suspect that this reaction is no more independent of the 'climate of opinion' in which it has developed than was the outlook against which it has taken place. Some words of Archbishop Temple on this subject, written eight years or so back, imply as much:

'If the security of the nineteenth century, already shattered in Europe, finally crumbles away in our country, we shall be pressed more and more towards a theology of Redemption. In this we shall be coming closer to the New Testament. We have been learning again how impotent man is to save himself, how deep and pervasive is that corruption which theologians call Original Sin. Man needs above all to be saved from himself. This must be the work of Divine Grace.'

Assuredly. In an age which has seen modern civilization led through the frustration of World Depression to the mass intoxications of Nazism, the horrors of Belsen, and the unleashing of the atomic bomb in a cause conscientiously believed to be righteous, we have indeed needed and do still need to be recalled to these basic spiritual realities. But it is not without significance that it is from Germany, where moral nihilism has gone farthest, that the strongest rejections of any social function for the Church have come. When we are told by an ultra-Barthian that 'we must learn to recognize that there is no one form of State life, of economics or of any other social order, that is more in the spirit of the Gospel than another', then we must surely be led to wonder whether a church which abdicates so conscientiously all claim to influence or pronounce upon the character of the social order within which the lives of its children have to be carried on and their duty to their neighbour to be done, has not had its share in preparing the moral chaos within which it found itself at length forced to struggle for very life.

It is necessary, I think, to distinguish between coming closer to the spirit of the New Testament, as we must ever strive to do, and so envisaging our task and our responsibility as to confuse them with those of the Primitive Church. After all, 'the security of the nineteenth century' has *not* 'finally crumbled away in our own country', at any rate; the possibility envisaged by Temple in 1938, which two short years later loomed as so hideous a probability, did not in God's mercy materialize. Britain was spared, not, we may be sure, for her own merits, but because God had work for her to do, but this work she will never accomplish unless her Church embraces such a responsibility of illumination and leadership as our late archbishop seemed uniquely to incarnate in himself. No one saw more clearly that in social as in personal life the essence of sin was, as St. Athanasius said, the erection of means into ends. 'If', wrote Temple in *Christianity and the Social Order*, 'what has true value as a means to an end beyond itself is in fact being sought as an end in itself, the Church must rebuke this dislocation of the structure of life and if possible point out the way of recovery. It is bound to "interfere" because it is by vocation the agent of God's purpose, outside the scope of which no human interest or activity can fall.' No one perhaps has ever done more than Temple to establish the validity of the Church's concern in the social sphere, and it was largely owing to his own work in this respect that he was able to say, in his supplement to the *Christian News-Letter*, written in the last year of his life, that 'among Christians who have seriously and thoughtfully faced the historical situation with which we are dealing there is, as I have proved by testing, an observable convergence'. Here I believe the Archbishop to have been right, and the character of this 'convergence' is worth our recollection. It is 'for God Who has spoken', for Neighbour; for Man as rooted in Nature; for History; and for the Gospel and the Church. In several of these respects the social outlook of the Christian community to-day is notably different from that most characteristic of it in previous decades. It is more consciously theocentric; it sets more store upon man's immediate environment and his functional associations, home, community and workplace; it has recovered some understanding of the idea of Natural Law; it apprehends that the truth about society is not primarily to be discovered in abstractions but that 'it is in history that the ultimate meaning of existence is both revealed and actualized'; it founds itself not on a sanctified humanism but on the revelation of God in scripture and on the redemptive function of the Church. Temple may somewhat have exaggerated the degree to which this convergence has actually been achieved and, by implication, the number of those affected by it. But in noting the existence of this tendency he was certainly right, and the features of it which he specified are of the highest significance as indicating an authenticity in the Christian social movement such as it has never before displayed on anything like the same scale. It marks, I would further suggest, if not a 'return to Maurice', at least a development along lines which he would have strongly approved and one for which his teaching offered clues which were, in the last century, too seldom followed up.

But if there is convergence there are divergences also, such as are sometimes of a more fundamental character than is generally realized. Agreement on the existence of a social function for the Church does not guarantee unanimity upon what the essential character of that function is. Some would limit the role of the Church to the encouragement of an acceptance of civic responsibility and the fulfilment of vocational tasks and opportunities 'in a Christian spirit', which spirit is commonly regarded as sufficiently exemplified in the exhibition of as high a level of integrity and altruism as established conventions allow. Such an outlook betrays a complete failure to understand what is the prophetic responsibility of the Church in respect of the social order whose purposes and performances she is ordained to judge. What it demands is indeed necessary so far as it goes, and no degree of dissatisfaction with either the ends or the means of the social order can excuse the individual Christian from his obligation to do his best, morally and intellectually, in the situation he finds imposed upon him. Social idealists have too often been disposed to make what is conveniently dismissed as 'the system' an alibi for neglect of an initiative which it lies within their power to take; by making the most of existing opportunities they may raise the level of civic or industrial practice. But since this consecrated individualism in social relations has been in every decade more and more clearly revealed as inadequate, it no longer constitutes a truly responsible outlook upon the social problem. The most significant divergence to-day is between those who assert that there is, *in esse* or *in posse*, a Christian sociology, and those who contest the validity of the claim as involving an invasion of the autonomy of the social sciences and a wilful flouting of sociological authority by a preference for 'less enlightened to more enlightened thought'.

I endeavoured to trace in the last lecture, so far as time permitted, the evolution of thought which led to the demand, made in the 'basis' of the League of the Kingdom of God, for a formulation of 'a Christian sociology consonant with the needs of the age', and to attempts to suggest its elements. It arose partly from a suspicion of the validity, or adequacy, or both, of the social movements and prescriptions for which the support of the Church was being claimed by enthusiasts, both within and without her borders, but still more from a re-examination of the sources and 'title deeds' of Christian social doctrine. The sponsors of this new effort, as one of them wrote later, 'no longer content to select from among contemporary social programmes the one that most attracts them and endeavour to enlist for it the support of organized religion', were 'looking to their own movement to supply something which, in a society not acknowledging Christian inspirations and sanctions, they cannot hope elsewhere to find'. The first and somewhat tentative crystallization of their ideas was presented in the volume, *The Return of Christendom*. No doubt it was partly the title of this book which led to the suggestion that the essential idea of the group which produced it was to 'go back to the Middle Ages'. This suggestion was quite unfounded; the basis of the book was clearly and explicitly credal and biblical. But when the writers came to the period in which a 'Christian Sociology' was an actual, historical phenomenon, and its concretization in accepted theory and general practice a primary feature of the 'Ages of Faith', they did not think it merely romantic or fanciful to look to these things for clues to a social doctrine of permanent significance. The quest of what was to become known as the Christendom Group was in essence for an 'autochthonous' sociology, growing from its own Christian roots in dogma, in tradition, and in the approximations of history as influenced by ideas and principles consciously related to the Church's interpretation of the nature of man and the purpose of human order. Thus, they argued, in

the words of a new voice which at once underpinned and reinforced their conclusions in the following decade, the twentieth-
century Church may 'contribute something which earlier ages
of the Church failed to do owing to their limited experience of
the rise and fall of civilizations, namely an insight into the causes
of social instability and collapse. She will then', added Dr.
Demant, 'be able to explain, as well as to proclaim, that a
religious climate is indispensable for the survival of the frail
flower of civilization. That is to say, she may learn to save
civilization precisely as she learns to become disentangled from
its assumptions.' This was indeed the fundamental point implicit in the challenge of the Tractarians, though too many of
its implications remained unexplored by them, and have remained so, with less excuse, by the great majority of their successors to this day.

Now it is clear that this call for a Christian sociology could be
—and likely that it would be—contraverted, as soon as it could
no longer be ignored, by those Christians whose sociological
convictions did not appear to them to demand any disentanglement from the assumptions they shared with the 'progressive'
forces of the day. Of the most obvious objection to the whole
position—that it claimed a relevance to a situation in which the
Church was the home of a minority for a notion evolved in an
age in which her authority was universally acknowledged—less
was heard than might have been expected. The objection which
was forthcoming was more fundamental; it was not the feasibility but the validity of the claim that was to be challenged.
Three characteristic criticisms may be, though all too briefly,
adduced. Mr. John MacMurray, in a review of the volume
Prospect for Christendom in the *New Statesman*, objects to the whole
notion as authoritarian in an illegitimate sense:

'A theology which finds its first principles in an authoritative
revelation is committed to a pattern of personal life which is
eternally right, and which must be independent of the changes in
the functional ordering of human relations brought about by
technological advances. . . . This is the crux of the conflict between science and religion. . . . These writers . . . do not see that

a dogmatic theology must frustrate their effort to supply a Christian sociology. . . . There is no possibility of relating the developing, experimental theory of science to a theory of man which is eternal, antiquarian [!] and 'received by faith'. . . . What Christianity provides is the dynamic principles of personal community . . . they determine patterns of personal life only when combined with a particular set of technological possibilities.'

Such a position appears to me to cut the ground from under not only the Christendom Group, but the whole Christian social movement, and lead to a mere empiricism.

Mr. Ronald Preston writes from a position less at variance with what seem to me to be the fundamental postulates of a credal religion, but with an equal scepticism as to the reality and the possibility of any specifically Christian form of society. The attempt to maintain that Christian doctrine leads forward to this, he declares:

'is bound up with a particular view of natural law and of the relation of secular learning to the Queen of the Sciences, maimed by an absence of the insight that we owe to Protestantism, and ultimately of course to the Bible itself, that all social systems fall short of the absolute demands of the Gospel.'

That they must so fall short no Christian could deny, but the acknowledgment of this truth should not drive us into the sort of moral and social relativism which Mr. Preston seems to deduce from it. The true question is not whether all social effort is impaired by human limitation and corrupted by human sin. It is whether there is not a difference in degree rather than in kind between a period which understands and accepts a Christian interpretation of man and society, and one which denies this, or ignores it, or simply fails to grasp what it affirms and what it implies.

This question of in what sense, if any, the 'ages of Faith', in virtue of exhibiting and developing a theocentric civilization, have a unique significance for Christian sociology, is involved in the strictures of Mr. Donald MacKinnon who stands much nearer to the Christendom Group than the writers so far quoted, yet constitutes himself its watchful critic. Mr. MacKinnon, writing in *The Student Movement*, having accused the Group, though with no very obvious warrant, of regarding history after the sixteenth century as a rake's progress, continues:

'We have to face the fact how much real solid achievement has attended the gradual de-Christianization of our frame of references. . . . We may like, ignoring the spiritual pride in ourselves that we encourage thereby, to try to turn the contemporary breakdown of civilization to apologetic purposes; it is far harder to seek to trace what God is saying to us in the long hard way He has brought our world since the sixteenth century. He has not guided it so far to minister to the pride and superiority of Christians but rather to disclose perhaps, in the light that shines in the darkness of the Cross, that truly He is a God who hides himself.'

From these deeps, says Mr. MacKinnon, the 'Christendom' writers turn aside. They may perhaps be forgiven for doing so. A not unnatural reluctance to declare the inscrutable purposes of God in a period of unexampled transition such as ours, in which we are so much immersed that we cannot hope confidently to assess its significance, even as judged by earthly standards—such reluctance need not be attributed to spiritual pride or medievalist escapism. Assuredly there are dangers in trying to 'turn the contemporary breakdown of civilization to apologetic purposes', and the injudicious anxiety of some Christian apologists to score points at the expense of secular humanism may only result in making the Christian vindication of what is truly human more difficult. It is not spiritual pride, however, but the observation of inescapable facts and our bounden Christian duty in face of them, which require us to point out that the 'solid achievement' lauded by Mr. MacKinnon, not without some justification, has proved, and is every day proving, exceptionally and increasingly precarious. Wars; slumps; ecological disturbances with consequent peril of famine; social revolt; undermining of the family unit; psychological maladjustment, mania and suicide—all these disintegrating forces have become endemic within it. This does not necessarily invalidate all or most of what has in fact been achieved, but it does suggest that man has become the victim of that achievement precisely because he has had no theological principles by which to master it and no historical guidance from a more Christian era in the light of which to discriminate in its application. This being so, Dr. Peck is surely justified in pointing out that,

'between the man of our time and the Gospel an "iron curtain" has descended, and he deems the Gospel irrelevant. What we have to show him, with overwhelming force and cogency, is that the forces which have produced this singularly comfortless and frustrated modern world, and now threaten to end it and mankind with it, are precisely the same forces as led Western man to disregard the Faith as the guide of life. They are the forces which made modern London, Berlin, New York, produced two world wars, and left the farms and fields of England desolate. The Christian doctrine of man calls us to a great reversal of all this.'

What has to be made clear is that the direction which things have taken since the sixteenth century is not the only consequence of scientific discovery and technological development imaginable. The modern world has gone astray not because it is modern and not medieval, but because with the loss of any supernatural criterion by which social development could be assessed and controlled, it has been dominated by a mixture of anthropocentric pride and sociological fatalism. 'Our moral and political problems', says Dr. Demant succinctly, 'largely arise out of the failure of progress to meet men's fundamental needs.'

The issue is obscured, however, if it is represented as involving a glorification of Catholic 'tradition' at the expense of 'the insight that we owe to Protestantism'. No doubt the Catholic sociologist will claim that a sacramental theology, a relation of the Faith to what is valid in the idea of Natural Law, an emphasis upon the Christian life as essentially corporate, and familiarity with the notion of the Church as exercising authority and discipline over her members—that all this gives him a basis for social doctrine more secure than the approach to the problem characteristic of those who do not derive from this tradition.

I am not now concerned with the validity of this claim. I am concerned, on the one hand, to ask whether Luther and Calvin, viewing western civilization four hundred years after their own day, would not be at least as much alarmed as would Dante or Aquinas by the most characteristic upshots of the Enlightenment as they have developed since the middle of the seventeenth century. And I would suggest on the other, that very many if not most Catholics, of whatever obedience, would be ready to lament, so far as they had been brought to appreciate it, the implicit abdication of social responsibility involved in the type of religion most characteristic of the Counter Reformation. If Catholics should be disposed to glory in the resources latent in their most authentic insights and traditions, they should be the more ready to confess their failure through so many decades, and even centuries, to draw upon them. All have sinned and come short of the glory of God; and all of us have to labour today against the enormous obstacles imposed by a society deformed from any semblance of a natural order as a consequence of the failure of religion to show men how to relate their activities and purposes to a supernatural interpretation and an intelligible end.

I have cited these divergences, upon which I have been able to touch all too briefly, not because I find in them discouragements to be realistically if unhopefully accepted. I have set them forth because I believe that if they are faced in a mood suffused by the theological virtues (a vital qualification) the controversies arising from them may lead to a more profound understanding by all parties of the issues raised. We may learn from such discussions not merely how to arrive at a theoretical synthesis, but as one of the Christendom Group critics has desiderated, 'how to express political responsibilities in a confused and frustrated society' and how to base present policy on current possibilities. It may well be that the search for 'clues' among the features of a theocentric social order has made the practical policy of the Christendom Group appear, as Mr. Daniel Jenkins has declared, 'astonishingly remote from life as lived in characteristic modern England', yet it may also be that much of that life is equally

The Lessons of a Century

remote from—and resistant to—any Christian interpretation of man and society. 'It has yet to be shown', says Dr. John Baillie, inquiring into *What is Christian Civilization?* 'that mass society, in anything like the form in which we now know it, is capable of developing *any* true sense of community, or that the chill impersonality of it can ever be spiritualized into a Christian togetherness with one's neighbours.' 'My contention is', he continues, 'that the disturbance caused by the Industrial Revolution is quite as potent a cause of the Church's changed situation as the disturbance caused in the intellectual life by the closely connected and roughly coeval movement known as the Enlightenment.' If that is true, as I myself believe, it is not surprising that attempts to state the conditions of a valid Christian life within the framework of the contemporary achievement are apt to appear as either unrealistic on the one hand or inadequate on the other. It may be that the Catholic sociologist is prone to adopt too sceptical or grudging an attitude to the affirmations most characteristic of a social analysis made in the name of 'science'. But it is true also that the conscientiousness with which the scientist commonly works within his chosen frame of reference, and the objectivity which he honestly believes himself to achieve, may blind some Christian social enthusiasts both to the often anti-Christian character of his assumptions, and to the essentially speculative nature of his confident, but often very transient conclusions. The very term 'social sciences' may easily obscure the degree to which human and volitional factors enter into the field being surveyed, and betray students into forgetting that generalizations about how men, as persons or in groups, may act most efficiently may involve unrealized assumptions about the primacy of the ends which those persons and groups exist to pursue. In short, we may say that if one party to the elucidation of Christian social doctrine and policy must beware of appealing to the past for a degree of authority which can never inhere in the essentially contingent character of historical phases ('all times are corrupt', as Mr. T. S. Eliot once bluntly reminded us), another party must be cautious in appealing to the 'most enlightened thought' of the present for an authority which can only be conceded to the modern outlook by those who share in full measure its most characteristic assumptions. And to say that these are at variance with the Christian interpretation of life and of man is surely something of a *meiosis*.

Yet in dwelling at so much length on certain divergences which now manifest themselves among those who are taking most seriously the task of elucidating Christian social doctrine and policy for the present age, I run the risk of underestimating both the profound 'convergence' noted and elaborated by Temple, and the extent to which Christians can and do unite to reinforce, to inform and to clarify the efforts of reformers to achieve their more immediate social objectives. It is interesting to note how many of the 'social evils' stigmatized at Malvern only half a dozen years ago have begun to be tackled by ambitious programmes on the main lines of which all parties are more agreed than the legitimate and often salutary controversy between them suggests. Housing, Education, Security of Employment, Improved Health services and Social Insurance were all the subject of resolutions passed at Malvern; in regard to all of them energetic policies have been set on foot, often in the first place by the Coalition Government. The implementation of such policies raises questions upon which Christians have every right to differ, and may do so in good faith and with constructive results. But behind many of such policies for 'social reform' there lies a larger question. How far are measures proposed to embody them valid in themselves, and the registration of a developing communal sense consciously experienced and genuinely welcomed? Or how far, on the other hand, do they represent the fatalistic resort to a state power to rescue a disintegrating order from the consequences of the decay of the organs through which a healthy society would, more or less spontaneously, function? This is a very large question indeed, calling for a degree of patient discrimination and study such as Christian reformers have not for the most part devoted to it. Its existence, and the existence of analogous problems lying just below the surface of our political and social life, raises a further, practical question. Despite the many societies, leagues and less formal groups occupying themselves with Christian social theory and practice, have we not yet to find the best way, first of mobilizing Christian thought upon such issues, and secondly (but of perhaps more obvious urgency, since a good deal of thought is, however dispersedly, going on) of making an effective impact upon the public consciousness? It has been informally suggested that if the 'convergence' detected by Temple is as striking as he indicated, the time may perhaps be ripe for the formation of a body analogous in purpose to the Fabian Society when it was established at the end of the 'eighties, not as a political party, but as a nucleus first for the crystallization of a practicable socialist policy, and secondly, for the permeation of society with socialist ideas. There is always a certain danger in seeking examples for Christian action in the secular sphere, but if the caution suggested by this reservation is borne in mind, the proposal may have value as indicating a step forward in the effort to relate Christian principle and political action. For to-day it is time not only to dig, but to build.

It would not be appropriate in this lecture to stress my own opinions about the elements of a Christian social policy. But there is one aspect of the existing situation which demands a reference because it raises questions about which many in the Christian social movement are now somewhat concerned and perplexed. From the days of Ludlow and Kingsley down to those of George Lansbury and Conrad Noel, that movement felt itself called in some measure to identify itself with what was proclaimed to be the cause of the workers. Leaders of the movement may not have felt able to associate themselves explicitly with all that was being specifically demanded by the workers' leaders; they may sometimes have cast doubt upon their policies and reproved their conduct. But they did feel, and commonly say, that here was an oppressed class, whose grievances called not only for sympathy but for redress, and whose status in the community required to be changed. But in this day of Labour Governments and gigantic industrial unions the situation may appear to be transformed; the great mass of the organized working class does not seem to lack opportunity to express or power to realize its cherished aims. In what sense then, if any, can we still see in the 'workers' an oppressed class calling for our especial championship? We have always to beware that we do not find ourselves lingering on traditional battlefields from which the conflicts in which our aid is most urgently required have moved away. As Professor T. M. Taylor pointedly observed to the 1946 Summer School of Christian Sociology, 'it is easy to be wise in the business of a hundred years ago, but who are the climbing boys of 1946?' (Some may find their closest analogy in those unhappy children in our public institutions in regard to whom a recent report made such disturbing revelations; others may think the fate of the aged in such places equally discreditable to a period so ready to congratulate itself on the efficiency of its State-sponsored 'welfare'.)

The organized workers of to-day, unskilled no less than skilled, are in a vastly better material situation than they were in the hungry 'forties, or even in the thirties of this century. We may rejoice that they are, and that Christian effort has had so large a share in helping them to become so. Yet in one fundamental respect their situation is essentially the same as it was when Ludlow first began to work for their liberation. For whether State servants or not, they are still the hirelings of a wage system, divorced from the responsibilities of ownership, with no share in control of the elaborate operations with which their fortunes are mysteriously entangled, and little, if any, say in the conduct of their working lives. They are in 1946 what they were in 1846—'hands', their status still that of a proletariat; it is in virtue of their character as such that their more revolutionary champions claim to exercise a dictatorship in their name. But it was the rejection of this 'sort of washed-out slavery' which Ludlow demanded, and it was to transcend it that the Christian Socialists founded their little associations a century ago. The challenge was re-stated some thirty years back by the national guildsmen with whom the leaders of the Church Socialist League made significant alliance. Surely it is in respect of this unfulfilled aspiration that the Church's social movement has still to associate itself with the workers' cause, even though the numbing effect of two centuries of proletarianism has obliterated for only too many of our people the memory and the hope of ownership, and the appetite for initiative, responsibility and choice. For these things are essential attributes of man as Christianity understands him; 'progress' is meaningless and 'reform' misunderstood unless it brings the workers nearer to an achievement of them.

It is significant that any effort on our part to work for such an enfranchisement of the employee will cut across the conventional controversies of Right and Left, and the same is true of two other subjects upon which it is being increasingly realized that a Christian word demands to be spoken. These are the rescue of the monetary system from bondage to financial abstractions, and the protection of the land and of the rural community which lives by it. There is a disposition in allegedly progressive circles to represent these concerns as inspired by mere idiosyncrasy and as involving an irresponsible challenge to what is postulated as the 'most enlightened thought'. It is not explained, however, why Christians to-day should be required to accept the claim of economic experts to lay down the conditions within which social development has to be sought with any more submission than Wordsworth and Southey or Kingsley and Maurice were prepared to display a century ago. It was failure to master the problem of Usury in an expanding economy which went far to wreck the Church's traditional sociology, and until financial assumptions are made subordinate to economic realities, there will be small hope of establishing a Christian sociology for to-day. There can, of course, be no specifically Christian money system, but there is a Christian obligation to demand a correct one, and to point to clues in the Church's traditional teaching on the subject to suggest the requirements to which it should conform. Whatever else the Just Price may mean in the modern world, it must surely imply such a level of prices as will make it possible for the people of a nation to buy all that they desire of what they have been able to make or exchange. But a problem arises here as to economic priorities, for we must recognize the need for securing primary production against the forces which

militate against it in a world of mass-producible gadgets. It is no
merely animistic piety, still less sentimental romanticism, which
has led to the re-affirmation of the symbiosis summed up in the
phrase, 'Church and Countryside'. It is a conscious return to
what the Church has always intuitively known, though sometimes allowed herself to forget, that first things must come first,
that economically speaking the production of food is the first
thing, and that this is a process which imposes a way of life of its
own, to be in its essentials jealously preserved. That way of life
has indeed its dangers and limitations, as it has its characteristic
beauties and rewards; and the Church stands in the village as
much to guard against pagan superstition and narrow self-
sufficiency as it does to vindicate the life of the countryman
against invasion and corruption from the alien forces of a
spurious 'science' and a hypertrophied urbanism.

'To-day', said Professor Haldane sixteen years ago, 'the ex-
ternal conditions of life in civilized communities differ more
from those of 1830 than the conditions of 1830 from those of
Noah's flood.' If this is even approximately true it may be suspected that we have little to learn from looking back a century
to a period when a railway train was still a novelty and what
would then have been called a flying machine the merest fantasy. But the problems of what we call, in a mood nearer to
despair than to hope, the 'era of atomic energy', though they
introduce important new factors into the human situation, do
not fundamentally alter the mission of the Church in the sphere
which we have been surveying in these lectures. Here the changes
which matter most are not spectacular ones, and I must be
content to indicate only two. The first was remarked upon in the
previous lecture, namely that whereas 'in the nineteenth century
the mere fact of identifying the Church with any social, i.e.
anti-individualist trend, was a salutary gesture . . . to-day a
movement is no longer *ipso facto* to be welcomed because it is a
social movement'. The importance of this change for us can
hardly be over-estimated. It will move us, on the one hand, to a
profound concern for the vindication of the person amid the

too fatalistically accepted social pressures of our time. But we must be careful, on the other, not to be stampeded into any position which involves a loss of grip upon the truth of human interdependence, with all the forbearance and self-forgetfulness that this demands for the success of any truly social experiment, qualities which Christian example even more than Christian precept has at once an obligation and a power to foster among men. The other change I would have you notice is the gradual transformation of the Church's social movement from the effort of a conscious minority into the diffused concern and responsibility of the whole body. The social movement *in* the Church of England is now in principle, and in some measure in practice, the social movement *of* the Church of England. Something of zeal and zest is apt to be lost in such a transition; just as there is no longer in the old sense an oppressed class and a progressive movement to claim our unqualified allegiance, so it is less exciting to sit upon a Church Assembly Commission to hammer out the Church's answer to a social problem than to stand upon a platform and denounce the bench of bishops for their callousness in face of it.

It is constructive leadership rather than critical denunciation that is called for from us now. That we have reached such a situation is due, as I emphasized at the beginning of this lecture, to the devoted labours of those who went before us in this movement. But in striving to serve our day and generation we may not only take inspiration from their achievements; we may take warning from their limitations and failures. The Tractarians crippled the effect of their magnificent challenge because they failed to appreciate all that was involved in the disentanglement from secularism which they preached. The 'Christian Socialists' weakened their impact upon the Church and delayed the development of the movement they set on foot, partly because they identified their ideas too much with the little experiments they initiated to exemplify them, and partly because they allowed Maurice's suspicion of all 'systems' and societies to restrain them from the organization necessary to secure that unfamiliar truth is spread and understood. The Guild of St. Matthew limited its influence because it relied too exclusively on 'shock tactics' and identified itself too completely with a mood of revolutionary defiance certain to antagonize many whom a more persuasive propaganda might have won. The Christian Social Union did much to supply this defect, but, as we have seen, while it 'claimed for the Christian Law the ultimate authority to rule social practice, it omitted to explain what the Christian Law was', and thus never found what would give it a unity, a certainty and an energy equal to the situation by which it was confronted. The Church Socialist League achieved a much to be desired contact with the organized working class, but it committed itself too recklessly to its political formulas and electoral fortunes. Too much importance has not, of course, to be attached to particular crystallizations in a movement which goes forward not so much in spite of the failures of this or that group, but by learning the lessons which those failures reveal. But such lessons have not necessarily to be learnt in this hard way, and much may be gained to-day if the Christian sociologists associated with or inspired by the Christendom Group will ponder Maurice's criticism of the Tractarians, that they 'opposed to the spirit of the age the spirit of a former age instead of the ever-living and acting spirit of God', and their critics will consider how easy it is for the reforming zeal born of a desire to act within the situation in which God has set us to become corrupted by an implicit acceptance of the terms in which a secularized 'enlightenment' is bound to mis-state it.

There is indeed a tension which such a movement as ours can never escape. For we have at the same time to act within the situation of our times and to stand away from that situation and strive to view its demands in the light of the eternal purposes of God. This will never be an easy task at any time, and we may perhaps be pardoned if we sometimes feel it to be an almost too exacting one to-day. For we live not only at a moment of exceptional discouragement, when the appalling strains and ardours of a terrible war do not seem to have won for the world any hope of repose or plenty or security, but under the shadow of a destruction more ghastly than man has ever known. We have even to live with the possibility of an 'End of the World' brought about not by the Lord of history as a preliminary to His second coming among men, but as the consequence of man's exploitation for the purposes of domination of the very fabric of the earth itself. Death may indeed be the gate of life, but murder and suicide, on a cosmic as on an individual scale, are alike mortal sins; and an end of civilization thus precipitated would be a fearful, though not illogical, culmination of a history begun with the sin by which Paradise was lost. But the Christian must be brave enough to face these possibilities, not with a mere stoicism, confronting the worst that time can do, but with a true heroism, accepting in faith whatever eternity may offer. And it may be that such a mood among us will after all avail to save the faith of civilization in itself, as ten just men would have saved Sodom from its fate. We are not the first generation in Christian history to feel the weight of our time hang heavy upon us. The 'Year of Revolutions' may seem a slight thing to men of this century who have endured so much and are threatened by worse, but its convulsions disturbed fearful souls in 1848, who were rebuked by Maurice in words with which this course may come to an appropriate end:

'Away then with that cowardly language which some of us are apt to indulge in when we speak of one period as more dangerous than another; when we wish we were not born into the age of revolutions, or complain that the time of quiet belief is past, and that henceforth every man must ask himself whether he has any ground to stand upon or whether all beneath him is hollow. We are falling into the temptation when we thus lament over it. We are practically confessing that the Evil Spirit is the Lord of all; that times and seasons are in his hands. Let us clear our minds from every taint of that blasphemy. God has brought us into this time; He and not ourselves or some dark demon. If we are not fit to cope with that which He has prepared for us, we should have been utterly unfit for any condition that we imagine for ourselves. In this time we are to live and wrestle, and in no other. Let us humbly, tremblingly, manfully look to it, and we shall not wish that the sun could go back its ten degrees, or that we could go back with it. If easy times are departed it is that difficult times may make us more in earnest that they may teach us not to depend upon ourselves. If easy belief is impossible, it is that we may learn what belief is, and in whom it is to be placed. If an hour is at hand which will try all the inhabitants of the earth, it is that we may learn for all to say, "Lead us not into the temptation" of our times; that so we may be enabled with greater confidence and hope to join in the cry of every time, "Deliver us from Evil".'

NOTES AND REFERENCES

Lecture I

A DOORSTEP IN QUEEN'S SQUARE: 1846

PAGE 13. The first quotation on this page and that on page 14 are taken from C. E. Raven, *Christian Socialism: 1848–1854*, who on p. 58 refers to *Life and Letters of F. J. A. Hort*, i, p. 154. For a vivid description of Ludlow in later life see Scott Holland, *A Bundle of Memories*, pp. 281–2. The following quotations are from *Life of Frederick Denison Maurice*, by F. Maurice, vol. i, chap. xxii. The house, No. 21, one of the few in the square remaining in its original state, was still standing, much as it must have done when Maurice first occupied it, ninety-four years later. It was much damaged by blast in an air-raid which destroyed some neighbouring property, and appears unlikely to be reconstructed. A plaque recording Maurice's residence there from 1846 to 1856, when he moved to No. 5 Russell Square, was undamaged.

PAGE 16. Quotation here is from G. C. Binyon, *The Christian Socialist Movement in England*, p. 33, who refers to *The Crisis*, 11th May 1833.

PAGE 17. Carlyle's verdict is quoted by H. Wilson Harris, *Caroline Fox*, p. 112.

PAGE 19. It is interesting, however, to find his mother writing to him in December 1830, with reference to the rioting of agricultural labourers in the district round Southampton: 'I cannot but think that this rising of the people, these midnight fires, have been very necessary to awaken us to a sense of the dreadful sin of poor labourers having been for many years obliged to work hard for scarcely enough wages to buy them potatoes. . . . High time for something dreadful to rouse persons from such wickedness. Though we have many crying, dreadful national sins, yet the obvious one pointed out at this moment is that the hire of the labourer is withheld.' F. Maurice, *Life*, i, p. 115. No doubt these thoughts took root in Maurice's mind. Five years later he gave as a reason for leaving his country curacy at Bubbenhall for the chaplaincy at Guy's Hospital, 'I am not skilful in suggesting improvements in the temporal condition of the poor, a serious deficiency in the country, but one that will not affect me there'. *Life*, i, p. 186.

PAGE 22. The quotation is taken from *The Age of the Chartists*, by J. L. and B. Hammond, p. 220, who quote extensively from the 'Official Census of Religious Worship', referred to in this paragraph

PAGES 22–3. The quotation here is from S. C. Carpenter, *Church and People: 1789–1889*, pp. 212–13.

PAGE 25. Carlyle, in his *Life of John Sterling*, says that the remark quoted here had 'evidently borne upon Church conservatism in some form', but this does not help us to decide whether Sterling was reproaching the parish priests of his time for not struggling for charity and justice or for contending for 'reactionary' causes and their own interests. But the sentence would hardly perhaps have 'survived on the wings of grinning rumour' (to quote Carlyle) unless the former more significant suggestion was implied.

PAGE 29. This characteristic and well-known stricture by Carlyle is taken from his *Life of John Sterling*.

PAGE 31. The quotations from Mill will be found in his Essay on Coleridge in *Dissertations and Discussions*, vol. i.

PAGES 32–3. The quotations from Bentham are from his *Principles of Legislation* (1876 edition), p. 133 and p. 119.

PAGE 35. Newman's admission was made in a private letter to Charles Marson. See his *God's Co-operative Society*, p. 71.

Lecture II

PROPHETS, PRIESTS AND POETS

PAGE 40. The quotation is from Dr. Peck's Hale Lectures on *The Social Implications of the Oxford Movement*, pp. 32–3.

PAGE 41. The title of Wilberforce's book is worth quoting in full; he called it *A Practical View of the Prevailing Religious System of Professed Christians in the Higher and Middle Classes in this Country contrasted with Real Christianity* (1797): the passage here cited is quoted in R. Coupland's *Wilberforce*, p. 195.

PAGE 43. For Wade see Binyon, op. cit., pp. 36 and 43. He was described by the contemporary radical journal, *The Pioneer*, which, says Binyon, 'might almost, in a sense, be called a Christian Socialist paper', as 'the only one of the beneficed servants of the Most High who had consistency and virtue sufficient to enlist himself in the cause of poverty and oppression'. Binyon also gives some account of Minter Morgan and Dr. William King.

PAGE 47. I am indebted to Dr. Stephen Liberty for permission to quote from a letter written to him in 1916 by Gordon Wordsworth, grandson of the poet. 'I take it he lost his faith in the political or parliamentary regeneration of mankind, but never his faith or hope in a social regeneration. He was *au fond* of an intensely practical nature, and no practicable scheme was before the world. He re-

Notes and References

mained a prophet, but circumstances and temperament prevented his being an initiator or an organizer. Besides hope like this, passionately felt, might dread a second disappointment.'

PAGE 48. But Wordsworth at any rate was neither sentimental about the past nor pessimistic about the future. He said to Caroline Fox in 1844, 'Railroads and all the mechanical achievements of this day are doing wonders for the next generation, indeed it is the appropriate work of this age and country and it is doing it gloriously. That anxious money-getting spirit, which is a ruling principle in England . . . is doing much by exhausting itself. We may therefore look forward with hopeful trust.' Wilson Harris, *Caroline Fox*, p. 183. Wordsworth's optimism, at a moment when the great majority of the upper classes went in terror of Chartism, is somewhat surprising, but optimism, often of an irrational sort, is a common characteristic of the aged. Wordsworth was then seventy-four.

PAGE 48. The letter quoted here is dated 1st March 1833, and is reproduced in *Life and Correspondence*, edited by C. C. Southey, vol. vi, p. 200.

The second extract on this page is from Southey's *Life and Correspondence*, vi, p. 58, and is quoted in the *Christian Socialist*, i, p. 79. I owe this reference to Dr. Raven's *Christian Socialism*, p. 48.

PAGE 49. The full title of the book is *Sir Thomas More: or Colloquies on the Progress and Prospects of Society* (1829). A valuable article dealing with this book, by Fr. Martin Jarrett-Kerr, C.R., appeared in the *Nineteenth Century and After*, Oct. 1942; vol. cxxxii, No. 788.

'He believed, and he consistently maintained, that it was the business of the State to provide what we now call "social services". Poverty was not to him, as it was to too many of the economists of his day, an act of God, deplorable but irremediable: it was an evil that could be greatly lessened, or even abolished altogether. . . . A century later the wheel has come full circle. Our sympathies lie with Southey rather than Macaulay.' Simmons, *Southey*, p. 152. Macaulay's essay on Southey, which is in form a review of the *Colloquies*, appears in vol. ii of the 'Everyman's Library' edition of his essays.

Dr. Raven notes that Dicey says of Southey that 'he is to us the prophetic precursor of modern collectivism'. (*Laws and Opinion in England*, p. 225.) Raven, *Christian Socialism: 1848–1854*, p. 48.

PAGES 50 and 51. The quotations here are from the edition of 1839, pp. 386, 403–4, 409, 417.

PAGE 51. Dr. Gloyn's book, *The Church in the Social Order*: A Study of Anglican Social Theory from Coleridge to Maurice (Pacific University Press, Oregon) is particularly valuable for the massive array of quotations cited from the writers with whom it deals.

PAGE 53. Newman's poem here quoted first appeared in *Lyra Apostolica* (1836) and is reprinted in *The Poems of Cardinal Newman*, 'Sacred Treasury' edition, p. 217.

Newman's dictum is taken from his *Parochial and Plain Sermons*, vol. vi, No. xxviii, sermon on 'The Danger of Riches'. Quoted by Ruth Kenyon, essay on 'The Social Aspect of the Catholic Revival', in *Northern Catholicism*, edited by N. P. Williams and Charles Harris. Another example is quoted by G. O'Brien, *Economic Effects of the Reformation*, p. 82: 'Cardinal Newman heaped invective and contempt upon the dictum of a contemporary economist that "the endeavour to accumulate the means of a future subsistence and enjoyment is to the mass of mankind the great source of moral improvement"—an observation which Newman described as "so very categorical a contradiction of our Lord, St. Chrysostom, St. Leo and all the Saints".' (*The Idea of a University*, p. 90.)

PAGE 54. Wilberforce's precise words were: 'The poor have the advantage, that if their superiors enjoy more abundant comforts, they are also exposed to many temptations from which the inferior classes are happily exempted.' *A Practical View*, p. 314.

PAGE 55. Marx's notable judgment was contained in his *Inaugural Address* to the International Working Men's Association (the 'First International') 1864. See Max Beer, *A History of British Socialism*, vol. ii, p. 216.

PAGES 55–7. The quotations are from the original edition of *The Ideal of a Christian Church* (1844) pp. xv, 31, 55, 32, 470–1, 467, 48, 338, 386.

PAGE 58. The quotations here are from Charles Whibley, *Lord John Manners and his Friends*, vol. i, pp. 66 and 107.

While Maurice wrote (13th May 1840) of Carlyle's 'wild, pantheistic rant', a month later we find him saying, 'I have seen something more of Carlyle lately, and feel increased interest in him, his utter unrest is, on the whole, a cheering, though a sad, symptom.' *Life*, vol. i, pp. 283, 284. The paradox contained in this judgment represents a characteristically Maurician outlook. Maurice could see the value of the 'unrest', but at the same time lament the uncertain dogmatic basis from which it proceeded and which promised no happy conclusion for the man who manifested it, and he could sympathize with the strain which such a situation involved for Carlyle.

PAGE 59. The passage is quoted in A. P. Stanley, *Life and Letters of T. Arnold*, p. 157.

PAGES 60–1. The quotation is from *The Condition of the Working Class in England in 1844*, English edition, 1892, Preface, pp. vi–vii.

Lecture III

THE SEVEN YEARS: 1848–1854

(a) *1848 and Charles Kingsley*

PAGE 65. The letter is given in full in *Charles Kingsley: His letters*

Notes and References

and memories of his life, edited by his wife. 15th Abridged Edition, 1885, vol. i, p. 97. [The references here throughout are to this edition, which though somewhat condensed from the original and larger work, contains some matter not included therein.]

PAGES 66–7. This passage will be found in *The Kingdom of Christ*: Everyman edition, vol. ii, p. 321.

PAGE 67. Maurice's question is taken from one of his *Sermons on the Prayer Book*, that preached on 3rd Dec. of that year. The passage from which this sentence is taken is given in the *Life*, vol. i, p. 484. How great was the effect of the events of 1848 upon thoughtful and religious minds is well suggested by a passage in an article by Dean Church, written in the *Christian Remembrancer* for July of that year and reprinted in his *Essays and Reviews*, p. 343.

'Chaos is for the present the recognized condition of Europe. Conflict, convulsion and overthrow belong to that condition. They affect us only like any other phenomena with which life has made us acquainted. Not so these outstanding and incredible tidings which used to come in the gloomy mornings of February and March, more trying to our faith even than to our fears or hopes, like the shocks of an earthquake to persons who have never felt one. We, the children of tranquil monotony and unbroken peace, gravely doubting whether war was henceforth a possibility, found ourselves in a moment the contemporaries of a revolution in very deed accepting the traditions of 1793, and not hesitating before any of its consequences. We found ourselves at once a historical generation.'

He adds, however:

'the bewilderment attending this novel transformation has worn off. We have recovered our breath and can look about us.' Maurice, we may note, never lost his. Church here notes thus early a fact lately observed by Archbishop David Mathew, that 'few moods slid away more rapidly than the revolutionary sentiments of 1848'. (*Acton: the formative years*, p. 95.)

Church's article contains many interesting passages, in which the question, 'how will the Church shape her course' in face of 'the multitudes who throng round her, accepting her poetry, but despising her creed' is, if somewhat sketchily, discussed. He concludes (p. 400):

'As it is certain that God's providence does not sleep, it may be that under this tempest of the wrath of man, the gradual and slow growth of good is going on, which in spite of ever new evils, we seem to discern even here. But—whether this heralds the last storm or whether, just as amid these overflowings of ungodliness which made our fathers afraid, much was working which God has turned to good for us, so now things may be growing wherewith the indulgence of an over-ruling Providence shall bless our children—we, at any rate, may take refuge in the thought, not new to us, or resorted to for the first time in perplexity, that "God's government is a scheme imperfectly comprehended".'

Maurice to Temple

PAGE 67. On the Sunday following the day on which Maurice received Ludlow's letter, Maurice had reached the petition, 'Give us this day our daily bread'. In the course of this sermon these passages occur:

'Beneath all distinctions of property and of rank lie the obligations of a common Creation, Redemption, Humanity; and these are not mere obligations to be confessed when the others are satisfied. They are not vague abstractions, which cannot quite be denied, but which have no direct bearing upon our actual daily existence; they are primary, eternal bonds, upon which all others depend; they are not satisfied by some nominal occasional act of homage; they demand the fealty and service of a life; all our doings must be witnesses of them. The Church proclaims tacitly by her existence—she should have proclaimed openly by her voice—that property and rank are held upon this tenure; that they can stand by no other. Alas! she has not spoken out this truth clearly and strongly here or anywhere. She has fancied it was her first work to watch over the protection of those who would have protected themselves well enough without her, provided she had been true to her vocation of caring for those whom the world did not care for, of protecting them continually, of fitting them to be citizens of any society on earth, by showing them what is implied in the heavenly filial citizenship into which God has freely adopted them. Failing in this duty, she has become powerless for the one she ignominiously preferred. She can give but feeble help to the rich in the hour of need, because she ministered to them with such sad fidelity in their hour of triumph and prosperity. She can scarcely make her voice heard against schemes for reducing all things to a common stock, for establishing a fellowship upon a law of mutual selfishness, because she has not believed that the internal communion, the law of love, the polity of members united in one Head, of brethren confessing a common Father, was a real one—has left people to fancy it was only a fine dream, a cruel mockery, incapable of bringing any tangible blessings. . . . Pp. 65–6 (edition of 1848).

'If we pass continually in our streets creatures of our own flesh and blood, who have a look of hunger and misery, without being able to determine whether it is a greater sin to withhold that which may save them from death, or to give them what may lead to the worst kind of death; if a thousand social problems which we once supposed were of easy solution, present themselves in new and embarrassing aspects, tempting us to pass them by altogether and then forcing upon us the reflection that they must settle themselves in some way, whether we forget them or not; if we hear masses of creatures spoken of as if they were the insects we look at in a microscope, and then are suddenly reminded by some startling phenomenon that each one of them has a living soul; then, before we become mad, or escape into an apathy that is worse than madness, let us ask ourselves whether we have yet prayed this child's prayer as we would have a child pray it, in simplicity and truth.' (Pp. 66–7.)

The sermon, however, will be found most impressive if read as a whole, and as part of the notable series to which it contributes. Maurice was fully conscious of the social reference of his course, and in the 'Advertisement' with which he prefaced the sermons on their publication that summer, declared that: 'I wished these Sermons to connect the Lord's Prayer with the thoughts which are most likely to be occupying us at this time. If they lead any to ask themselves how their study of passing occurrences may be made more serious, and their worship more real, my purpose in publishing them will be answered.'

PAGE 69. The quotations here are given in the *Life of Kingsley*, vol. ii, p. 162. The second is from the preface to *The Gospel of the Pentateuch*.

PAGE 70. This letter will be found in the *Life*, vol. ii, p. 247. It is curious to recall that these are the verdicts of one who was not only a Christian teacher but the Professor of Modern History at Cambridge for some years.

Kingsley's enthusiasm for the 'Norseland' carried him to fantastic extremes of nonsense as e.g. 'The Church of England is wonderfully and mysteriously fitted for the souls of a free Norse-Saxon race; for men whose ancestors fought by the side of Odin, over whom a descendant of Odin now rules.' *Life*, vol. i, p. 203. Conversely, his contempt for Latin culture was equally unbalanced. A few sentences farther on in the same letter (January, 1857) he writes: 'I can only believe that if they [the Italians and Spaniards] had been capable of anything higher [than Catholicism] God would have given them something higher.' In this, as in some other matters, Kingsley could 'only believe' what his perverse strain of Victorian insularity prompted him to believe.

PAGE 71. The phrase 'Muscular Christian' was already current at this time and had been applied to Kingsley, as he suggests in writing to Maurice in 1857: 'I have to preach the divineness of the whole manhood, and am content to be called a Muscular Christian, or any other impertinent name, by men who little dream of the weakness of character, sickness of body and misery of mind by which I have bought what little I know of the human heart.'

PAGE 71. Kingsley seems to have been conscious that his old colleagues may have had some suspicion that he was deserting them. He wrote to Tom Hughes in 1855: 'You may have fancied me a bit of a renegade of late.

'Still in our ashes live their wonted fires, And if I have held back from the Social Movement, it has been because I have seen that the world was not going to be set right in any such rose-pink way, excellent as it is, and that there are heavy arrears of *destruction* to be made up before *construction* can even begin; and I wanted to see what those arrears were. And I do see a little. At least I see that the old phoenix must *burn*, before the new one can rise out of its ashes.'

It is a little puzzling to know what was in Kingsley's mind in writing thus. He was not one to welcome 'revolution', which in any case looked less likely than ever by 1855. He was probably chiefly concerned to excuse himself from taking a hand in the patient work of Hughes and Ludlow, for which indeed he had neither the temperament, the training nor the opportunity.

PAGE 74. The quotation here is from *Alton Locke*, p. cxvi (edition of 1884).

PAGE 76. For the determination here recorded see *Life of Kingsley*, vol. ii, p. 88. He had written five years earlier (1854), 'Those who fancy me a "sentimentalist" or a "fanatic" little know how thoroughly my own heart is for physical science . . . or how, again, my theological creed has grown slowly and naturally out of my physical one'. (Ibid., vol. i, p. 299.)

PAGES 76–7. The quotations are from the edition of 1888, pp. 187, 219, 210.

PAGES 77–8. The letter here referred to is given in the *Life*, vol. ii, p. 138.

PAGE 78. For the quotation here see the *Life*, vol. ii, p. 277.

(b) *Maurice and 'Christian Socialism'*

PAGES 79–80. Quotations from Raven, *Christian Socialism: 1848–1854*, pp. 134–5.

PAGE 81. Quotations of Dr. Ramsey from an article in *Theology*, Jan. 1945, p. 3 (What is Anglican Theology?'), and from *The Gospel and the Catholic Church*, p. 216.

PAGE 82. The dictum will be found in *Life of Maurice*, vol. i, p. 219. In his letters Maurice is always returning to this theme. Examples are to be found in the *Life*, vol. i, pp. 506 and 535. But Maurice always thought of reconciliation as 'the destruction of compromise'. In Dec. 1849 he wrote to Ludlow that Julius Hare 'wishes to make everyone comfortable in the Church; and I want no one to be comfortable in it, so cross-grained am I. Yet I seek for unity in my own wild way.' (*Life*, vol. ii, p. 30.)

PAGE 83. C. F. G. Masterman's observation is made in his biographical study of Maurice ('Leaders of the Church' series: Mowbrays), which, though written forty years ago and affected by the 'progressivist' climate of that time, is still the only substantial account of critique of Maurice's life and significance that we have. The official *Life*, published as long ago as 1884, is of course indispensable; but it is chiefly valuable for consisting largely of extracts from Maurice's copious correspondence. His son made no attempt at any critical estimate of his father's work and message.

PAGE 85. This very important letter is given in full in the *Life of Maurice*, vol. ii, p. 137.

PAGE 85. For Max Beer's judgment see his *History of British Socialism*, vol. ii, p. 181.

Notes and References

PAGES 86. This letter is in *Life of Maurice*, vol. ii, p. 35.

PAGE 88. The letter is in *Life of Maurice*, vol. ii, p. 32.

PAGE 89. This striking verdict of Ludlow on the wage system is quoted in Raven, op. cit., p. 249.

PAGE 90. For information about the 'Redemptionists' see G. D. H. Cole, *A Century of Co-operation* (1945), p. 101.

PAGE 92. The hymn, *O God of Truth*, is No. 440 in *Hymns Ancient and Modern* and No. 449 in *The English Hymnal*.

Lecture IV

SEED GROWING SECRETLY: 1854–1884

PAGE 95. Maurice's tract was in the form of a dialogue, a very favourite method with him. Here is a characteristic extract, which has an interesting bearing on the Christian doctrine of Vocation:

'A. Perhaps you would not be quite confounded by the ordinary argument that if kings exercise their functions by this grace [of God], all doctors, soldiers, lawyers, cotton-spinners, journalists, handicraftsmen, exercise their functions by the same grace?

'B. Confounded by it! It is a logical conclusion from my premises. It is the very principle I am most anxious to maintain. When we thoroughly grasp it I believe we shall become a righteous and a free people, able to be witnesses of righteousness and freedom to the ends of the earth. If we let go the half faith we have in it, instead of seeking to deepen and expand it, I see no alternative for us but the acceptance of the most slavish doctrines into our hearts and of the actual bodily slavery to which such doctrines always lead at last.' (p. 56) [This Tract is No. x in the second volume.]

PAGE 97. The letter is in *Life of Maurice*, vol. ii, p. 617.

PAGE 98. The description of Fraser as 'prince and leader' is by J. W. Diggle, in his book on *Bishop Fraser's Lancashire Life*, p. 22. This biographer adds that 'He was not only the chief Churchman in Manchester—he was also Manchester's Premier Citizen. He threw himself, heart and soul, into the civic life of his diocese. Mayors and Corporations were not less interesting to him than Archdeacons and Rural Deans.' Fraser described himself as 'a churchman of the school and type of Richard Hooker'.

The other quotations here are from Thomas Hughes, *James Fraser, second Bishop of Manchester*, pp. 234, 232.

Fraser declared (1884) that 'Bishops had to do daring things', ibid., p. 323.

PAGE 99. Bright's combination of sincere idealism and thoroughgoing commercialism strikingly typifies the dominant mood of Victorian liberalism. The afterglow of this mood is reflected in the towns which remain as relics of the period. A modern writer records of one of them [Middlesbrough], 'the atmosphere of years of forced and awkward growth will soon be felt; the background of Victorian compassion and cruelty, of aspiration fogged by commercialism that belongs to this over-populated, half-decayed place.' John Piper in *Cornhill*, Dec. 1945, pp. 432–3.

PAGE 100. The facts given here are set out by E. L. Woodward, *The Age of Reform*, p. 586. He adds, however, that in 1870, 'a far greater number of Englishmen than in 1815 belonged by occupation and surroundings to an industrial proletariat. In these circumstances it would be idle to talk of fraternity; Englishmen of different classes were unable to sit at the same table without a sense either of patronage or awkwardness', p. 607. From any genuinely egalitarian standpoint the nineteenth century in Britain was assuredly not a period of progress.

PAGES 101–2. The quotations are from R. C. K. Ensor, *England, 1870–1914*, pp. 137–8.

PAGE 104. For Dr. Lowther Clarke's judgment see the essay on 'English Church Life in 1850', included in his book, *Eighteenth Century Piety*, p. 147.

PAGE 104. Mr. Hollis's essay on 'The Meaning of Anthony Trollope' appears in the composite volume, *For Hilaire Belloc*, edited by Douglas Woodruff. There were undoubtedly serious limits to Trollope's knowledge of developments within the Church of England of his day. A writer in the *Church Quarterly Review* for April, 1945, points out that there seems to be a 'time lag' in his pictures of things ecclesiastical; 'Trollope thinks in terms of the parsons he knew in his youth.' Article on 'Fiction and the Oxford Movement', by Andrew L. Drummond, p. 43.

PAGE 107. The quotations here are taken from Philip Guedalla, *Palmerston*, p. 347.

PAGE 108. The quotations from Miss Constance Smith are taken from an essay on Shaftesbury in *Christian Social Reformers of the Nineteenth Century*, edited by Hugh Martin, p. 83. The Hammonds' definitive biography is well known. Miss Higham's shorter study is published by the Student Christian Movement.

PAGE 109. The quotations here are from an article on Charles George Gordon by Graham Seton Hutchison in *Church Quarterly Review*, Jan.–March, 1945, pp. 77–8.

PAGES 110–11. For the particulars given here I am indebted to Bro. George Every, S.S.M. See, in this connection, his review of Miss Georgina Battiscombe's study of C. M. Yonge in *Theology*, Jan. 1944, p. 17. There were lesser-known novelists of the same school as Charlotte Yonge. In Mrs. Linton's *Lizzie Lorton* (1866) Margaret Elcombe thinks of establishing 'a kind of Christian Socialism on a High Church basis'. And in Disraeli's late novel, *Endymion*, 'we have the picture of slum life irradiated by Anglo-Catholic influence'. See article in *C.Q.R.* for April, 1945, to which reference has already been made.

Notes and References

Also *The Novel and the Oxford Movement*, by Joseph Ellis Baker (Princeton, 1932).

PAGE 111. The extract is from Pusey's sermon on 'Almsgiving' in *University Sermons*, which is quoted by W. G. Peck, *The Social Implications of the Oxford Movement*, pp. 67–8.

PAGE 113. The extract is from Pusey's book on *The Councils of the Church* (1857), quoted by Ruth Kenyon in her essay on 'The Social Aspect of the Catholic Revival', in *Northern Catholicism*, edited by N. P. Williams and Charles Harris. Miss Kenyon points out that 'long before he [Pusey] wrote those words' he had applied himself 'to pioneer work along these lines' by the foundation of churches in slum parishes, beginning with St. Saviour's, Leeds.

PAGE 113. The quotations relating to Stanton and Dolling are taken from G. C. Binyon, *The Christian Socialist Movement in England*, p. 102. The incident concerning Dolling occurred at a date (1890) later than the period covered by this lecture. Headlam had declared that 'the land was the Lord's and therefore could not be in any absolute sense the landlords',' whereupon 'there was some applause in the church and much commotion afterwards in the town'. (Portsmouth.) See also F. G. Bettany, *Stewart Headlam*, p. 118.

PAGE 114. This description of Osborne is that of his biographer in the *Dictionary of National Biography*. The following is a sample of Osborne's vigorous style, taken from a letter written to *The Times* in the first year of the period covered by this series of lectures [1846]. Osborne suggests that *The Times'* Commissioner to Ireland should be sent to six or seven English counties, 'that he may show the condition of the peasantry on the estates of some of the largest and wealthiest proprietors in this country—men cognizant of every feature of the condition of those, by the sweat of whose brow their broad acres are cultivated—men who know of, and have abetted, for their own selfish ends, a system of tyranny and exaction which has produced a state of hideous moral and physical destitution, equal to any he has unveiled in the worst parts of the sister country. In Ireland the peasantry are at least tolerated in their misery, they are left undisturbed in it. Here, Sir, the poor have, in but too many districts, daily proof that their numbers are considered an intolerable nuisance —a nuisance to be put down by every exercise of the ingenuity of those whose power, unfortunately, is fully equal to the carrying out of their cruel ends.

'Their wages have been brought below the *minimum* of healthy existence and the poor-rate has for ever to preserve a nice balance between absolute and partial destitution. The villages in which they dwell have been turned into dirty undrained lanes, bordered with hovel homes, whose outward evidence of physical want and filth form a speaking label of the moral destitution and moral filth to be found within; so crammed that the air in which the night's rest is sought is at least as foul as the conditions under which alone that rest can be taken. . . .

223

'That the presence of your "Commissioner" would create a panic in the "halls" and "parks" I doubt not. . . . I should like him to compare the after-public-dinner practice of the great owner with the after-breakfast practice of the steward's office. . . .'

The Times, 19th Jan., 1846.

PAGE 115. For Gore's declaration see the Convocation of Canterbury Report for 1918, p. 275, quoted by D. O. Wagner, *The Church of England and Social Reform since 1854*, p. 175. Dr. Prestige in his *Life of Gore*, referring to Gore's feelings at this time, records him as writing in 1925, 'The Squirearchy was not by any means a bad lot, nor the clergy, but they lacked imagination. . . . We always seem to see the truth about things when it is too late.' (p. 17) Prestige further notes (p. 17) that in its review of the year 1874, *The Church Times* compared Arch's work sympathetically with the Peasants' Revolt under Richard II, and regretted 'that no clerical champion had come forward from the outset, like John Ball, to direct this more peaceful protest against rural injustice'. Yet as this lecture makes plain, there were in fact several such.

PAGES 115–16. The quotations are from the *Church Congress Report*, 1873, pp. 27, 30–3, 34.

PAGE 119. Toynbee's words are from a passage quoted by Beatrice Webb in *My Apprenticeship*, where reference is made to p. 318 of Toynbee's Lectures on *The Industrial Revolution of the Nineteenth Century in England*, but I have been unable to trace the passage in the 1908 edition of these lectures. Mrs. Webb finds the origin of the social ferment of the eighteen-eighties in 'a new consciousness of sin among men of intellect and property', 'a collective or class consciousness, a growing uneasiness, amounting to conviction, that the industrial organization which had yielded rent, interest and profit on a stupendous scale, had failed to provide a decent livelihood and tolerable conditions for a majority of the inhabitants of Great Britain'. (*My Apprenticeship*, p. 179.)

PAGE 119. Riley, who became interested in social philosophy while working as a commercial traveller, subsequently became a journalist and was a worker for progressive causes in Bristol in the early 'seventies. There are some particulars about him in *An Account of the Labour and Socialist Movement in Bristol*, published in Bristol, 1929, pp. 13–15.

Lecture V

'THE BANNER OF CHRIST IN THE HANDS OF THE SOCIALISTS': 1884–1914

PAGE 122. The quotations from *The Rock* will be found in H. C. Shuttleworth, A Memoir edited by G. W. E. Russell (1903), a most useful source of information for the period under consideration.

Notes and References

PAGE 122. R. C. K. Ensor, *England 1870–1914* (p. 112) notes it as 'symptomatic that the word "unemployed" used as a noun is first recorded by the *Oxford English Dictionary* from the year 1882, the word "unemployment" from 1888'. 'Before the end of 1887 trade was working towards another boom. But England was not the same afterwards. There was "never glad confident morning again" for the workshop of the world' (p. 111).

PAGE 123. In view of Shuttleworth's partial identification with 'Morell', it is perhaps only fair to quote the judgment recorded in Russell's *Memoir of Shuttleworth*, that 'the applause that would have ruined many another man never seemed to do him the least hurt', which is not the impression 'Candida' conveys to us of the effect of applause upon her husband! Shuttleworth was a prototype of the athletic sort of cleric who began to appear for the first time in Anglo-Catholic circles at the end of the 'seventies. Russell thinks he was 'the first to combine chasubles before the altar with flannels before the stumps'. Op. cit., p. 19.

PAGE 124. Morris's lines are from 'All for the Cause', first published in *Justice*, the S.D.F. weekly periodical, 19th April 1884, and reprinted in *Poems by the way* (1891), and in vol. ix of Morris's *Collected Works* (1911), p. 185.

PAGE 124. The story of these stirring events has been told in many social histories. There is a particularly good account in Godfrey Elton, *England Arise*, chapter vi. See also H. M. Hyndman, *The Record of an Adventurous Life*, chapter xxiv. Linnell lost his life on 20th Nov. 1887.

PAGE 128. 'In the gasworks the resident engineer hails one of his workmen. "Thorne, what is this Socialism I hear you are always talking about to the men?" Thorne knows that Socialism is his dream of a fuller life. But the engineer will want definitions. So he pulls out of his pocket a copy of John Burns's speech from the dock [after the riots of November, 1887]. With one foot on a pile of coal he twists himself so that the uncertain light of the retorts falls upon the ill-printed page. "Socialism is a theory of society which advocates a more just, orderly and harmonious arrangement of the social relations of mankind." He cannot help declaiming the words. Yes, but the engineer will want definitions. He turns the leaves and finds one which will do. But what sticks in the engineer's mind is perhaps those first vaguer words . . ." A more just arrangement . . ." ' Elton, op. cit. p. 214, based on Will Thorne, *My Life's Battles*, pp. 62–3.

PAGE 128. Hancock's famous sermon is reproduced in *The Pulpit and the Press, and other Sermons* (1904), pp. 31–40.

PAGE 130. For the quotations in this paragraph see F. G. Bettany, *Stewart Headlam*, pp. 43–4, pp. 62, 64. The telegram was sent to Bradlaugh in 1880 while he was in prison, to which he had been committed for his defiance of the House of Commons' ruling over the oath question. It ran, 'Accept my warmest sympathy. I wish you good luck in the name of Jesus Christ, the Emancipator, whom so many of your opponents blaspheme'. Mr. Bettany, with some justification, describes the telegram as 'strangely injudicious, especially in its terms' (op. cit., p. 60), but the episode, in its quixotic and generous defiance of what opinion might require from one in his position, is altogether characteristic of Headlam.

PAGE 132. Hancock's sermon on 'The Social Carcase and the Anti-social Vultures' will be found in *The Pulpit and the Press*, as also that on 'The Banner of Christ in the hands of the Socialists'.

PAGE 134. Champion's utterance is given by Binyon, op. cit., p. 129, quoting from an account of the social disturbances of 1886–7, written by Bernard Shaw.

PAGE 135. The quotation is from an article on 'Christian Socialism, Past and Present', in *The Commonwealth*, December, 1926, pp. 374–5.

PAGE 136. For Scott Holland's days at Eton see Stephen Paget, *Henry Scott Holland*, pp. 9–18.

PAGE 137. G. K. Chesterton, *Autobiography*, p. 168.

PAGE 140. The passage in which Maurice so describes himself is from a letter to Kingsley: 'I am a hard Puritan, almost incapable of enjoyment, though on principle justifying enjoyment as God's gift to his creatures, and though I try to feel no grudge against those who have that which my conscience tells me it is not a virtue but a sin to want'. *Life*, vol. ii, p. 261. Cf. a much earlier passage (*Life*, vol. i, p. 281), 'if I could dare, which I do not, to think of anything as pleasant in itself apart from some moral law (in this case I hope not wanting)'. This grave scruple was expressed with reference to a suggestion for a visit to Switzerland!

The references to Westcott here are from Arthur Westcott, *Brooke Foss Westcott*, vol. ii, p. 131, and Joseph Clayton, *Westcott* (Mowbray's 'Leaders of the Church' series), p. 33.

PAGE 141. See Chesterton's delightful poem describing the impression made upon a matter-of-fact citizen of a meeting held by the C.S.U. in Nottingham in the early nineteen hundreds and addressed, *inter alia*, by Holland:

> He said the human soul should be
> Ashamed of every sham,
> He said a man should constantly
> Ejaculate 'I am'.
> . . . When he had done I went outside
> And got into a tram.

With which lines the poem, very appropriately, concludes. *Autobiography*, p. 168.

There is a most moving account of the sceptical phase in Chesterton's early life in his *Autobiography*, chapter iv, 'How to be a Lunatic'.

The reaction against 'Incarnational' theology is well exemplified in an article by J. V. L. Casserley on 'The Interpretation of Catastrophe' in *Christendom*, vol. iii, No. 30, June 1938. 'Too long has the neat and cosy sacramentalist incarnationalism of a comfortable Church blinded us to the essential puritanism, the austerity, the ascetic element which loomed so large in the original Catholic Faith and without which *the soul cannot be free*. The sufferings of the coming time may at least restore to us that rigid Christian self-discipline whose claims so many of us have ignored' (p. 123).

PAGE 142. The quotation here is from an illuminating passage by Ruth Kenyon, in her essay in *Northern Catholicism*, on 'The Social Aspect of the Catholic Revival', p. 394.

PAGE 145. Gore's remark is quoted from his chapter on 'Holland and the Christian Social Union', in Stephen Paget's *Henry Scott Holland*.

PAGE 147. Gore's characteristic stricture on the Church of England is quoted by Prestige, op. cit., p. 265. The phrase occurs in a letter written to D. C. Lathbury while Gore was Bishop of Birmingham.

PAGE 147. Scott Holland's recollections of Ludlow will be found in his book, *A Bundle of Memories*, pp. 281–2.

The references to Enid Stacy are from an article written after her death by A. L. L.(illey), in *The Commonwealth*, October, 1903, p. 321.

PAGE 148. Adderley, who was one of the best propagandists the movement ever had, put his knowledge of the 'idle rich' class from which he sprang to good effect, especially in his satiric novels, one of which, *Stephen Remarx*, first published in 1893, was still selling in a twelfth edition a dozen years later.

PAGE 150. A book which reflected the influence of Bussell, and combined an attack upon plutocracy with a good deal of suspicion of collectivist tendencies and a leaning towards what was afterwards to be known as 'Distributism', was *Politics and Religion*, by Gabriel Gillett. Published as early as 1912, this book foreshadowed a type of social criticism which was later to become predominant in Anglo-Catholic sociology. To-day, says the author, 'everything is made easy for the rich and difficult for the poor in almost exact proportion to their poverty. If there were a strong public opinion in favour of wider distribution, changes in our laws might be made in a contrary direction. In addition to the much more graduated taxation of great incomes we might legislate deliberately to favour small owners and small investors. . . . Some policy of that kind is the only sane alternative to collectivism. . . . Such a policy would be immensely popular, appealing as it would both to the conservative and democratic instincts of the people; for it would be a conservative policy in refusing to aim at something which has never been tried on a large scale, and a democratic policy in securing for the ordinary man the opportunities of a larger life.' (pp. xvii–xviii)

PAGE 151. It is interesting to find Stewart Headlam expressing his anxiety about the influence of bureaucratic ideas and of 'busybodies' generally in an article on 'Socialism and Personal Liberty' in *The Optimist* for October, 1911, pp. 169–78. Writing of the famous Minority Report of the Poor Law Commission, he says, 'Mr. and

Mrs. Webb's scheme would, in my opinion, if carried out in its entirety, bring into being a monstrous gigantic "servile state", under the espionage and dominance of a few carefully selected "intellectuals".' (p. 170) An article in the same journal, for July 1912, by the present writer, declares that 'we see society menaced by the Servile State on the one hand and Syndicalism on the other, and it is that which leads us to declare that we are standing not on the threshold of Utopia, but between the Devil and the deep sea.' (p. 100) By this date the mood of optimistic progressivism which had long characterized the Christian social movement was 'on the way out'.

PAGE 151. Widdrington's article appeared in *The Commonwealth*, April, 1927. Mr. Binyon (op. cit., p. 138) declares that 'so far as I have been able to discover, the first occasion on which anyone used the expression "Christian Sociology" was at the Church Congress of 1887 when Bishop Alexander, of Derry and Raphoe, contributed a paper on "Christianity and Socialism" in which he "urged that the staff of theological professors might profitably be increased by the endowment of a chair of "Christian Sociology".' Sixty years later this admirable suggestion has still to be adopted, so far at any rate as Great Britain is concerned.

PAGE 151. Temple's article appeared in *The Economic Review*, 1908, pp. 190 *et seq.* I owe this reference to D. O. Wagner, op. cit., p. 270.

Lecture VI

'NOT TO BUILD BUT TO DIG': 1914–1946

PAGE 151. The quotations from Dr. Demant are from his essay on 'The Tragedy of War and the Hope of Peace', in the Oxford Conference volume on *The Universal Church and the World of Nations* (1937), p. 171.

PAGES 162–3. The extracts are from *Christianity and Industrial Problems* (1918), p. 7, para. 8, and p. 105, para 167a.

PAGE 164. This definition of a priest is given in *Geoffrey Studdert Kennedy*, a Memoir by his friends, p. 185. For similar thoughts of a young admirer of Studdert Kennedy on the same theme, see *Basil Jellicoe* by Kenneth Ingram, p. 138.

PAGE 165. The quotation is from Kennedy's book, *The Word and the Work*, pp. 65–6.

PAGE 169. Bishop Weston's stirring address, 'Our Present Duty', is No. xxiii in *Report of the Anglo-Catholic Congress, 1923*, pp. 185–6.

PAGE 171. Gore's address will be found in *The Proceedings of COPEC*, p. 212.

PAGE 173. The quotations from Mr. Bevin's speech will be found in *Hansard*, vol. 419, No. 81, cols. 399, 402. (Debate of 12th February 1946.)

Notes and References

PAGE 175. The Archbishop's speech is reported in *Hansard*, vol. 64, col. 49.

PAGE 176. The book here referred to was described as 'An Outline for Christian Thought and Action, submitted to the Christian Social Council by its Research Committee'. The sentence quoted appears on p. 12.

PAGE 177. The substance of the passage here quoted from *The New Age* was reproduced in Dr. Demant's book, *This Unemployment: Disaster or Opportunity?* (1931), pp. 17–18.

PAGE 180. The quotation here is from a vivid picture of Oxford in the early 'Thirties given by Michael Barsley: *The Wolf at the Door*, p. 131.

PAGE 185. The quotation from Dr. Peck is from his important essay on 'William Temple as social thinker', in the volume *William Temple: an Estimate and an Appreciation*, by six writers (1946), p. 60.

PAGES 185–6. Temple's verdicts on the Conference will be found in the volume *Malvern: 1941*, p. 215 and pp. 220–3.

Lecture VII

THE LESSONS OF A CENTURY

PAGE 192. Lest an emphasis upon the physical and psychological strain of mass-production be attributed, as it often is, to an academic outlook upon the subject, the following letter from a woman worker, which appeared in the *News Chronicle* a few years back, may be usefully quoted:

'As one who, at eighteen, went and worked in a factory for a long time, I am absolutely certain the deadly monotony of the repetition work is responsible for *all* the trouble.

'Long hours standing in the same spot left one aching, stiff and weary in every limb, and no girl's body is suited to this treatment.

'By the time one left one was too tired and limp to do anything but sit and dream—mainly of the day when one might escape. The appalling monotony of the work made every five minutes seem an hour, and the day endless.

'It is impossible for anyone who has not experienced this hell of boredom to realize the devastating effect it has on the most wholesome body or the most determined brain.

'Born a country girl, readily able to do a hard day's work on a farm, I returned enfeebled in mind and body, and it took a long time to recover. Although I have now to some extent lived it down, the experience has undoubtedly affected me adversely for life, both mentally and physically.' See also *Democracy and Industry*, by Constance Reaveley and John Winnington (1947) who write from first-hand experience of mass-producton work.

PAGE 192. Note in connection with the lack of interest here remarked on the following passage: 'It is credibly reported that Christian students in our universities and colleges, unlike their predecessors a generation ago, are eager now to study the Bible and dogma, but display little, if any, interest in the discussion of political and social questions. This change may at first sight gratify the theologian, but it ought not to do so for long. There is something radically wrong with Bible study that induces pietism or absorption in religious interests. One way of counteracting this tendency is to . . . show that the Bible itself is a manual of politics.'

Editorial in *Theology*, October, 1946, p. 289.

PAGE 193. The first of these philosophical issues is stated in the words of Mr. Donald MacKinnon, reviewing the volume *Prospect for Christendom* in *The Student Movement*, November–December, 1945, p. 30.

PAGE 194. Temple's words are quoted from his introduction to the Report of the Doctrinal Commission, *Doctrine in the Church of England* (1938), pp. 16–17.

The 'ultra-Barthian' quotation here cited is from Gunther Dehn, *Man and Revelation*, English translation, p. 157 (quoted by John Baillie, *What is Christian Civilization?* p 33).

PAGE 197. The accusation of a 'preference for less enlightened to more enlightened thought' is made against the contributors to the volume, *Prospect for Christendom*, by Mr. Eric W. Brewin in a review of the book in *Theology*, Sept. 1945, p. 207.

PAGE 108. The quotation is from *God, Man and Society* (1933), p. 44.

PAGE 199. Mr. Preston's words are quoted from an article on 'A Century of Anglican Social Thought', in *The Modern Churchman*, March 1943. Mr. Preston continues: 'Consequently the Christian task is always to work for the next step forward in the light of the possible alternatives open at the time. To know these involves a good deal of general and specialized knowledge which is not specifically "Christian" and on which opinions differ; hence the conclusion which emerges from such a process of reflection cannot be labelled "Christian". There is bound to be an element of uncertainty.' This is on the whole true, but betrays a misunderstanding of the claim of the Christian sociologist, which is not that he is either entitled or competent, as such, to pronounce upon the details of specific secular programmes or policies, but that he has to make plain what are the social norms to which a society striving to embody the Christian truth about man must strive to approximate.

PAGE 201. The sentence quoted from Dr. Demant is from his *Christian News Letter* Supplement. April 3rd, 1946, p. 10. The whole argument of this discussion of 'The incompetence of unaided virtue' is of the first importance in the consideration of the matters dealt with in this lecture.

PAGES 206–7. Far the most thorough and radical attempt known to me to work out what ownership by the workers might mean in an industrial society is contained in Mr. Paul Derrick's lately published book, *Lost Property*, which deserves the attention of Christian sociologists. The relevance of the monetary problem for Christian Sociology is well argued by Dr. V. A. Demant in an essay on the subject in his book, *Christian Polity*.

PAGE 208. For elaboration of the fundamental basis of the Church's concern with rural life, see *Earth and Heaven: the Theology of the Countryside*. Pamphlet by David G. Peck, published by the Council for the Church and Countryside.

Page 211. The quotation from Maurice is from his *Sermons on the Lord's Prayer*, pp. 100–1.

SELECT BIBLIOGRAPHY

The emphasis is on the word 'select'. The books here listed are for the guidance of the general reader; those wishing to make a closer study should refer to the bibliographies in Dr. Raven's *Christian Socialism, 1848–1854* and D. O. Wagner's *The Church of England and Social Reform since 1854*. Most of the books are listed in relation to the Lecture with which their subject-matter is particularly concerned, but in a number of cases they cover the field dealt with in more than one lecture. An asterisk indicates the most indispensable books.

Articles in periodicals are not included here, though they were often of some importance at the time. Some of the most influential leaders of the movement did the greater part of their writing in journals rather than books. A number of these were not primarily writers at all, and their impact was chiefly made by the spoken word; this is particularly true of Stewart Headlam, Conrad Noel, Studdert Kennedy and Basil Jellicoe.

GENERAL

*s. c. CARPENTER: *Church and People: 1789–1889*.
RUTH KENYON: 'The Social Aspect of the Catholic Revival: 1833–1933', in *Northern Catholicism*, edited by N. P. Williams and Charles Harris.
*G. C. BINYON: *The Christian Socialist Movement in England*.
*G. M. YOUNG: *Victorian England: Portrait of an Age*.
Oxford History of England:
E. L. WOODWARD: *The Age of Reform* [1815–1870].
R. C. K. ENSOR: *England: 1870–1914*.

LECTURES I AND II

F. D. MAURICE: *The Kingdom of Christ* [1838] (Everyman's Library edition: 1938).

*F. MAURICE: *Life of Frederick Denison Maurice* [1884].

(This book, which is principally built up from Maurice's corre-spondence, is indispensable to any understanding of the man and of those he inspired.) [Also for Lectures III and IV.]

C. K. GLOYN: *The Church in the Social Order*: A study of Anglican social theory from Coleridge to Maurice. (Pacific University Press: Oregon, U.S.A.)

*W. G. PECK: *The Social Implications of the Oxford Movement.* (The Hale Lectures, 1933: delivered at Seabury-Western Theological Seminary, U.S.A.)

*W. G. WARD: *The Ideal of a Christian Church* [1844].

R. COUPLAND: *Wilberforce.*

Ed.: G. D. H. and MARGARET COLE: *The Opinions of William Cobbett.*

G. K. CHESTERTON: *Cobbett.*

S. T. COLERIDGE: *Lay Sermons* [1816–17]. *The Constitution of Church and State* [1830].

R. SOUTHEY: *Sir Thomas More, or Colloquies on the Progress and Prospects of Society* [1829].

J. SIMMONS: *Southey.*

R. OWEN: *A New View of Society* [1813].

T. CARLYLE: *Sartor Resartus* [1838]; *Chartism* [1839]; *Past and Present* [1843]; *The Life of John Sterling* [1851].

S. SAGAR: *Round by Repentance Tower* (a Christian critique of Carlyle).

J. L. and B. HAMMOND: *The Age of the Chartists.*

LECTURE III

*C. E. RAVEN: *Christian Socialism: 1848–1854.* [The definitive study of the movement.]

*F. E. KINGSLEY: *Charles Kingsley: His Letters and Memories of his Life.* [1876: Abridged edition, 1879.]

*G. KENDALL: *Charles Kingsley and his ideas.*

C. KINGSLEY: *Yeast* [1848—in book form 1851]. *Alton Locke, Tailor and Poet* [1850]. *Two Years Ago* [1857].

F. D. MAURICE: *Sermons on the Lord's Prayer* [1848].

C. F. G. MASTERMAN: *Maurice* (Mowbray's 'Leaders of the Church' series, 1906).

CLAUDE JENKINS: *F. D. Maurice and the New Reformation.*

G. D. H. COLE: *A Century of Co-operation*, especially chapter vi.

LECTURE IV

*D. O. WAGNER: *The Church of England and Social Reform since 1854.* [Columbia University Press: U.S.A.] (Also for Lectures V. and VI.)

E. WINGFIELD-STRATFORD: *The Victorian Tragedy.*

Select Bibliography

J. L. and B. HAMMOND: *Lord Shaftesbury.*
F. HIGHAM: *Lord Shaftesbury.*
T. HUGHES: *James Fraser.*
B. F. WESTCOTT: *The Gospel and the Resurrection* [1866].

LECTURE V

E. WINGFIELD-STRATFORD: *The Victorian Sunset. The Victorian Aftermath.*
GODFREY ELTON: *England, Arise!*
T. HANCOCK: *Christ and the People* [1875]. *The Pulpit and the Press* [1904].
*F. G. BETTANY: *Stewart Headlam.*
J. CLAYTON: *Westcott* (Mowbray's 'Leaders of the Church' series).
*S. PAGET: *Henry Scott Holland.*
H. S. HOLLAND: *A Bundle of Memories* [1915].
G. L. PRESTIGE: *The Life of Charles Gore.*
J. ADDERLEY: *Stephen Remarx* [1893]. *In Slums and Society* [1916].
C. MARSON: *God's Co-operative Society.*
CONRAD NOEL: *Autobiography* [ed. Sidney Dark].
M. GOBAT: *T. C. Gobat: His Life, Work and Teaching.*
ROGER LLOYD: *The Church of England in the Twentieth Century,* vol. i.

LECTURE VI

Christianity and Industrial Problems: Fifth Report of the Archbishops' Commission [1918].
G. A. STUDDERT KENNEDY: *The Word and the Work.*
Geoffrey Studdert Kennedy, by his Friends.
*A GROUP OF CHURCHMEN: *The Return of Christendom* [1922].
The Proceedings of COPEC [1924].
K. INGRAM: *Basil Jellicoe.*
V. A. DEMANT: *God, Man and Society. Christian Polity. Theology of Society.*
Malvern, 1941. The Life of the Church and the Order of Society. (Conference Report.)
*W. TEMPLE: *Christianity and the Social Order* ('Penguin Special').
W. G. PECK: *William Temple: An Estimate and an Appreciation.* (Essay on Temple as a social thinker.)

LECTURE VII

Ed. M. B. RECKITT: *Prospect for Christendom* [1945].
(The reviews of this volume give perhaps the best insight as yet obtainable into the issues which sometimes unite and sometimes divide the Christian social movement to-day.)

Maurice to Temple

J. BAILLIE: *What is Christian Civilization?* [The Riddell Lectures, 1945.]

*Christian News-Letter. Supplements by W. Temple (29th Dec. 1943) and by V. A. Demant (3rd April 1946).

SOME PERIODICALS

(The dates given do not necessarily cover the whole life of the journals concerned, but indicate the period during which they were of importance for our subject.)

For Lecture III
   Politics for the People: Weekly, May–July, 1848.
   The Christian Socialist: Weekly from Nov. 1850, which became in 1851 *The Journal of Association*, ending June 1852.

For Lecture V
   The Church Reformer (Guild of St. Matthew). Monthly 1883–95.
   The Commonwealth: Monthly, 1896–1929.
   The Economic Review.
   (Both the above were founded and long edited by Henry Scott Holland.)
   The Optimist: Quarterly, 1906–13.
   (This journal, which was edited by Samuel Proudfoot, was from July 1909 to April 1911 known as *The Church Socialist Quarterly.*)
   The Church Socialist: Monthly, 1912–17; Bi-Monthly, 1918–21. (The organ of the C.S.L.)

For Lecture VI.
   The Pilgrim: Quarterly, 1920–27. Edited by William Temple.
   Christendom: A Journal of Christian Sociology. Quarterly from March, 1931.
   The Christian News-Letter: Fortnightly from October 1939. (Founded by Dr. J. H. Oldham.)

INDEX

Index

Index

Index

Index

Index

Index

Index